*The
Complete
Guide to
Walking
in Canada*

Also by Elliott Katz

The Complete Guide to
Bicycling in Canada

ELLIOTT KATZ

The Complete Guide to Walking in Canada

Illustrated by
Helga Schleeh

GREAT NORTH BOOKS

Cover design by Tania Craan
Interior design by Robert Burgess Garbutt
Maps by Samuel Daniel
Printed in Canada by Gagne Printing Ltd.
Cover photo by Alex Pytlowany/Masterfile

ISBN 0-920361-03-X

Published in the United States by:
   Great North Books
   P.O. Box 507, Station Z
   Toronto, Ontario
   Canada M5N 2Z6

Distributed in the United States by:
   Firefly Books Ltd.
   250 Sparks Avenue
   Willowdale, Ontario
   Canada M2H 2S4

To my parents,
Jack and Silvia Katz

PREFACE

CANADA'S magnificent natural areas are best experienced on foot. In the outdoors you can discover many uncrowded areas of spectacular beauty that provide a precious respite from city stresses and that can only be explored by walking, hiking or backpacking.

Even at popular natural attractions, a path can lead away from the crowds. At Moraine Lake in the Canadian Rockies (its picture appears on the back of our twenty dollar bill), I walked three kilometers along the serene lake's edge and was free of the tourist crowds.

In our increasingly hectic urban life, much of our time is spent indoors at work, shopping in malls or driving a car. We have to make a commitment to go walk outdoors and yet, stepping out in the Canadian outdoors is not only exhilarating, but physically and spiritually rejuvenating.

You can walk along the surf-washed, unspoiled beaches of Vancouver Island's west coast where the setting sun haloes rocky headlands and Pacific gray whales swim offshore, or retrace the footsteps of the Klondikers of 1898 over the Chilkoot Pass. The peaceful backcountry of the lush Coast Mountains, the lofty Selkirks and the majestic Rockies are best explored on foot.

Across the prairie sea of land and the rugged lake and forest park belt to the north are trails first walked by Indians, explorers, fur traders and settlers. In Ontario's spectacular Lake Superior and Killarney regions, which inspired Tom Thomson, A.Y. Jackson and the other artists of the Group of Seven, hikers can walk along untouched stretches of the rugged shores of Lake Superior, and hike the white rocky ridges overlooking Killarney's turquoise lakes.

Walkers can enjoy the beauty of Quebec's autumn forest ablaze with color. On Baffin Island north of the Arctic Circle the violet gray Pangnirtung Fjord Mountains are the exclusive domain of backpackers and mountaineers.

Hiking is the best way to explore the red cliffs, highland glens and river meadows of Nova Scotia's Cape Breton Highlands, the fjords, flat-topped mountains and windswept treeless barrens of Newfoundland, and observe puffins, gulls and gannets dive for fish off the coast of New Brunswick.

To walk in the wilderness is to experience nature directly. On the trail you are immersed in the natural world and your senses rediscover the world around you. Your eyes feast on a mountain sunrise, silent, lofty ice-capped peaks, ponderous glaciers and snowfields, ancient, worn mountains, crystal-clear lakes, the blazing color of an alpine meadow in full bloom, the kaleidoscope of an autumn forest and glistening cascades. Your ears are soothed by quiet lagoons, coves and bays or awakened by thundering waterfalls. You can smell the perfume of a pine forest, the salt air of the ocean, and the delicate scent of wild flowers. You can cool your brow with icy mountain water. You feel the sun and wind on your face, and the exercise of hiking makes you alive to the sense of blood flowing through every part of your body, which is why hikers are comfortable on a cool day wearing just shorts and a shirt. Walking lets you appreciate the solitude, silence and simplicity of a world with few signs of technology.

Whether you want to walk on an interpretive trail with explanations of the natural phenomena, go on a day-hike or do an extended backpacking trip, this book contains the needed information. "Getting Ready", covers the basics of equipment and techniques. The second part, "Where to Walk, Hike and Backpack in Canada", is a comprehensive guide to trails in Canada. The opportunities are as diverse as Canada's geography, ranging from gentle rambles near cities to rugged wilderness treks. American visitors can reach most of Canada's trails within a day's drive or a short airplane trip. Pick up this book and discover the exciting footpaths in every region of Canada.

Contents

PART ONE

Getting Ready

How to Use
Part One

WALKERS, hikers and backpackers, will find useful information in this section on "Getting Ready." The following chapters are oriented to conditions in Canada, but most of the information and suggestions apply also to hiking in other countries.

The introductory chapter, "Walking" discusses the physical and psychological benefits of setting out on foot and how to walk in the backcountry. Hikers outfitting themselves will find the basic information they need in the chapters "Equipment" and "Food and Cooking Gear." Anyone hiking during bug season will find tips on how to avoid being attacked by the bloodthirsty pests in the "Biting Insects" chapter. "Routefinding" covers how to find your way with a topographical map and compass, and how to order Canadian maps.

Parents who hike with their children will find suggestions in "Children." "Winter" is for hikers who want to extend the season through the winter.

Part One concludes with an important discussion on "Preserving our Natural Environment"; we must make every effort to leave the backcountry unspoiled for future generations.

1
Walking

WALKING is as natural to the human body as breathing. It is one of the first things a child wants to learn, and if an elderly person has to give it up, it's with much sadness. But for most of our lives we take walking for granted, and the magnificent benefits of physical and mental health that walking can give have often been overlooked.

Walking is good exercise

Walking can help prevent heart disease and improve your circulation. When you are sedentary, blood collects in the lower part of your body, depriving the brain and upper body of blood. The heart muscle has to work harder to maintain circulation. When you walk, the muscles of the feet, calves and thighs give the blood an extra push that lessens the load on the heart and helps to lower blood pressure. Walking also aids the respiratory system and digestion.

People who suffer from insomnia will sleep better after hiking. Charles Dickens cured his insomnia with nightly walks. If you are inactive, when you go to bed your mind is tired but your body is not. After a day on the trail your body is truly tired and sleep comes easily.

A walk in unpolluted air will improve your appearance, put color in your face and help to give you a clear complexion.

Walking helps overweight people reduce fat by burning up extra calories.

The psychological benefits of walking are just as important as the physical benefits. Bertrand Russell wrote: "Unhappy businessmen, I am convinced, would increase their happiness more by walking six miles every day than by any conceivable change of philosophy."

When the mind is tense, angry or feels a painful emotion, the muscles in the body become tense, which can cause headaches, backaches, high blood pressure and insomnia. Walking at a steady pace releases the tension in your muscles, relieves the physical pain and causes the mind to relax.

Walking in nature clears the mind, leaving it open to ideas and solutions to problems. Plato expounded his philosophy while walking in an olive grove.

Pace and Rhythm

Walking is the symphony of a relaxed mind and body. Rhythm is just as important in walking as it is in music. An hour of disjointed stop-and-go city walking is often exhausting, but hiking at a steady tempo you can keep going for several hours without becoming tired.

When starting out, amble down the trail at an *adagio* (leisurely) tempo. As the muscles loosen, speed increases and you gradually work up to an *andante* (moderate) pace. When walking on flat ground the tempo can often be brought up to a brisk *allegro con alma* (with spirit, soulfully) without getting out of breath. Singing a song (in your head or aloud) is a fun and effective way of keeping a steady rhythm while walking: a march for a sprightly step to cover distance or a long ballad for leisurely ambles.

Novice hikers often keep an erratic pace. They race down the trail in the morning, soon tiring themselves out, and don't enjoy their wilderness experience. Like the fabled tortoise who beat the hare, the hiker who keeps a steady pace will cover a greater distance and be less tired at day's end than the Speedy Gonzales who makes several jackrabbit starts and soon drops from exhaustion.

Distance

Set realistic goals. It's better to underestimate the distance you'll walk than to try to go too far.

When planning a trip, take several factors into account. Your physical condition is an important one. If you're out of shape you may find 25 kilometers on the first day a little too ambitious. As you walk your muscles tone up, and you'll gradually find yourself able to walk farther and faster and be less tired at the end of the day.

The terrain is also an important factor in calculating the distance for your trip. A rigorous kilometer-long three-hundred-meter climb over a mountain pass takes a lot more out of you and a lot more time than a five-kilometer ramble through gently rolling fields. Don't forget to consider the weather: warm days and dry trails are faster and easier than slogging through ankle-deep mud.

The times given in guidebooks are usually an average for experienced hikers under good conditions. Some, it may seem, were set by marathon runners. If you've just come from the city you might double the given times for the first day or so until you know how your hiking times compare with the guidebook's.

Another important factor is what you want to accomplish on the trail. If your desire is to set a record for covering a trail in the least amount of time, your only concern is walking and you'll have little time for looking at flowers, wildlife and the views. On the other hand, if your main interest is nature you may stop often to look at a plant or flower, identify an animal's tracks, marvel at the flight of geese or gaze at mountain vistas, and will likely cover just a few kilometers a day. Most walkers fall somewhere in between these two extremes. They like to look at a map and see the distance they've covered, but also like to take relaxing breaks on mountain summits and other lookout points, enjoy a refreshing waterfall and occasionally stop to look at wildlife and flowers. When planning the distance of your trip take into account time for rest stops and enjoying scenery.

Walking Uphill and Downhill

Approach hills with slow, short steps and avoid long strides. As the grade gets steeper, slow your pace but keep the rhythm steady. Keep your energy output at a comfortable level. Frequent rests may become necessary.

Slowly but surely you reach the top. Once there you'll most likely be faced with a downhill stretch. You may have thought going downhill is a breeze compared to going uphill, but you may find going down is actually more tiring.

Hiking down a hill, especially with the extra weight of a full pack, requires that you expend energy to hold yourself back against the force of gravity. Going downhill may be easier on the heart and lungs than an uphill climb, but it is harder on the knees, ankles and feet. When faced with a stretch of downhill, shorten your stride and slow down to reduce the wear on these vital parts of your walking equipment. Make sure your boots are laced tightly to reduce the chance of blisters forming from your feet sliding forward in your boots.

Rest Stops

After reaching an open mountain summit, cascading waterfall, alpine meadow in full bloom, refreshing stream or other scenic spot, you may feel like taking the load off your shoulders and resting. Rest stops are a good time to adjust boots, put on or take off sweaters and have something to eat and drink. The frequency of rest stops is a matter of personal preference and varies considerably among individual hikers. Many hikers average a rest stop about once an hour. If you find that you need to rest very often, try walking more slowly.

2

Equipment

MODERN equipment has made exploring Canada's natural areas on foot more accessible and enjoyable. Of course, the right equipment for you depends on what type of outings you plan. For a day-hike, a day pack with some extra clothing, hiking shoes, and food may be sufficient. An overnight backpacking trip involves more equipment such as a sleeping bag, backpack and tent. Aching feet or a sleepless night can be the result of not using the equipment that is right for you.

When shopping for equipment keep in mind the duration of your trip, the weather conditions at the time of year you're going and your personal experience. This chapter tries to give you the basics to help you make a good choice.

Outfitting yourself doesn't have to be expensive. You can equip yourself well with moderately priced gear. It's a good idea to buy a quality brand to reduce the possibility of problems with poor workmanship. If problems do occur almost all of the quality brands are guaranteed, some offering lifetime guarantees. Cheap equipment is likely to be uncomfortable or even painful and you'll probably want to replace it as soon as possible.

If you need new equipment, don't go out and buy it all in one day. Buy one piece of gear at a time and think about each purchase carefully, considering all the alternatives, and decide if you really need it before you spend your hard-earned cash.

The expense of outfitting a family with growing children can be reduced by making some things at home. Once outgrown, equipment can be passed on or traded among several hiking families.

Footwear

Proper shoes or boots are one of the most important parts of a hiking outfit. You can have the best gear on your back, but if your boots are torturing your feet, walking is difficult and the hike becomes miserable.

Comfortable walking shoes are sufficient for most day outings. Hiking shoes are suitable for most hiking trails where you won't encounter snow or wet conditions.

For all-round backpacking with relatively heavy loads on rough trails, mediumweight hiking boots are best. Lightweight trail shoes are suitable for short hikes on gentle trails. The heavyweight mountaineering boots bought by many unsuspecting hikers who mistakenly believe that extra cost and bigger boots make for better hiking, is too much boot for backpacking. Their stiff soles are intended for climbing and take forever to break in. Remember, 500 gm (1 pound) on the feet is like 2,500 gm (5 pounds) on the back.

Mediumweight boot

Lightweight boot

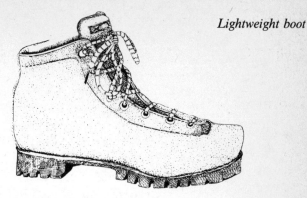

Selection

Decide what kind of footwear you need before you go shopping. The types of trails you plan to tackle will decide what weight of boots you buy.

Hiking shoes are flexible, comfortable and easy to break in. They have less padding or reinforcing than boots, but do provide some support and protection, and are suited to hiking with light packs on gentle trails.

The mediumweight hiking boots weigh between 1.5 and 2 kg (3 and 4½ pounds) a pair and are the right choice for most people who hike rocky and muddy trails, and occasionally traverse snowfields. The sole on mediumweight boots is less flexible than on trail shoes to provide protection from rocks and the upper is padded and more rigid for more support.

Fit

The most important consideration in selecting footwear is fit. On an average day's walk you may lift and pound your feet onto the ground more than 10,000 times. If your heel chafes and creates a painful blister it can keep you off your feet for several days.

Visit a hiking equipment shop that has several lines of footwear, and try on as many pairs as you can until you find a pair that fits. Wear the socks that you intend to wear on the trail.

Hiking shoes can be fitted in much the same way as regular shoes. Boots, because of the increased chance of chafing and blistering, require more careful study. A boot must be long enough so that when it's laced snugly your toes do not hit the front while walking downhill producing sore and blistered feet. A general rule when fitting boots is to stand in the unlaced boot and push your foot to the front. The length is about right if you can insert one finger down behind the heel. Another test for length is to lace up the boots tightly and slide your foot forward to simulate walking downhill with a heavy pack. The toes should not push against the front. If they do, or if your toes feel pinched, the boot is either too short or too narrow.

Slide your foot back and lace the boot tightly. Make sure that the boot feels as if there is room for your feet to swell—as they will after a long trek—and for the addition of a pair of socks. You should be able to wiggle and curl your toes. The ball of the foot should be comfortably snug and should not roll around when you stand on the edge of the sole. Walk with your boots. If your heels move up and down very loosely, the boot is too long, or too wide at the heel. There is often some slight lifting of the heel, which won't chafe your foot. Too much lifting, however, and the foot rubs on the boot, forming a painful blister.

Take your time fitting boots. Finding the best fit is a time-consuming process. Be sure that the boots you buy are a comfortable fit. When a boot feels right, try a size smaller and a size larger. If you are not satisfied with any boot in one shop, try another. Be sure that you have the right fit before you hand over the cash, because most shops will not exchange boots that have been worn outside. Your first trip with the new boots is not the time to find out if they fit.

Children's footwear

Children's feet are tender and require the same protection as adult feet. Since children outgrow footwear rather quickly, outfitting them with hiking shoes or high-topped running shoes with some tread is probably the best route. Buying boots every year can be just too expensive. To save money, boots and hiking shoes can be passed down to younger children and traded with other families.

Breaking in new footwear

Start breaking in new shoes or boots before heading out on the trail. It's especially important when backpacking, as the extra weight of your pack increases the pressure on your feet, which may cause blisters to form. After buying the boots, check the fit at home by wearing them indoors. Then go on longer walks outside. Be sure to wear the socks you plan to wear while hiking. Always check that the tongue is straight. Leather has a memory and the tongue will stay in the same position once the boot is broken in.

Hiking shoes are broken in relatively quickly, but it takes 50 to 100 kilometers of walking to break in most boots. The boots will stretch slightly with use and conform to your feet. While the leather is stiff you should be on guard for tender spots or blisters on your feet. When the boots have molded to your feet, blisters are less likely to form.

Boot Care

Every so often leather boots should be treated with a dressing to preserve the leather and to help keep the water out. The type of dressing depends on the tanning process used on the leather. Most hiking boots are chrome-tanned, and a silicone wax waterproofing protects the leather without softening it the way oil and grease will. Either warm the boot slightly or apply the wax in a melted state.

Always clean mud and dirt off your boots as soon as you return from a trip and treat them with waterproofing. Dressing should be applied only to clean, dry boots. Brush off the loose mud, and wash off the ground-in dirt with saddle soap. Let the boots dry before applying the waterproofing dressing.

Boots should always be dried at room temperature. If your boots get soaked, stuff them with newspaper and let them dry slowly in a cool, well-ventilated room. Never try to dry boots near a fire, heating duct or oven. Exposure to direct heat cracks leather, shrinks the uppers, and breaks down the bonding materials used to secure soles and midsoles to the uppers of the boot, causing them to separate. After you've cleaned and treated your boots, store them in a cool, dry place.

Foot Care

Pounding on the trail all day can be hard wear on feet fresh from the city, especially if you're carrying a heavy backpack. At the end of the hiking day, slip on a pair of sneakers, moccasins or other lightweight shoes to give your feet a rest from your hiking boots.

There are several ways to help prevent friction and possible blisters on your feet. Keep your toenails short. This will prevent a nail rubbing the skin of a neighboring toe. In hot weather, stop often and wash your feet in a stream, or just air your feet. If you know from experience that certain parts of your feet are prone to blistering, protect them with tape or moleskin before heading out.

If you feel a hot spot on your foot, stop immediately and cover the chafed area with moleskin or molefoam. Also, pull up your socks, remove pebbles, tighten laces or whatever adjustments are necessary to prevent more hot spots.

If a blister develops, immediate treatment is necessary. Cover a small blister with moleskin. If it's large and full of liquid, you may have to drain it to relieve the pressure and pain. Sterilize a needle in a match flame, apply antiseptic to the blistered area, and carefully puncture the blister on the edge, not on the top. Drain the liquid by pressing the blister gently, apply more antiseptic, and, if you must continue hiking, put some gauze on it and cover it with a piece of moleskin to prevent further irritation. Always carry moleskin or molefoam with you on a backpacking trip. Should you need it for a hot spot or blister, you'll think the moleskin is worth its weight in gold.

Packs

Natives, explorers and fur traders were the first to roam North America with their homes on their backs. The Natives hauled heavy loads with packboards strapped to their shoulders. The *voyageur* fur traders adapted Native packboards to carry heavy loads of furs over portages. Hikers wandering self-sufficient in the wilderness need to carry a minimum – the bare necessities that provide food, warmth and shelter in some type of conveyance that will keep the items together and leave their arms and heads free.

Modern equipment has eliminated much of the pain and agony formerly associated with backpacking. With the right pack you should be able to carry supplies and equipment comfortably and not feel like you have become a pack horse or some other beast of burden.

Although a pack is worn on the back, because we walk upright we don't carry the weight on our backs like a horse or other pack animal. The older packs suspended the weight from your shoulders away from your back, putting vertical pressure on the spine and strain on the back muscles. Modern packs have hip belts, which transfer the weight to the hips.

Daypacks

For day hiking there are numerous designs of daypacks, belt pouches and fanny packs available. Belt pouches and fanny packs are suitable for carrying lunch, water bottle, map, guidebook and compass. They're light enough to bring on trips when you plan to set up a base camp and explore the area on day hikes.

The frameless teardrop packs are larger and have room for a sweater, jacket and poncho. They can comfortably carry loads up to 9 kg (20 pounds). Most have a waist belt keeping the pack close to your back preventing it from shifting and throwing you off balance, which is especially appreciated when skiing, cycling or rock climbing.

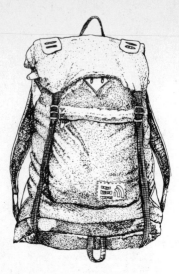

Rucksack

Internal Frame Packs

Unlike the older rucksacks which hung away from the back and pulled on the shoulders, modern internal framepacks have incorporated the advantages of an external frame pack's more comfortable suspension system, while holding the weight close to the wearer's center of gravity. The full-size packs tend to be narrower and not as high as external frame packs, making it easier to hike through thick bush and for travel. Some of the internal frame packs can be converted from backpack to hand-held luggage for easy handling at a hotel or airplane, an advantage if you're combining hiking and travelling.

The development of the padded hip belt has reduced the strain on shoulders and back and has made carrying a pack much more pleasant. This has made hiking more attractive to people who do not see themselves as rugged broad-shouldered *coureurs de bois*.

When setting out on the trail, keep the belt tight to take as much weight as possible off your shoulders. A hip belt with a quick-release buckle allows you to jettison the pack quickly in case of a fall, preventing the momentum of the weight on your back from causing serious injury. If you fall while fording a

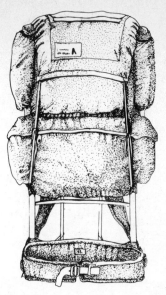

Framepack (with hip belt)

swift stream with the pack belt secured around your hips, the weight of the floating pack can hold you face down in the water. As a safety measure, always unbuckle the belt before crossing streams, walking on logs or stretches of terrain with slippery footing.

External Frame Packs

For trips of three to ten days on marked trails, a frame backpack has the advantage of carrying the weight high, close to your back and near your center of gravity. The rigid frame allows an efficient transfer of weight to the hipbelt. With the hipbelt and shoulder straps done up tightly, more than 75 per cent of the weight should be carried by the hips, and the remainder on your back and shoulders.

Some companies have different sizes of frames for different sizes of people. Be sure to get a comfortable fit that won't hit your thighs.

Pack frames are equipped with nylon mesh backbands to

hold the pack away from your back and distribute the weight evenly over your back. The backband should be kept tight to keep the crossbars from pressing into your back. Shoulder straps should be 6 to 7½ cm (2½ to 3 inches) wide, padded with Ensolite or other material that won't bunch up, and covered with nylon. The length of the strap can be adjusted.

Most packs made by quality manufacturers incorporate good quality frames and comfortable suspension systems. If you can't afford one of these packs and have to settle for an economy model with a straight frame and simple web belt that does not transfer weight to the hips, you can purchase a hip belt separately and attach it to the pack in place of the web belt.

Packbags

Most bags are made of coated nylon, which is generally waterproof and will keep the contents dry unless the pack is dropped into a stream. In very wet weather it's a good idea to protect the bag with a raincover, poncho or plastic. A large garbage bag makes a good rain cover which will last two or three days.

The style of the bag depends on your needs and personal preferences. Most popular among backpackers is a packbag that extends for three quarters of the length of the frame with room at the bottom for strapping on a sleeping bag and pad. Some packbags are one undivided large pocket opening from the top, which are good for carrying bulky items. The packbag divided horizontally into two pockets with zipper across to the lower pocket is more popular as it's easier to reach equipment at the bottom of the pack. Front-loading packbags have one or two compartments with zippers on three sides that open the entire back providing quick and easy access to every nook and cranny of the pack.

Big side pockets are handy for items that you want to reach quickly such as water bottle, trail snacks, rain gear, moleskin and toilet paper, and to stow sweaters you've shed while walking. Zippers on all pockets and compartments should be strong, dependable and covered with rain flaps. Nylon-coil zippers are preferred, as metal zippers tend to freeze and are difficult to operate in winter. Most top-loading packs have a map pocket on the storm flap.

Buy the size of bag needed for the length of the trips that you plan to take. A bag that is too large may tempt you to fill it up with unnecessary "just might come in useful" gadgets. A packbag's capacity is often indicated in cubic centimeters or inches. Bags suitable for general backpacking of up to a week or ten days average from 24,600 to 65,550 cm^3 (1,500 to 4,000 cubic inches). Expedition bags are up to 82,000 cm^3 (5,000 cubic inches).

Most quality framepacks have lash points for strapping gear on the outside of the pack, and include provisions for optional frame extentions to increase the carrying capacity of the pack.

Children's Packs

When a child is old enough to walk entirely on his own without being carried he usually wants a pack of his own so that he can feel like a full participant in the hike. A daypack is a good first pack.

A child's fully loaded pack should not weigh more than one quarter the child's weight. A pack stuffed with a sleeping bag or down-filled clothing appears large in size without being heavy and gives the child the feeling he is participating fully. Buy a pack that will be comfortable. Avoid the cheap, poorly constructed packs that will cause nothing but misery for the child and discourage him from going hiking again.

When parents feel that a child is strong enough, they can buy a framepack and bag for him. Several companies manufacture small backpacks designed for children.

Loading Your Pack

Stow heavy items such as cookware, stove, food and tent high in the bag and close to your back to put the center of gravity high, and keep most of the pack's weight pushing downward on your hips and not pulling on your shoulders. Lighter equipment—sleeping bags and clothes—should go at the bottom of the pack.

For ski-touring and cross-country travel through thick bush, the center of gravity should be kept low to make it easier to keep your balance on rough footing.

Get into the habit of keeping items in the same place in your pack. It makes packing and finding small items easier, especially when setting up camp in the dark.

Sleeping Bags

After a full day on the trail there is nothing worse than a miserable night awake and shivering in a sleeping bag you thought would keep you warm. You can always tell who was cold at night. They are the ones who were up at dawn, gathered wood and started a fire to warm up. Lacking a good night's re-energizing sleep, they then plod along the trail with no enthusiasm or spirit.

A sleeping bag that will keep you warm at the coldest temperatures that you're likely to encounter in the region and time of year that you hike is a necessity, not a luxury. Don't scrimp on a bag, or you'll curse yourself on a cold night and probably soon buy a better one. But don't go overboard and buy a super deluxe expedition bag rated to minus 40°C (−40°F) if the coldest time of year that you plan to hike in is late fall and early spring when there is only an occasional night below freezing. The expedition bag will be extra expense and weight and will be uncomfortable as it is just too hot. If you plan to take up winter camping you'll need another bag or you can use your regular sleeping bag with another bag or a liner.

The outdoors boom has produced a proliferation of sleeping bag manufacturers who are bringing out a flood of varieties of sleeping bags with different insulation, construction and shape. Making a choice isn't all that difficult. You should have no problem if you buy a bag with the desired temperature rating made by a reputable manufacturer, from a reliable hiking shop where they know their equipment.

Sleeping bags do not produce any heat on their own. They conserve your body heat, trapping it in the dead air space created by the bag's insulation and preventing that body heat from being carried away by wind or absorbed into the cold ground. The total thickness of the sleeping bag's insulation is known as the bag's loft, and is a fairly good indicator of a bag's temperature range; it is a good criterion for comparing insulating qualities of several sleeping bags.

The U.S. Army Quartermaster Corps research data gives an idea of minimum thickness of insulation needed to keep warm while sleeping at certain temperatures. These figures apply in windless conditions.

Temperature	*Loft*
C°	centimeters
4°	3¾
−1°	4½
−7°	5
−12°	5¾
−18°	6¼
−23°	7
−29°	7½
−34°	8¼
−40°	9
−51°	10

A sleeping bag with 15 cm (6 inches) of loft has 7½ cm (3 inches) of insulation around the body. When shopping around you'll probably find bags with 15 cm (6 inches) of loft rated to around −7°C (20°F). This rating takes into account wind, dampness, individual metabolism and allows for the comfort desired by most hikers. Because of the difference in hikers and conditions, temperature ratings should not be taken as gospel but used as basis of comparison.

The type of insulation influences the price and weight of the bag. Any material that keeps air from circulating away from your body is an insulator. It is the thickness of the insulation, not the weight or type that determines the degree of warmth. But for a sleeping bag to be suitable for backpacking it must be lightweight and pack to a small size for carrying. The only insulations that meet these requirements are down and the new synthetic polyester fills.

Insulation Fills

Until a relatively short time ago the only type of sleeping bag that was lightweight, warm and small to pack was filled with goose down. Down is the fluff that grows close to the skin of waterfowl. It traps air more efficiently than any other available material, providing more loft per gram, and allows the moisture given off by the body to pass through. The average person gives off about one half liter (one pint) vapor each night, and if this moisture accumulated it would reduce the effectiveness of the insulation. Down bags also stuff small for carrying. With the increasing demand for goose down and the trend to slaughter geese for eating before they reached full maturity, the quality of down deteriorated. Some manufacturers began using duck down which is less expensive, and it is now generally accepted that duck and goose down are equal in quality.

The synthetic polyester fills, Hollofil II and Polarguard are now a popular alternative to down. A synthetic filled bag does not absorb water directly into the structure; so, if it's drenched, it will still keep you warm and will dry out from your body heat alone. If a polyester bag becomes soaked, wring it out and you'll sleep warmer in it than in a wet down bag. When down gets wet it loses almost all its loft. Sleeping in a wet down bag will be colder as the dampness will conduct your body heat. This advantage should definitely be considered if you plan to use a tarp or other minimal shelter while hiking in rainy or humid areas, a description that fits many parts of Canada. Unlike down, polyester does not compress underneath your body weight. It still provides some insulation beneath you. Polyester also costs less, which is an important consideration for hikers on a limited budget. Compared to the synthetic fills, down is lighter for the same amount of warmth and when packed occupies 25 per cent less space than a polyester bag of the same weight. When weight and space are important considerations, such as on extended trips, you may opt for a down bag.

Construction

After deciding between down or polyester, and the temperature range you want for your bag, other differences in sleeping bag construction aren't earth-shattering.

Shell Fabric

Almost all sleeping bags are constructed of rip-stop nylon or tafetta nylon. Both materials are light, strong, wind resistant and allow water vapor to pass through. When you climb into your bag the nylon feels cold, but it quickly warms up to your body heat.

Cut

Many bags have a differential cut, meaning that the inner shell is smaller than the outer shell. This allows the fill to loft more evenly around the bag preventing cold spots caused by protruding knees or elbows pressing the inner shell against the outer shell.

The space-filler cut has both shells the same size. The theory behind this approach is that the inner shell drapes over the body reducing the amount of space that has to be heated.

Baffles

Several construction methods are used to keep down distributed evenly around you and prevent it from shifting and lumping up in certain spots, such as the bottom of the bag, leaving other areas unprotected. The simplest and least expensive method is sewn-through construction, in which the inner and outer shells are sewn directly together. Each seam has no insulation and is a cold spot.

To eliminate these cold spots, most down bags are constructed with vertical baffles sewn around the bag connecting the inner and outer shells. The baffles are usually of a light nylon material that prevent the down from moving inside the bag and allow the down to loft. The three basic patterns of baffles are square box, slant box and overlapping V-tubes. The simplest is square-box construction which is a series of straight walls separating the down. Slant-box construction uses longer offset baffles that partially overlap each other and is considered better than square box as it allows the down to expand more. Most down sleeping bags have slant-box construction. Overlapping V-tubes are small triangular compartments that interlock, and are considered the most efficient construction to insure a uniform distribution of down in the bag. They require about twice the amount of baffling material making the bag heavier and more expensive.

Polyester comes in rolls of batting and does not have the shifting problem of down. The inexpensive synthetic-fill bags use a sewn-through batting construction and are only suitable for camping in warm weather. Most of the better quality bags use double-quilted (also known as laminated) construction that consists of two sewn-through batts with the seams staggered so that one batt's thin area is covered by the thick part of the other.

Zippers

For ease in getting in and out of the bag, and for ventilation control, the sleeping bag should have a durable zipper. Nylon zippers are self-lubricating, do not freeze up, and are lighter than metal. Sleeping bags with full length and across-the-foot zippers can be joined together if the zippers are compatible, and if their occupants are also. To join sleeping bags with zippers

Square-box construction

Slant-box construction

V-tube construction

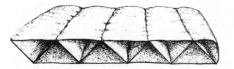

only on the side, one right-hand and one left-hand zipper is required. If you want to be able to snuggle with your loved one, buy sleeping bags made by the same manufacturer to insure that they have the same type and size of zippers. In quality bags, the zipper is covered by a draft tube to keep out cold drafts.

Styles

Sleeping bags come in several shapes. The most common style for backpacking is the mummy bag. They are lighter and warmer because they have snug fit and less air space for your body to warm up. The barrel bags, also called the semi-mummy, have more room around the shoulders and hips, allowing elbows and knees to move around while you're sleeping and are preferred by hikers who think that they will feel claustrophobic in a mummy bag. Because an unprotected head will lose a lot of heat, the mummy and the barrel bag have built-in hoods with drawcords to protect your head. On warm nights the hood can

Sewn-through polyester-fill baffles

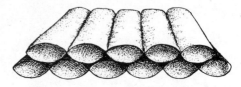

Double-quilted or laminated baffles

be left flat, and on cold nights the draw cord is pulled tightly with only your nose exposed. If your nose is cold, breathe through a sweater, but don't breathe through your bag, as it will absorb moisture. The rectangular bags are heavier, not as warm as the mummy bags and are suited only for short summer trips.

Sleeping bags are carried in a nylon stuff sack. Though the material is treated to make it waterproof, it is a good idea to line the stuff with a plastic bag to insure absolute protection in a downpour.

Children's Sleeping Bags

While the child is a baby, he can snuggle in his parents' double sleeping bag or if the parents prefer single bags, in one of their bags. When the child reaches a certain size this becomes impractical and he requires his own sleeping bag. Several manufacturers produce sleeping bags for children. Synthetic-filled bags with flannel liner are best for children who are possible bed-wetters. An economical child's sleeping bag can be made by shortening an old bag to the desired length.

Sleeping Bag Care

Keep the bag dry, especially if it's a down-filled bag. Never lay it directly on the ground where moisture can be absorbed.

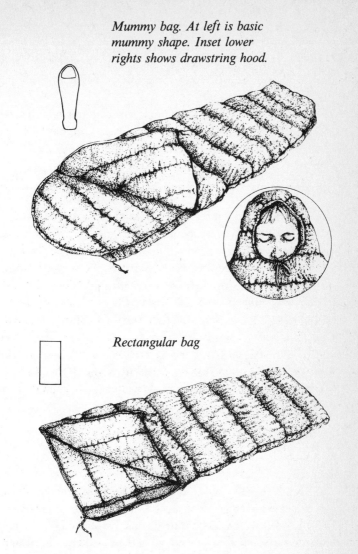

Mummy bag. At left is basic mummy shape. Inset lower rights shows drawstring hood.

Rectangular bag

There should always be a waterproof layer such as a groundsheet or tent floor between the sleeping bag and the ground. In the mornings, while you're eating breakfast and getting ready to break camp, open the bag and let it air out and dry in the sun to remove the night's accumulation of body moisture.

Sparks from campfires can melt holes in the shell fabric. Take care to keep your sleeping bag a good distance away from the fire. If a hole in your sleeping bag occurs, patch it immediately with rip-stop tape or, if you don't have any, use ordinary tape, to prevent losing any down.

Leaving a bag stored in a stuff sack for long periods of time can cause the down to lose its resiliency. Keep the bag in a dry place where it can remain lofted.

Sleeping Pads and Sleeping Bag Covers

The ground is the source for much of the cold discomfort that someone in a sleeping bag feels. For insulation, a 1-cm (⅜-inch) closed-cell foam pad is usually sufficient for summer conditions. However, it provides a small amount of comfort. The Therma-a-Rest sleeping pad is made of open-cell foam which is warmer and much more comfortable. They are also more expensive than closed-cell foam pads.

Sleeping bag covers help protect the bag from wind and moisture, and are generally used by hikers who require extra protection when sleeping under a tarp or in a snow shelter. The top of the cover is breathable rip-stop or nylon tafetta and the bottom is coated with waterproof nylon that serves as a groundsheet. They can also be used as a makeshift tent.

Hammocks

Some hikers who don't like sleeping on the hard ground bring a light-weight backpacking hammock made of nylon netting. Hammocks are especially handy when sleeping on rocky hills where there is no flat ground. Just find two trees spaced the correct distance apart and tie one end of the hammock to each tree. If there's a possibility of rain, rig a tarp over the hammock. For hiking in buggy country, look around for army surplus jungle hammocks that are enclosed with mosquito netting.

Clothing

It isn't necessary to spend a fortune on hiking apparel. Most of the clothes needed for summer trips can probably be found among the clothes you already own. Thrift shops and army surplus stores have good bargains for durable outdoor clothing.

The type and quantity of clothing to bring, like other equipment, depends on where you'll be hiking, the length of the trip, the time of year, your metabolism and other factors based on your experience. In most of Canada, summer days are usually warm, and you'll probably want to hike in shorts and a T-shirt. Evenings are cool and you'll need long pants, a long-sleeved shirt and a sweater or light jacket to keep warm and for protection against biting insects which will come out to feast on hikers in early evening.

Weather can range from sweltering, humid days in thick forest to cold, pelting rain on a windy mountaintop. When selecting clothing, try to have the least amount of clothing that will allow you to be comfortable in the conditions you're likely to encounter. The system most efficient for weight and warmth is to wear many layers of light clothing, rather than one heavy garment. This enables you to regulate your comfort by adding or removing layers as the weather and your activity change. When you're moving and producing heat you'll roll up sleeves, undo the collar and change into shorts, or whatever is just enough to keep you warm. When you stop you'll soon cool off and want to slip on a sweater or windbreaker and put on a pair of long pants.

Headwear

A good hat should be carried the year round for protecting the head against cold, wind, sun or rain. The head and neck are the most important portion of the body in regulating body heat. Unlike the rest of the body, the flow of blood to the brain is constant regardless of changes in air temperature, and as a result the head radiates more heat than the rest of your body. Up to 50 per cent of your body heat can be lost through an uncovered head and neck. If the head and neck are cold, the other extremities such as feet and hands will also be cold.

A wool hat, balaclava, tuque or watch cap will keep you warm, and uncovering your head will help cool you. A hat allows you to regulate your body heat simply and quickly instead of taking your pack off and removing a sweater, and repeating the process as the weather cools.

In hot weather, an uncovered head under scorching sun can make you dizzy and lead to heat stroke. A cotton hat keeps the sun off your head and provides ventilation. Sunhats with wide brims keep the sun out of your eyes, and off ears and nose. Bandanas are versatile and can be used as sun hats or to protect the back of the neck from sunburn.

Socks

Proper socks reduce friction between boot and foot, cushion feet from the constant pounding of walking, keep feet warm and absorb moisture. Socks made largely of wool are best for hiking, as wool wicks sweat away from the foot, keeping it relatively dry. The socks should be several centimeters higher than the boots. To last longer, the socks should have nylon reinforcement at the heels and toes or be a cotton and nylon blend; 80 per cent wool, 20 per cent nylon is a common blend.

Some hikers wear one light and one heavy sock on each foot. The lightweight inner sock eliminates the itchy feeling of the heavy wool. Other hikers wear two medium weight socks. Experiment with different combinations and use the one that suits you.

When socks get wet, many hikers try to dry them over a fire. This is time consuming and often results in burn holes and charred socks. If you have the time and want to dry wet socks over a fire, position the socks a safe distance away from the flame and check them regularly. Another way to dry socks is to put them close to you in your sleeping bag and let body heat dry them. This method is very effective, but don't try to dry more than a few items at the same time or the dampness will make you cold in your bag. On a sunny day, you can also spread wet socks on rocks or tie them to the outside of your pack while hiking.

If you have to do a lot of slogging through very wet terrain with 15-centimeter mud and don't want small lakes in your socks, there is a way of keeping some sense of dryness on your feet. Put a plastic bag between the inner and outer socks, or on top of the outside layer. Fold the bag carefully to avoid wrinkles that will press into your foot. Your feet will remain warm and dry except for perspiration, most of which will be absorbed by the inner layer.

Underwear

The regular cotton underwear that you wear in the city is sufficient for almost all summer backpacking. Cotton absorbs sweat; nylon does not, and soon becomes clammy. A cotton T-shirt doubles as an undershirt on cool days. For cold weather long bottoms and long-sleeved tops are needed. Two types of underwear are popular with hikers. Thermal underwear is made of wool with a nylon outer layer and a cotton inner layer. Fishnet underwear provides insulating dead-air space when used with a shirt worn over it, and it also allows perspiration to evaporate. This type of underwear is made of wool-nylon or cotton-polyester blends.

Pants

Loose-fitting pants of durable material—denim, corduroy or hard-finish wool—are most desirable for hiking. Avoid cuffed or flared pants as they can catch on rocks or underbrush and cause you to fall. Pants that fit tightly at the hips and knees make walking more tiring. Many hikers always wear shorts for the freedom of movement and ventilation. In cool weather, you can add more layers to the upper part of your body and, combined with the heat generated by walking, your legs will be warm. In wet weather long pants become heavy with water and more energy is required to lift each leg. When you're wearing shorts in the rain, your legs will be warm as long as you're moving and you'll have a dry, warm pair of pants to slip into when you reach camp.

Long pants are needed for warmth on cool evenings, for cold rest days, for protection from biting insects, poison ivy and poison oak, and when travelling in rough thick bush, so you won't scratch your legs to shreds.

When hiking in winter or in wet chilly areas such as British Columbia's coastal rainforests where you're guaranteed to get sopping wet at least once during your trip, wool pants are a godsend as they will keep you warm when wet.

To keep your pants up you'll need a belt or suspenders. Some hikers find that the pack's padded hip belt presses a leather belt into their skin, and prefer keeping their pants up with suspenders.

Shirts and Sweaters

After the head, the chest is the most important part of the body in regulating body heat. The layer system is generally applied here. The first layer is usually a cotton T-shirt and if it's a hot day that's probably all you will wear on your torso. Cotton absorbs perspiration without feeling clammy. If the weather is very hot and humid, you may prefer to go without a shirt. On real scorchers, however, it's advisable to wear a T-shirt to prevent sunburn.

The second layer will be a cotton-flannel, chamois or light wool shirt with long sleeves and long tail. The long sleeves protect the arms from insects. When you get warm you can roll up the sleeves, unbutton the front and pull out the tail. As it cools down, you roll down the sleeves, button up the front and tuck in the tail.

The next layer is a medium-weight sweater, which is preferred to a heavy sweater, as it is more versatile. Pullover sweaters with crew necks are the most common, turtleneck shirts may be too hot on the back of the neck while your chest may be cold without a sweater. V-neck sweaters should be avoided as they won't protect the top of your chest. New sweaters of 100 per cent virgin wool are expensive, and you might want to check with parents, friends, and second-hand clothing stores for an old wool sweater. Wool's ability to keep you warm when wet makes a wool sweater a necessity.

Wind Shell Clothing

The shirt and sweater layers create dead air space which is what keeps you warm. An outer layer comprising a wind parka or anorak is needed to prevent the wind from penetrating and cooling the dear-air space.

Wind clothing is usually windproof and water repellant. Until recently, wind clothing could not also be waterproof as the material must breathe to allow body moisture to pass through. If the moisture can't escape, it condenses and you're soon drenched in perspiration. Clothing with Gore-Tex laminate is both waterproof and breathable.

Nylon wind parkas are the simplest and lightest. Nylon wind pants are also available and are useful on windy mountain

Wind parka

ridges. The wind shell parkas made of a blend of cotton and nylon, 60 per cent cotton and 40 per cent nylon, are durable in rigorous conditions. This fabric combines the comfort, moisture and water-repellancy of cotton, and the strength and wind resistance of nylon.

One style of wind parka opens with a two-way nylon zipper covered with a storm flap with snaps. The zipper should reach to the chin, and the hood should have a drawstring to adjust the opening around the face. The parka should also be equipped with a drawstring at the waist, and an elastic or Velcro closing on the cuffs. The other style of wind shell is a pullover known as an anorak, which doesn't have as good ventilation as the open front design.

Wind parkas usually abound in patch pockets, with two cargo pockets, slash pockets for hands and two breast pockets, most with Velcro-closed storm flaps.

Poncho

Raingear

A poncho that covers both you and your pack is the best bet for hiking in a downpour. Because a poncho is open at the side, it provides good ventilation, reducing internal condensation. Almost all ponchos have hoods, eliminating the need for a separate rain hat; they also keep the water from running down your neck.

A few ponchos have sleeve extentions to help keep your arms dry. Ponchos of coated nylon are the lightest. The rubberized cloth ponchos are heavier but still preferred by some hikers. The cheap vinyl plastic poncho may be a worthwhile buy when you're starting out and need a lot of other expensive gear such as boots, pack and sleeping bag, but don't expect one to last more than a few trips, after which it will have more holes than anything else.

In a pinch, ponchos can also be used as groundsheets, but

Cagoule

this should be avoided—they tear easily and wear on the material makes it less waterproof. Ponchos equipped with grommets can be rigged as shelters for lunch stops on drizzly days.

A hip-length nylon-coated rain jacket should not have any seams directly over the top of the shoulder. If the zipper in the jacket is left open, it provides some ventilation, but for strenuous hiking rain jackets tend to be too hot.

A cagoule is like a waterproof, loose-fitting anorak that reaches to the knees. It is good protection against rain but has little ventilation.

Waterproof rain pants have little ventilation and can only be used comfortably for standing around camp. They are handy to walk through thick underbrush that has just received a heavy rainfall when you can ventilate the upper part of your body to make up for the lack of ventilation in your legs. A better solution is to walk in short pants.

Gaiters

To keep water and mud from pouring over the top of your boots or soaking your socks and the cuff of your pants, wear a pair of gaiters. Made of nylon, canvas or a cotton-polyester blend, gaiters come in several sizes and cover the gap between the pants and boots.

The long gaiters, 40 to 45 cm (16 to 18 inches), cover the bottom of pant legs. If you hike in shorts during the rain the long gaiters will keep the calves of your legs warm and dry, and leave your knees unhindered. The short gaiters—18 to 23 cm (7 to 9 inches)—keep your socks dry and water and mud out of your boots.

Mittens

Wool mittens are good to have when you're up in the mountains in early spring or late fall. When days can be chilly you don't want to keep your hands in your pockets all the time. They're essential for winter trips. Mittens are warmer than gloves because they keep the fingers together.

Insulated Clothing

For additional warmth on cool Canadian mornings and evenings or for treks on tundra or windy alpine ridges, most hikers carry a down or synthetic-filled jacket or vest. Down is warmer and packs smaller than the synthetic polyester fills, but when down becomes wet it loses virtually all its insulating value making it mostly suitable for cold, dry conditions.

Polyester will keep you warm when it's wet, and dries very quickly with body heat. Although it doesn't pack as small as down, on summer trips there should be enough room in the pack. It is preferable to wear synthetic-filled clothing on trips in areas where conditions are likely to be wet, which includes a large part of Canada.

The shell on insulated clothing is usually either rip-stop nylon or 60/40 cloth. A down-insulated sweater has long sleeves, reaches the hips, is lighter and takes up less space than a wool sweater. The insulated jackets and parkas extend over the hips. They contain more insulation than a sweater to keep you warm at colder temperatures. Vests keep the torso warm, and are suitable for temperatures that don't require a jacket or when you're engaged in a vigorous activity. They allow unrestricted arm movement, which is especially appreciated in cross-country-skiing.

Children's Clothing

Always bring at least one complete change of clothing for each child and a good supply of extra socks. Some of the child's clothing should be in bright colors like red or yellow so that if the child wanders off he will stand out and be easier to find. It may be difficult to locate rain pants and other gear in children's sizes. Clothing is one area where making gear is relatively simple and can save a lot of money.

Shelter

There are a few places in Canada where one can confidently backpack without carrying some sort of shelter. There may be occasions when you can sleep out under the stars, but most of Canada, particularly the mountainous regions, the coasts and the Canadian Shield are subject to frequent rain or are plagued by bloodthirsty mosquitoes and blackflies that make sleeping out unprotected, unpleasant, if not downright miserable. Tents provide that little haven from the elements. With the increase in the number of hikers, it's necessary to carry a tent even on trails that have cabins or shelters, as they may be full when you arrive.

Tarps and Tube Tents

If a regular tent is too expensive or if you hike alone and find a tent is too heavy and provides more shelter than you require, a tarp or a tube tent may be more suited to your needs.

Tarp shelters can be made to suit most situations. They provide protection against wind and rain, though not as much as a tent, and mosquitoes are still free to bite the parts of your

One way of setting up a tarp shelter

Another way

body sticking out of your sleeping bag. The tarp should be opaque; a color that reflects sunlight, preferably a translucent white and not transparent plastic.

The polyethylene sheets sold in hardware stores are completely waterproof and make very inexpensive tarps that will last for a few trips. Get the 0.1 cm (4 mil, .004 inch) thickness. The lighter sheets tear easily and plastic thicker than this is unnecessary weight. A tarp measuring 2-by-2½ meters (6-by-8 feet) is about right for one person.

There are several devices for attaching cord to plastic tarps which make the plastic tarps more versatile and easier to set up. Visklamps consist of a metal ring and a rubber ball, and operate on the same principle as a garter. Versa-ties use a disc instead of a ball. Before these items were marketed, hikers would wrap a small stone or stick and tie it off. Use a strong lightweight cord such as braided white ⅓-cm (⅛-inch) nylon cord of 250-kg (550-pound) test strength.

If the tarp tears, and you can't use it anymore, pack it out. Because of the plastic sheet's low price, you may feel generous and want to lighten your load by leaving the sheet at the last campsite in case future hikers need extra shelter. Don't. Every hiker should carry his own shelter, and those who follow you will see anything you leave behind as litter.

On longer trips, where extra strength and dependability is needed, carry a coated nylon tarp. They weigh less than plastic tarps and are less likely to tear in a wind or be punctured by sharp sticks. A rain fly from a double-wall, two-person backpacking tent makes a good tarp for one person. Good quality nylon tarps are usually made of urethane coated rip-stop and usually have grommets around the edge and other strategic points for ease in setting up.

Tube tents are .008 to .01 cm (3 or 4 mil) polyethylene in the shape of a tube. They offer good protection against rain and can be quickly set up. Rig a nylon cord through the tube and secure it to two trees to form the ridge line. The weight of your gear and you will anchor the floor down. The one-person size is about 3 meters (9 feet) long, 2½ meters (8 feet) around and the weighs about ½ kg (1¼ pounds). The two-person model is the same length, 4 meters (12 feet) in circumference and weighs 1 kg (2½ pounds).

Tents

Though they save weight, tarps and tube tents don't provide complete protection from the elements. If you try to sit out a windy rainstorm under an open tarp there's a good chance you and your equipment will get drenched. If you hike in areas where it often rains continuously for several days, get a roomy tent. You'll appreciate the space to dress, cook and store gear without going stir-crazy. A tent with good insect netting will provide the bug-free oasis necessary to preserve sanity.

Another advantage of a closed tent is privacy. On popular trails, campsites can be very crowded, and the privacy of your own tent is appreciated. If you're planning to set up a base camp and take day hikes you can stash all your gear inside the tent, more secure and more tidy than leaving your gear around camp.

The tent should keep you dry, comfortable and warm. Before buying a tent, decide what type will fill these needs best for you. Some people tend to buy more tent than they need and pay for it not only in higher costs but added weight. A mountaineering tent with snow flaps and frost liner is just not needed for summer backpacking use. Don't carry more than 1½ kg (3 pounds) of tent per person. A two-person tent should weigh around 3 kg (6 pounds). Anything weighing much more is too heavy.

Breathable flytent

Things to look for in a backpacking tent include a waterproof floor that extends up the sidewalls for several centimeters to keep out ground moisture and insect netting on all doors and vents. If you want to keep your gear inside the tent, there must be enough room to accommodate it. If you keep your pack outside, cover it with your poncho.

Almost all modern backpacking tents are made of 54-gm (1.9-ounce) rip-stop nylon. Unlike cotton which was used in older tents, nylon does not mildew when wet, doesn't wick water and is lighter. Cotton is half as strong as nylon meaning a cotton tent of equal sturdiness will weigh twice as much as a nylon tent.

A single-wall, waterproof nylon tent will keep out most of the rain, but because the inside of the tent is warmer than the outside, moisture from your breath and body, which cannot penetrate the waterproof single wall, will condense on the inside of the tent. Good quality tents use a double-wall construction that has a coated nylon fly over an inner tent of breathable nylon. The fly keeps the rain out and the inner tent allows moisture to escape. If you already have a single-wall tent you can add a rain-fly to it. A fly also keeps the tent cooler on hot days.

If you plan to do most of your camping below the timberline, this is the type of tent you'll need. The rule for other equipment applies to tents also: Don't buy more than you need; it will just be an unnecessary expense and extra weight.

3

Food and Cooking Gear

WALKING, hiking and backpacking burn calories. Tasty energy-boosting food is essential for physical and psychological well-being.

For a day trip, pack some sandwiches, fresh vegetables and fruit, cheese and some quick energy trail snacks. Make it a picnic outing. Since you're carrying only one or two meals, the weight of the food is not as crucial, but do avoid litre or larger jugs of juice or other drinks.

The type and quantity of food taken on a backpacking trip depends upon the length of the trip and personal taste. On overnight or weekend trips, fresh vegetables and fruit, canned food and other relatively heavy food can be carried without discomfort. A trip longer than three or four days requires that food be selected for its light weight. Otherwise, the load becomes unbearable. Important criteria for selecting food for a backpacking trip are weight, bulk, nutrition, cooking time and taste.

Nutrition

For trips of up to three weeks, one need not be overly concerned about having a balanced diet of carbohydrates, protein and fat. Though keep in mind that you will probably be burning more calories than normal and will require foods that provide energy.

A person of average weight and metabolism burns about 3,500 calories a day while hiking, but everyone has different energy needs and a general rule cannot be applied. It's best to bring the food you like and determine your needs from experience. How you feel is the best measure of how well you are eating.

Carbohydrates are quick-energy foods. Snacks consumed during rest stops on the trail should be high in carbohydrates. Dried fruits, chocolate, candy and other sweet foods, are high in sugar – one type of carbohydrate – and are favorite trail snacks. The starch in bread, rice, peas, corn and potatoes is another type of carbohydrate usually eaten with meals.

The fat found in meat, margarine and nuts is another source of calories. The body stores fat and can convert it into heat energy very quickly when needed. On cold days, especially on winter trips, add extra margarine to your morning oatmeal for the extra heat it will provide.

Protein, found in meat, fish, eggs, milk and cheese, produces energy that lasts longer. Owing, however, to its molecular structure, protein consumes calories in its conversion into energy.

Salt is needed in your food to prevent dehydration. Your body releases salt in perspiration and urine. When you exert yourself hiking and perspire more than usual, you lose more salt which needs to be replaced.

Weight and Bulk

On trips longer than five days, food is probably the heaviest part of your outfit, and the weight and bulk of food are important considerations. You may wish to dine like a gourmet every night, but remember that you have to fit it into your pack and carry the weight.

The heaviest ingredient in food is water, weighing 1 kg/litre (8 pounds per gallon). By using dehydrated and freeze-dried food, and other foods that are normally low in water, you can plan for about 1 kg (1½ to 2 pounds) of food per person per day.

Cooking Time

Meals that are simple and quick to prepare are most desirable on most trips since hikers usually want to spend most of the time hiking and exploring, not cooking. Instant oatmeal, porridge and granola are quick and filling breakfasts for days when you want to get an early start. On rest days, the morning can be filled frying pancakes. Lunch is usually a short stop on the trail and the meal should also be simple and quick to prepare. A meal of instant soup with sandwiches of salami, cheese, peanut butter or honey is filling, and provides energy for the afternoon's hike.

The cooking time for supper can be a little longer; a half-hour wait is reasonable. Any longer and famished hikers may start a full-scale revolution against the cook. Also, meals that have to be cooked for a long time consume more fuel, an important consideration on long trips. Fresh Beef Wellington and *coq au vin* are definitely out.

Flavor

Hiking in clean air makes food taste better and meals more enjoyable. Hikers often find that foods that did not appeal to them at home become delicious while in the backcountry. When planning a trip's menu try experimenting with new foods, but be sure also to carry foods that you know you like. Bring a few of your favorite spices to make bland freeze-dried dinners more exciting.

Lightweight Supermarket Food

Before going to a hiking gear shop and shelling out money for the expensive foil-wrapped backpacking dinners, check supermarkets and health food stores for foods that are lightweight and can be had at a much lower cost. Complete menus can be assembled with supermarket food, though it will be heavier and bulkier than freeze-dried food.

Granola, instant oatmeal, cream of wheat, pancake mix with raisins and other dried fruit, powdered milk and fruit juice crystals are some of the foods suitable for breakfasts on the trail. Quick lunches can be made with rye, pumpernickel or other heavy bread, crackers, margarine, cheese, salami, sausage, beef jerky, sardines, tuna, salmon, herring kippers, corned beef, peanut butter, jam, honey, and instant soups. Lightweight suppers can be made with dried soup, bouillon cubes, spaghetti or macaroni, rice, bulgur, buckwheat and other grains, instant potatoes, the canned meat and fish listed above, and dried vegetable flakes. Many of the instant meals (usually marketed for busy working people) can be made by adding hot water, and are suitable for the trail. Some of the seasonings that add life to one-pot suppers are curry, chili powder, onion flakes and green-pepper and red-pepper flakes. Coffee, cocoa and tea with sugar and powdered milk make good hot drinks.

It is more difficult with supermarket food than with pre-packaged freeze-dried food to calculate the amount you'll need. Again, experience is the best guide. Many of the outdoor cookbooks indicate amounts and are helpful in planning complete menus with supermarket food. (Several cookbooks are listed in the suggested reading at the end of this chapter.)

Dehydrated Food

Most commercially produced lightweight food sold in hiking equipment shops has had its water removed by either dehydration or freeze-drying. Dehydration, the older of the two methods, has been a natural way of preserving food since man started to store food.

Dehydrated food is dried with hot air. The process removes 80 to 97 per cent of the food's moisture, shrinks the food and significantly reduces its weight. Hiking foods produced in this way usually cost less than the freeze-dried type.

Dried fruits, beef jerky and dried vegetable flakes are some of the foods produced by hot-air drying. Dried fruit and beef jerky can be eaten dry or rehydrated. Try soaking some dried fruit overnight and adding it to your morning oatmeal. Dehydrated vegetables should be soaked until almost completely rehydrated. The soaking time depends on the type and size of the vegetables. If they require more than 15 to 30 minutes, put them and some water in a plastic bottle several hours earlier and carry it in your pack. The same method can be used to reduce the cooking time of beans.

Hot-air drying is a relatively simple and inexpensive process and home food dehydrators can be purchased in many kitchen appliance stores. Home-dried foods are free of preservatives which are added to commercially prepared food to improve its appearance. Another advantage of having your own dehydrator is that you can dry foods not usually found in the dried foods section of supermarkets and backpacking equipment stores, such as cherries, cranberries, blueberries, strawberries, broccoli, beets and cabbage. Vegetables should be steam blanched before drying to stop the organic action that allows low-acid foods to spoil. Properly stored home-dried food should be edible for about a year. (Consult the suggested reading for books on drying food at home.)

Freeze-dried foods

Most of the foods packaged in bright aluminum foil or plastic envelopes and sold in hiking equipment shops are freeze-dried. The freeze-drying process is more expensive, but it tends to retain more of the flavor than does hot-air drying. Cooked or raw food, depending on the type, is frozen in a vacuum at a very low temperature, down to $-45°C\,(-50°F)$. The solid ice in the food is sublimated into the air, converted directly from a solid into a vapor without going through the liquid state. The original color, nutritional value and shape of the food is preserved. The product is very porous enabling quick rehydration.

A hiker who chooses to outfit his trip with a menu of freeze-dried food has an enormous selection awaiting him. Freeze-dried food can be purchased as complete meals or in separate portions of meat, vegetables and fruit. Due to the high cost of freeze-drying, manufacturers have concentrated on products with high food value, such as meat, poultry and fish. Most freeze-dried food will be palatable if the instructions for preparing it are strictly followed.

Some of the freeze-dried breakfasts available are eggs with bacon, cheese omelettes with apple sauce, sausage patties and granola with freeze-dried blueberries. Lunches include freeze-dried tuna salad, chicken salad and cottage cheese. The largest selection of freeze-dried meals are the dinners. The backcountry gourmet can choose from rib eye steaks, pork chops, beef stroganoff, chili con carne, chicken chop suey, shrimp creole, lasagna, beef almondine, chicken stew, beef stew, turkey tetrazzini, chicken with rice, tuna à la neptune, cheese romanoff, turkey supreme and spaghetti with freeze-dried meat balls. Vegetables available separately include freeze-dried green peas, green beans, carrots and corn.

To complete this freeze-dried smorgasbord with dessert, a hiker can have vanilla, chocolate or strawberry flavored ice cream, blueberry or raspberry cobbler, banana cream pudding or no-bake pineapple cheesecake with graham cracker crust.

Freeze-dried food manufacturers are notorious for being overly optimistic in the suggested number of servings marked on each package. A dinner intended for four servings will usually satisfy only two or three hungry hikers. One way to extend freeze-dried dinners is to add instant rice or noodles.

The empty aluminum foil pouches that remain after you've eaten their contents will not burn no matter how hard you try. Slip them into your litter bag and pack them out with the rest of your garbage.

Trail Snacks

Most hikers like to take a break about once an hour to rest, drink water and have something to eat. Foods high in carbohydrates are best for snacking on during rest stops. *Gorp* is the name that has been given to a snacking mixture containing some of these quick energy foods: raisins, currants, dates, peanuts, chocolate chips, dried fruit, coconut, roasted soybeans, pumpkin seeds, sunflower seeds, cashews, almonds, walnuts and other nuts. Mix the gorp in a plastic bag and keep it in a pocket that you can easily reach for on those short stops when you don't take your pack off. Quick energy snacks are easy to make. (See 'Suggested Reading' at the end of this chapter.)

Sprouts

An excellent way to satisfy the cravings for fresh vegetables that often develop on long backpacking trips is to eat sprouts which you can grow in your pack as you hike. Sprouts are the germinated seeds of a number of plants. They provide roughage, usually lacking in dehydrated and freeze-dried foods, and are high in protein, minerals and vitamins B, C and E. Alfalfa sprouts are easy to grow on a backpacking trip and taste delicious. They can be added to sandwiches, soups and omelets, and steamed with rice, bulgur and other grains. They are good as salads and as garnishes on macaroni, freeze-dried stews and casseroles.

To grow sprouts: Soak two tablespoons of alfalfa seeds (available in health food stores) overnight in a wide-mouth plastic bottle. In the morning drain the water and stretch a piece of nylon or cheesecloth over the mouth of the bottle, and secure it with a rubber band. Keep the bottle in a part of your pack where it will be out of the light but not cut off from air. The seeds must be kept moist and should be rinsed through the strainer twice a day.

At the end of the second day little sprouts will appear. On the third or fourth day expose the sprouts to sunlight by carrying them in a plastic bag on top of your pack. The sunlight produces chlorophyll, which rapidly turns the sprouts green. The sprouts are now at the peak of flavor and nutritional value, and are ready to eat. Start some of your seeds before leaving and the sprouts will be ready early in your trip. Mung beans, soybeans, mustard seeds and lentils are some of the many seeds that can be sprouted.

Water

On most of Canada's trails finding fresh drinking water should not be a problem. In areas where the purity of the water is questionable—if there is even just the slightest doubt—it's best to play it safe and purify the water. Boil the water for at least 20 minutes to insure killing all the bacteria, or treat the water with halozone tablets, which are available in drugstores and hiking equipment shops. Halozone gives the water a chlorine taste which can be masked with powdered juice crystals. Conscientious hikers should do their best to safeguard the water supply by not permitting anyone to wash themselves or their dishes in any lake, river or stream.

Fishing and Wild Food

The hiker's diet can often be supplemented with fish or edible wild plants. The lakes and streams along many of Canada's trails contain trout and other fish that hikers with angling equipment can catch and eat fresh. Telescoping and other fishing rods that attach to packs are available. Be sure to inquire about fishing regulations and licenses.

Hikers on trails along ocean beaches have long supplemented their food supply with fresh mussels, clams and other shellfish from the tidal pools. Before you start beachcombing, find out about red tides and possible local pollution that can make shellfish poisonous.

Edible wild plants gathered fresh from the wilderness are at their tastiest and most nutritious. Raspberries, blueberries, and cranberries are some of the many wild berries that can be picked and eaten fresh. Try boiling a cupful of berries to spread on pancakes. A crisp backcountry salad can be made of wild leeks, fiddlehead ferns, white trilliums and other edible wild greens. Edible mushrooms can be sauteed in margarine and add a gourmet touch to dinner.

If you are not absolutely certain a berry, plant or mushroom is edible, it's best to leave it alone. Study a book on edible wild food and learn a few of the safe, easily recognizable varieties that grow in the area you hike in.

Planning a Menu

Many beginning hikers worry about starving in the wilderness and as a result overload their packs with too much food. Carefully planning your menu in advance is the best way to ensure that you don't bring an excess of food or run short. Make a chart with three columns labelled breakfast, lunch and supper, and mark the days of your trip in the margin. Write the foods and amounts required for each meal in the proper space. Keep to simple one-pot meals, especially if you're cooking on a stove. Using the menu, draw up a shopping list and buy the food. Don't forget trail snacks.

Packing Food

Preparing meals on the trail will be easier if you organize the food at home. Carrying just the amount required of each food, rather than the whole box, reduces the weight and bulk of your load. Transfer the amount of dry ingredients required for each meal into individual plastic bags. For food that may be confused, such as sugar, powdered milk and flour, label the bags with masking tape. This process, which takes little time at home, is a great convenience on the trail. It saves fumbling around with a measuring cup at suppertime as darkness approaches. It also ensures that you will not run out of food because an over-enthusiastic cook used too much of one ingredient for one or more meals. Make sure you pack the food in strong plastic bags and close them with a twist tie—for there is nothing worse than opening your pack to come across your flour, salt, sugar and coffee in one rock-like clump stuck to your maps like hardened glue.

Food and Water Containers

Hiking equipment shops carry a large variety of plastic food containers. Plastic bottles can be used to carry grains, beans and other dry food. The poly squeeze tubes hold jam, honey, peanut butter and margarine. In cold weather, the contents of these tubes become hard and are difficult to squeeze out. Salt, pepper and other spices can be carried in small plastic bottles or in an old 35 mm film container. Egg carriers of durable plastic, in six- and twelve-egg sizes, are available for hikers who want fresh eggs in the morning. You can also carry eggs without the shell in a wide-mouth plastic bottle.

For carrying water while hiking there are several types of water bottles. The narrow-mouth poly bottles with attached screw-on caps are popular. Some hikers prefer the wide-mouth bottles that will fill with water more quickly, an advantage when you submerge the bottle in an ice-cold mountain stream.

A group of hikers may consider using a collapsible water carrier at camp. Available in 5-, 10- and 20-litre (1½- and 5-gallon) sizes, these water carriers enable you to get all the water needed for a meal at one time, eliminating frequent trips to the stream with a one-litre (one-quart) bottle.

Campfires

There is a certain romance associated with campfires. At the end of a day on the trail, after the tents have been set up and supper devoured, sitting around the fire is a relaxing way to pass the evening. The warm glow exuded by the fire draws hikers close together to talk about the trail, the next day's hike and thoughts on life. Some of the good memories associated with campfires are the group sing-alongs. Harmonicas, recorders, spoons and kazoos are some of the musical instruments suitable for hiking, and add to the enjoyment of backcountry concerts.

Many national and provincial parks discourage the use of

fires, encouraging hikers to carry backpacking stoves for cooking needs. Some parks have gone so far as to prohibit campfires. The large increase in the number of people in the backcountry has made these restrictions necessary. In the one kilometer radius surrounding campsites on popular trails, every shred of dead wood has been gathered and burnt, and there is virtually no firewood left. Hikers may find campfires are prohibited during hot, dry weather, due to the high risk of forest fires.

There are many backcountry areas in Canada that have a plentiful supply of deadfall where hikers can safely build campfires with a clear conscience. If you are hiking in such an area and decide to build a fire, begin by finding a safe site for a firebowl. Chances are there will already be one at the campsite, and you should use it rather than making another. If there isn't, collect stones and put them in a small circle to confine the fire, and clear a one-meter circle of all loose burnable material

around the firebowl. The safest place for a campfire is on rock, or on sandy or clay soil. If you must locate the fire on loam soil, line the bottom of the firebowl with rocks. Loam soil has roots and other organic material that will burn. The fire can smoulder along roots and, when it eventually reaches the surface, can cause a forest fire.

Collect a good supply of dry tinder and twigs. White birch makes excellent tinder as it burns slowly with a lot of heat even when damp. Take bark that has already fallen off the tree. Don't strip live trees. Crumple the tinder into a ball and put it in the center of the firebowl. Starting with the small twigs and adding sticks of gradually increasing thickness, build a teepee-shaped structure around the tinder. When this is completed, light the tinder. The flame should soon have the kindling and larger wood burning. If the fire requires air, blow gently at its base. Don't add more wood until the base of the fire is burning well as you might suffocate it.

Keep the fire small. A good campfire can be had using wood about three cm (one inch) in diameter, which is about the thickness of the length of your thumb. There is no need to weigh down your pack with an axe, hatchet, saw or machete, which will only scar the forest. Any wood that you can break in your hands or against a rock is suitable. Dead wood snaps easily when broken. Green wood is still living, does not snap and will not burn. Rotting wood usually contains moisture and burns poorly. Gather only enough wood to use during your stay.

Softwoods such as balsam, poplar, pine, cedar and spruce are easy to ignite and burn quickly, and are the best for starting a fire. Hardwoods are more difficult to ignite but burn slower, give off more heat and produce coals that are best for cooking. Once the fire is burning well add such hardwoods as birch, maple, elm and ash.

In wet weather, a fire is appreciated for its warmth and is often needed for drying out wet clothes. Starting a campfire under damp conditions may be more difficult, but it can be done. Begin by stripping the wet bark off dead wood and using the dry center from which you can shave slivers to use as kindling. If you still cannot get a fire started, pour a small quantity of gas from your fuel bottle to help ignite the kindling.

If you plan to use campfires in a wet area, bring a chemical fire starter such as the solid hydrocarbon fuel tablets, or a tube of fire ribbon, which is smeared on wet wood. Once ignited the tablets or ribbon burn for a long time.

The rules for putting out a fire should be well known. Drown the ashes with water and stir until they are cool to touch, and drench the fire-ring rocks. When breaking camp at a virgin campsite where you've made the firebowl, remove every trace of the fire by returning the firebowl rocks to their original locations and scattering the ashes and leftover wood.

Grates

Supporting pots over the fire can be a tricky business, as anyone who has crunched on the remains of pea soup scooped from the sand and stolen back from the ants already knows. It's often possible to arrange logs or stones so that the pots can balance on them, but extra care must be taken to ensure that the pots are steady and do not tip over, spilling your supper and putting out the fire in the process. A metal grate makes cooking on a fire easier and less worrisome. Backpacking grates sell for $5 to $6. One type has folding legs for better stability and weighs 340 gm (12 ounces). The other which is supported on rocks, weighs about 115 gm (4 ounces). Cake racks weighing 115 gm (4 ounces) and selling for around $2 in the kitchenware department of supermarkets make excellent lightweight grates.

Matches

Always carry a plentiful supply of matches in a moisture-proof container. If you expect to encounter wet and windy weather you may want to carry matches that are waterproof and windproof. You can make waterproof matches by dipping the head of wooden matches in melted wax. Scrape the wax off the tips before using them.

Safety matches have to be ignited on the striker panel on the matchbox. They won't light on any abrasive surface such as zippers, rocks, leather soles as strike-anywhere matches will. If you are bringing safety matches be sure to take the box with the striker.

Wrap an emergency supply of matches in plastic and keep them in your pack. Some hikers bring a butane lighter in addition to matches.

Stoves

Many hikers use stoves not only for ecological reasons but for convenience and to save time. With a stove you don't have to spend a half hour gathering wood and building a fire while you're famished. On rainy days, a stove is very advantageous and during very hot weather cooking over a stove is more pleasant than dealing with a hot open fire. The regulating valve found on most models gives you more control of the heat than cooking over a fire does. It permits you to boil water quickly, or simmer a freeze-dried dinner. Backpacking stoves can be divided between those that burn white gas and those that operate with a butane cartridge.

Butane Stoves

Butane cartridge stoves are the simplest to operate. The cartridges contain pressurized butane gas that vaporizes instantly when vented to atmospheric pressure. No priming, preheating or pumping is required. Just open the valve and light. Unlike white gas stoves there is no fuel to spill and butane burns quietly.

Butane does have disadvantages. The cartridges weigh more for the same amount of heating energy, and butane is more expensive than white gas and has a lower maximum heat output, which means a longer cooking time. As the butane cannister empties of fuel, the pressure and the stove's heat output decrease making the cooking time even longer. The

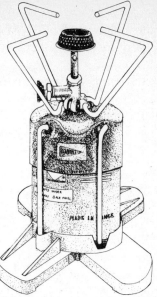

Bleuet S-200 butane stove

cartridge cannot be changed until it is empty. As butane freezes at −9°C (15°F) and does not operate effectively at temperatures below freezing, butane stoves are impractical for winter use.

The Gaz S200-S Bleuet stove was the first butane stove available and is the best known and the most widely sold. It costs about $25 and weighs 400 gm (14 ounces) without a cartridge. A butane cartridge lasts about three hours, weighs 100 gm (4 ounces) and costs about $2.50.

White Gas Stoves

White gas stoves are better suited for longer trips. They burn hotter than butane stoves and the fuel is cheaper. White gas backpacking stoves are manufactured by Svea, Optimus, Phoebus, Coleman and MSR. The traditional Svea 123, which weighs 510 gm (1 pound, 2 ounces), has a built-in windscreen and sells for $60, and the Optimus 8R which weighs 700 gm

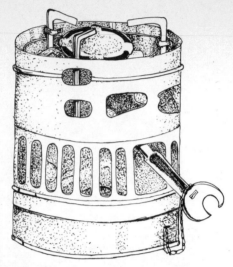

Svea 123R white gas stove

(1 pound, 9 ounces), is carried in a sturdy steel box and also costs $60. Neither has a built-in pump but an optional mini-pump manufactured by Optimus attaches to the fuel tank cap and increases the efficiency of the stoves during cold weather.

The newer stoves have built-in pumps and are lightweight for backpacking. Good examples of these are the Coleman Peak 1 at 1 kg (2 pounds) and around $60 and the MSR stove which uses a fuel bottle as the stove's reservoir. The MSR has a high heat output and weighs only 310 gm (11 ounces) about $60. Both the Coleman and MSR stoves are available in multi-fuel models which burn kerosene in addition to white gas.

The Optimus 111B, weighing 1½ kg (3 pounds, 8 ounces) and selling for $80 is better suited for winter camping and for large groups where the extra heating capacity is needed and the weight can be shared.

White gas stoves are noisier than butane stoves and, because they have more parts, are more likely to break down. Spare parts can be purchased, and it's a good idea to carry a spare burner plate and burner head. Problems with white gas stoves can be avoided by using the proper fuel. Blazo or Coleman fuel,

Optimus 8R

which are cleaner than white gas, are best. Automobile gasoline burns dirty and gums up the nozzle.

White gas is a liquid that is very flammable, and it should be carried in a metal leakproof container. The aluminum Sigg Fuel bottles, available in liter and half-liter sizes, fit easily into a side pocket of your pack, away from your food and clothing. A vented pouring cap, sold separately, makes pouring easier and eliminates the need for a funnel and eye dropper.

Operating a White Gas Stove

Lighting a white gas stove is a little complicated. The whole process centers around priming, the purpose of which is to heat the vaporizing chamber so that the fuel burns as a gas rather than in its liquid form.

To start a Svea or Optimus stove, first turn the throttle to the cleaning position. A needle will rise through the orifice and remove soot and anything else that can block the passage of the vaporized fuel. On older models, which have a separate cleaning needle, plunge it into the orifice several times. After this is done, turn the valve to the off position, remove the tank cap and fill the reservoir with fuel. A funnel makes pouring easier and reduces waste.

The next step is to prime the stove by heating the vaporizing tube located between the tank and the burner. Using an eye dropper, withdraw gas from the tank and fill the priming cup at the bottom of the burner. Close the tank and put the fuel bottle away from the stove. Ignite the fuel in the cup and let it heat the vaporizing chamber. When the flame is nearly out, open the valve. A roaring blue flame should come out around the burner plate. If this does not happen, it is probably because the gas in the vaporizing tube has not been sufficiently heated. Try priming the stove again.

The manufacturer's instructions with some stoves say to warm the tank in your hands, which will force some gas out of the nozzel into the priming cup, and then ignite the fuel after closing the valve. This method does work, but most hikers find filling the priming cup directly much more efficient.

Before taking your stove on a trip, practise lighting it a couple of times in the backyard at home to learn its idiosyncrasies. You should soon have filling the tank, priming and lighting the stove down to a simple routine.

Safety

All stoves and fuel should be treated with caution. Don't overheat the stove by insulating the tank, or preventing adequate circulation of air by using the Svea 123 with windscreen inside a Sigg Cookset. Keeping the regulating valve open the whole way will also overheat the stove. When a white gas stove is overheated the safety valve will blow, releasing gas vapor, which often immediately ignites.

The need to follow safe procedures when using a stove cannot be overemphasized. Don't use an excessive amount of gas to prime the stove. Fill the tank away from all open flames, and never when the stove is hot. If the stove runs out of fuel in the middle of cooking a meal, let the stove cool before refilling it. If a small flame remains when you've turned the valve off, just blow it out. Don't open the fuel tank to release the pressure; it will allow gas vapor to escape and ignite in a ball of flames.

Be extra careful when using a stove inside a tent. Ensure that the stove is stable so that it won't tip over and ignite your sleeping bag or the tent itself. Open the tent flap slightly, even if there is a blizzard outside, to keep a flow of fresh air into the tent to eliminate the danger of carbon monoxide poisoning and asphyxiation. It's safest to use the stove outside whenever possible.

Cookware

The size of the hiking group usually decides what pots and pans will be taken on a trip. A solo hiker can often get by with one small pot for cooking and eating. Parties of four or more usually require two or more larger pots.

The billies, kettles and cook sets sold in hiking gear shops are made of lightweight aluminum and are easy to clean. Many of the billies have tight-fitting covers that double as frying pans. The Sigg nesting pots have a 2-cm (¾-inch) wide handle that locks in an upright position for ease in lifting and pouring. The set of three pots have capacities of 1½, 2 and 3 1 (1½, 2 and 3 quarts) and weigh 250, 300 and 400 gm (9, 11 and 14 ounces). The Sigg tourist cook set is a compact kit combining a Svea 123 stove with pots of 2½- and 3½-l (1½- and 3½-pint) capacity, a lid that is also a frying pan and a pot gripper. A large variety of cook sets comprising a small pot, frying pan, plates and plastic cup, intended for one or two persons, are widely available.

If you need a good pan for frying pancakes or freshly caught trout, and find the pans included in cooksets inadequate, get a lightweight, non-stick aluminum frying pan. These weigh 360 gm (12 ounces) and cost about $15.

A pot-gripper is very handy for handling hot pots. The steel pot-gripper with a spring-loaded grip holds heavy pots best. This small item weighs 60 gm (2 ounces).

Eating Utensils

Many hikers limit their eating ware to a cup and a spoon. There are some instances, though, when a fork comes in handy: so you may want to carry one. An insulated plastic cup can be used for eating and drinking. Some hikers, particularly those who hike in large groups and prepare meals in one big pot, may find just a cup insufficient and also bring plastic bowls and plates.

A pocketknife, such as one of the Swiss Army knives, has many uses on a hiking trip, including cooking and eating. A knife equipped with two blades, can opener, reamer and corkscrew is sufficient for most backpackers. The fully equipped luxury models which include magnifying glass, scissors and a miniature wood saw tend to be too bulky and heavy for a shirt or pants pocket. If your knife doesn't have a can opener, get a separate one, such as the ½-ounce (15 gm) G.I. type.

Dishwashing

To wash dishes in the backcountry, you need a nylon or copper scouring pad to loosen the food off the plates, and a small amount of biodegradable detergent and hot water to cut grease. Heat water in the largest pot and use it as a wash basin.

Don't bother scrubbing the carbon off the bottom of pots used in a wood fire, as it holds and spreads the heat more efficiently. Carry the blackened pots in a stuff sack to keep the rest of your pack clean.

The dirty dishwater should be dumped on the ground, away from lakes and streams, preferably on soil that is deep enough to absorb and decompose the waste. Don't permit other hikers to pollute the water source with their dishwater.

Suggested Reading

The Hungry Hiker's Books of Good Cooking by Gretchen McHugh (Knopf).

The Expedition Cookbook, by Carolyn Gunn (Chockstone Press).

The One-Burner Gourmet, by Harriet Barker (Contemporary Books).

Gorp, Glop and Glue Stew, by Yvonne Prater and Ruth Dyer Mendenhall (The Mountaineers).

The Snack Bar Gourmet, by Marsha Eines (Firefly Books) focuses on making quick-energy trail snacks.

Supermarket Backpacker, by Harriet Barker (Greatlakes Living Press 1977).

The Well Fed Backpacker, by June Fleming (Vintage Books).

Putting Food By, by Ruth Hertzberg, Beatrice Vaughan and Janet Greene (New York: Bantam Books 1973), includes chapters on home food dehydrating and sprouting seeds.

4

Biting Insects

MOST hikers have a horror story to tell about camping during blackfly and mosquito season. They often go something like this: You have hiked from mountain top to lake, and now, tired but nearly content, you settle down for supper and to watch the sun shout its last hurrah for the day. But wait, what is that black cloud hovering yonder, emitting

buzzsaw-like sounds? Within seconds the sound has become a not-so-dull roar and there are monsters chipping and mangling every available pore. The next sound is your scream as you dash for your tent, all thoughts of food forgotten.

Biting insects are found in many of Canada's natural areas. Employing the proper defenses against these pests can mean the difference between an enjoyable outdoor experience and a nightmare.

Mosquitoes and Flies

A legend from the Canadian North on the origin of the mosquito says that Kitch Manitou, the nature spirit underlying the world and life, was angered when one day all the men married all the women. A universal honeymoon began and

Mosquito

there was no one to harvest the rice and corn. The angry spirit created the mosquito and sent forth swarms of the maddening bugs to work his will. All romance and intimacy disappeared and the honeymoon suddenly ended.

Mosquitoes, called flying piranhas by some, are encountered during the spring and summer, and are most active at dusk and at night, and during overcast days. Only the females bite as they require the blood to produce eggs. The irritating reaction in humans is caused by anticoagulant injected by the mosquito to thin the blood.

The itching is usually minor and temporary. The only disease known to have been transmitted by mosquitoes in Canada is equine encephalitis, a virus that fortunately is very rare. It is that buzzling sound and the swarm of mosquitoes around ears, eyes and nose that can drive hikers mad.

Although blackflies are widespread throughout Canada, the worst areas are northern Ontario, Quebec and the muskeg areas of the Canadian Shield. Ontario's Algonquin Park in June is filled with hungry bugs. It's not safe to yawn unless you desire a mouthful of pests. Unlike mosquitoes, blackflies attack only during the day and are most active at daybreak and at dusk. In warm and humid weather they feast all day.

Blackflies like to bite shaded areas of exposed skin such as

Blackfly

around the collar, hairline and under hat rims and sunglasses. They are very persistent and will penetrate beneath clothing and into the nose, ears and eyes. A bite from a blackfly is painless but irritation due to a histamine reaction from the fly's digestive juices usually sets in. The bites leave red bleeding spots, and can be severe enough to cause painful swelling requiring medical attention.

No-see-ums are flies so tiny that they can be mistaken for pieces of dust. Usually found in lowland areas, no-see-ums' bites give an itchy feeling all over. If perchance you find yourself snugly encamped in your bugproof tent yet feel ravenous hordes attacking your body, don't panic. Let the thoughts of poison ivy and fleas recede, and you will probably find that no-see-ums have snuck inside your haven. Your only hope is to move to higher, windier ground.

Horseflies and deerflies are large insects found in open woodlands, located near water. They attack only during the day, and their bite is very painful. Insect repellants are not effective against these flies, and they are best killed with a strong slap.

An important defense against biting insects is dressing properly. Loose clothing with a tight weave will protect most of your body. Long-sleeved shirts should be closed at the collar and wrists. Tuck the cuff of full-length pants into socks or boots. Headnets will keep the bugs from biting your face.

Dark colors attract mosquitoes and blackflies, so avoid black, red, blue and dark-brown clothing. Both bugs are very attracted to blue jeans. Wear light colors. White and yellow are best.

An effective insect repellant is vital to preserving one's sanity during blackfly and mosquito season. Repellants block the sensors on the insect's antennae and prevent the bugs from landing and biting. However, the pests remain only a few meters away swarming around you, and will land on untreated areas of your body.

Most insect repellants contain M, M-diethyl-meta-toluamide (diethyl toluamide or DEET for short) as the sole or one of the active ingredients. The percentage of active ingredients, which is indicated on the container, determines the strength of the repellant and the length of time it is effective. For broad range protection on a trip in the backcountry, use a repellant that contains the highest percentage of active ingredients.

Apply repellant evenly to all exposed skin and clothing, especially around the neck and waist. Liquid and cream repellant, are lighter, take up less space in your pack and are cheaper. The repellant should keep bugs off you for several hours unless it is washed off by water or perspiration.

What you eat can make you attractive to hungry insects. After eating bananas, for example, your skin exudes an odour that is very attractive to mosquitoes. If you eat garlic, however, the odour exuded from your skin keeps biting insects away—and perhaps your hiking companions also.

Floral scents attract bugs, so don't use colognes, scented soaps or shampoos while in the outdoors. Do wash though, as mosquitoes like warmth and humidity, and are more attracted to people who perspire a lot.

When choosing a campsite, look for a dry and open area that has a breeze to keep insects from clustering. Tall grass and thick woods should be avoided as they break the wind. Most important, stay away from areas with stagnant water where mosquitoes breed.

A smudge fire can help keep mosquitoes away from your camp. Green grass or green pine needles on a bed of glowing coals will produce thick smoke, and as the smoke drifts through the campsite the bugs will go elsewhere. Most important to the hiker is a good night's rest so shop carefully for a bug-proof tent. At night you can retreat into the insect-free interior for a peaceful sleep.

No matter how well prepared you are—dressed in light colors, bathed in repellant and smelling of garlic—some insects may get through and you may get bitten. Calamine lotion helps reduce the swelling and relieve the itch. A paste of baking soda and water is also effective. If abnormal swelling develops, consult a physician when you get back.

Ticks

Ticks are wingless parasites about five millimeters long that are found in open areas such as trails, clearings and the edge of forests. Of the 20 species in Canada, only the Rocky Mountain Wood Tick and the American Dog Tick bite humans. Encounters with them are most likely to occur in the southern interior of Alberta and British Columbia during spring and early summer. Rocky Mountain Wood Ticks are feared as carriers of Rocky Mountain Spotted Fever, but very few cases of tick-related diseases have been reported in Canada. The disease, which formerly was fatal, is now easily cured by antibiotics. Ticks are also associated with the spread of Lyme disease.

Ticks give a painless bite and begin to feed on your blood. When hiking in tick country, wear long pants treated with insect repellant and at the end of the day inspect your body and scalp. If a tick has dug into your skin, touching it with a drop of repellant, kerosene or gas may induce it to withdraw. If this doesn't work, hold the front part of the tick and pull slowly.

Tick

Should parts of the mouth remain in the skin, remove them like an ordinary splinter and treat with antiseptic.

Wasps, Hornets and Bees

These insects generally leave people alone except to investigate brightly colored clothing they mistake for flowers. Like mosquitoes and flies they are also attracted to perfumes and sweet scents. They will bite humans only when threatened. Hornet nests are located on the ground, and care should be taken not to disturb them. Wasps and hornets can sting several times. Bees lose their stinger in the wound. If you are bitten by a bee, remove the stinger by scraping across the skin with a knife.

To treat a sting, apply a cold compress and a baking soda paste. If you are allergic to the venom from these insects, consult a physician and carry medication to take in case of bites.

5

Routefinding

FINDING your way on well-marked trails is a simple matter of following the blazes or cairns along the well-worn path. A map and compass come into use for determining the distance to the next shelter, campsite or stream. When hiking cross-country or on poorly blazed trails, an accurate map and a dependable compass are essential.

In areas where several trails converge, which can cause

"What do you mean, you don't know?"

confusion, consult the map at junctions where the trail isn't clearly indicated. If you're hiking in a group, someone should wait at the junction to indicate the correct path.

If you lose the trail, stop and return to the last blaze if visible. If a blaze cannot be seen, two or three members of the party should spread out and look for the trail. If they can't find it, determine the group's location on the map and plot a route to the trail.

Practise using a map and compass in different situations. If you become lost or confused in the wilderness, these navigating techniques can get you out safely.

A hiker receives directions from park ranger in British Columbia's Mount Assiniboine Provincial Park. (B.C. Government Photograph)

Topographical Maps

Always carry a detailed map of the area you are hiking in. The 1:50,000 series topographical maps published by the Department of Energy, Mines and Resources indicate every dirt road, trail, stream, river, lake and cabin in the wilderness. The physical relief of the terrain is portrayed with contour lines; brown lines that join points of the same elevation. Widely spaced contour lines represent a gentle slope, while lines that are close together indicate a steep hillside or cliff. Valleys and concave slopes appear as a series of V-shaped contours that point upstream. Ridges and convex slopes are a pattern of downhill pointing Vs. A series of rough circles or closed loops represents a summit or hilltop.

With experience, you can look at a topographical map and have a mental picture of the land. For a backpacking trip get maps in advance and use them to plan your route, select campsites and organize a rough itinerary that will prepare you for difficult sections and give you some idea of landmarks.

The relationship between a distance on the map and the actual distance on the ground is known as the scale, In the 1:50,000 series, 2 cm on the map equals 1 km on the ground.

Include a 15-cm (6-inch) flexible plastic ruler in your map kit for measuring distances on the map. A cardboard ruler known as a "roamer," which indicates distances in miles and kilometres, is available from the Canada Map Office. It can also be used for pinpointing grid references. A map measurer, a mechanical device used for determining distance on a mapsheet, has a little wheel that is run over the course you wish to follow and the distance is indicated on the device's dial. The distance is as though the trail were flat; this can be deceiving in mountainous country.

When in the backcountry, carry maps in a clear plastic bag (such as a freezer bag with a zip-top seal) or a map case to keep them clean and dry. In windy or rainy weather, fold the map so it can be read without removing it from the case.

opographical maps for the entire country can be purchased from the Canada Map Office, 615 Booth Street, Ottawa, Ontario, K1A 0E9, telephone: (613) 952-7000. Request a Regional Map Index, available free of charge, for the region you are interested in. There are three indexes; number 1 covers Eastern Canada, number 2 is for Western and parts of Northern Canada, and index 3 covers the remainder of the North. Follow the instructions on the index to identify the maps you require. When you receive the maps, check the date that they were published. Older maps may be less useful in locating trails, as roads, trails and buildings constructed since that date will not be indicated.

Topographical maps can also be obtained from provincial government departments responsible for recreation, conservation and natural resources, and from map dealers. A complete list of suppliers is available from the Canada Map Office. Maps for national parks and provincial parks can often be ordered from park offices, but be sure to check in advance.

The Compass

Carry a dependable compass with you and know how to use it. The better compasses are liquid filled; the needle settles into position quickly and stays stable. Many compasses have sighting devices for taking precise bearings. Along with the four cardinal points—north, south, east and west—modern compasses have an azimuth, a 360°-marking system which allows for more accurate direction-finding. To keep your compass accessible, hang it around your neck with a string and slip the compass into your shirt pocket.

Most compasses have a pivoting needle that has one end marked with the letter *N* or colored red, black or blue to indicate north. The needle does not point to true north everywhere in Canada, but to magnetic north. The magnetic north pole is located on Bathurst Island about 1,560 km (970 miles) south of the true north pole. The compass needle points to true north only along the agonic line, which runs from Thunder Bay through Churchill to the magnetic pole. The difference in degrees between true north and magnetic north is known as the declination. The local declination usually is indicated in the margin of a topographical map. East of the agonic line you add the number of degrees of declination to the bearing, and west of the line you subtract. Some compasses have a small screw to make semi-permanent adjustments that save correcting for declination each time you take a bearing.

Navigating with a Map and Compass

The first step in finding your way with a map and compass is to orient the map. The easiest way is to line up the known landmarks with their symbols on the map. To orient the map

Place the compass edge on the map along the desired line of travel between your present location and your objective.

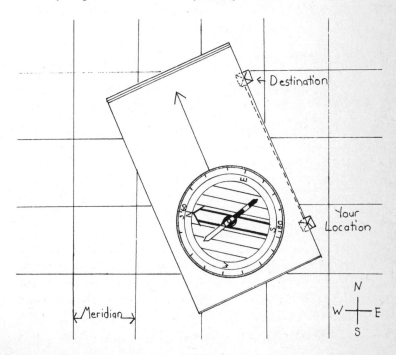

using a compass, place the compass on the map with the direction-to-travel arrow parallel with map north and the meridan lines on the map. Turn the map and compass together until the needle points to the number of degrees east or west of north which is the local declination. The map is now oriented. Be sure to keep the compass away from metallic objects such as belt buckles, knives, photo meters and lighters, which can affect the accuracy of the compass.

When the map is oriented the next step is to determine your location on the map. If you know your position relative to a distinct landmark such as a trail junction, bridge or mountain, this should be no problem. Make a point of observing the terrain you are hiking through. Count the number of creeks you

Turn the compass dial until the north-south lines on the base of the compass are parallel with the meridian lines on the map and the N on the compass points to north on the map.

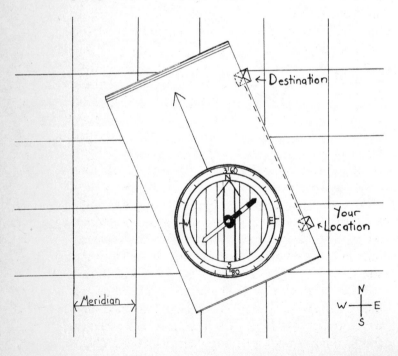

cross, the number of mountains you climb over and other distinct landmarks that can be identified on the map.

If you do not know your position on the map, you can use triangulation to determine it. This method involves taking a bearing on three natural features or landmarks that can be identified on the map. Make a line on the map from the first landmark at the same angle as your compass reading to that point. Repeat this procedure for two other features. The point where the three lines intersect on the map is your approximate location.

To take a bearing on a landmark, face the object and hold the compass with the direction-of-travel arrow pointing at the feature. Turn the dial on the compass until the needle is pointing to the *N*. The number of degrees indicated at the travel arrow is the bearing to the landmark.

To take a map bearing, place the compass edge on the map along the desired line of travel between your present location and your objective. Turn the compass dial until the north-south lines on the base of the compass are parallel with the meridian lines on the map, and the *N* on the compass points to north on the map. Without changing the dial setting, and keeping the compass horizontal, turn the entire compass until the needle points to north on the dial. Your destination is in the direction of the compass' travel arrow. To follow the compass bearing, look along the bearing, pick a landmark in this direction and hike there. When you reach this objective, sight with the compass to another landmark along the route and continue until you reach your destination.

A good practice when navigating with a map and compass is to establish a baseline, an unmistakeable feature that can act as a boundary of your trip area. A road, railway line, river, power line, cliff, lakeshore, sea coast, canyon or mountain range is suitable.

When aiming for a target located on a baseline such as a car, base camp, cabin or small lake, it is safer to make an intentional deviation, of several degrees in your compass bearing, than to follow the bearing directly to your objective. When you reach

Without changing the dial setting and keeping the compass horizontal turn the entire compass until the needle points to north on the dial. Your destination is in the direction of the compass' travel arrow.

your baseline following a bearing with an intentional deviation, you will know which way to turn to reach your objective. If you had set your compass bearing directly on your goal, a car for example, and you came out on the road around a bend and could not see the car, you would not know whether to turn left or right.

To measure the distance you have hiked, a pedometer can be used. This watchlike instrument is carried in a watch pocket or looped onto the belt. It operates on a rocker arm and spring principle. The length of your step is preset on the pedometer, and it counts the steps and totals the number of kilometers or miles covered by the wearer. As the length of a hiker's stride varies with the terrain, the pedometer gives only an approximate distance travelled.

Navigation by Natural Signs

On a clear night, true north can be found by looking at the sky and spotting Polaris, which is also known as the North Star. In latitudes below 60° north the bearing of Polaris is never more than 2¼° from true north. To locate the North Star find the Big Dipper and the two pointer stars on the outer lip. These stars point to Polaris which appears above the opening of the Big Dipper.

If you lose your compass, a watch and the sun can be used to tell direction. If daylight saving time is in effect, set the watch back to standard time. Place the watch flat and point the hour hand in the direction of the sun. South will lie halfway between the hour hand and 12 on the dial. Before 6 p.m. use the smallest angle shown and after 6 p.m. use the largest angle. At noon the sun will lie due south.

Suggested Reading

Be Expert with Map and Compass, by Bjorn Kjellstrom (New York: Charles Scribner's Sons, 1976), focuses on orienteering.

6

Children

DISCOVERING the natural world with children is a special experience. Time spent together in the outdoors is an opportunity for family closeness, a closeness not usually possible with the distractions at home, and on other types of outings. Parents will also find that they are recapturing some of the old thrill of discovery themselves, as they see flowers, insects and animals through the eyes of their offspring. Playing and learning go together in the outdoors, helping children and adolescents to become responsible and self-confident.

If children enjoy their hiking trips, they are more likely to develop an enthusiasm for wilderness activities and derive pleasure from them for the rest of their lives. But hiking can also be a terrible experience for both child and adult.

Hikes with children differ considerably from those exclusively for adults, and it's important that the children's needs be kept in mind. Parents, camp counselors, leaders of scout troops or of other youth groups should be aware of several important aspects of planning a trip that includes children.

At what age can a child start hiking? An infant can enjoy an outing from a carrier being carried by a parent. You can begin exploring short nature walks soon after your child can walk. For overnight or longer hiking trips, between five and eight years of age is a good time to start. The child can carry a small pack containing a sleeping bag, clothing and some food. Between the ages of nine and twelve, children are usually able

*Nature trail at Greenwater Lake Provincial Park, Saskatchewan.
(Saskatchewan Government Photograph)*

to carry more. It is for trips with children between the ages of five and twelve that the following is intended.

On the Trail

Adult goals on the trail are different from those of children. Your goal may be to reach a goal by a certain time and as group leader you march the children in line down the trail, making sure you keep to a schedule. A child's goal is to have fun. To make your children enthusiastic, see to it that their goal is accomplished.

Some parents fear that their children cannot endure the rigors of a hiking trip. After all, if Mom and Dad were exhausted after a short climb, how will their child do? Though they have less stamina, children are stronger and can usually walk farther than you think. Teach them to keep a steady pace rather than tearing down the trail.

Start with short hikes. If you want to do an overnight trip, try to schedule it for warm, dry weather, and when there are the fewest bugs. Mosquitoes and blackflies love children's tender skin. Since there are some bugs out during most of the summer, take proper precautions against biting bugs, by including insect repellants and proper clothing. (See the chapter on insects.)

The distance you plan to cover on an outing with children should be shorter and the pace slower than on adult trips. Choose a trail you are already familiar with. Until your children are older and more experienced hikers, avoid trips that involve bushwacking or scrambling over rocks.

Until children reach the age when they can carry their packs all day without complaining, it's a good idea to hike into a backcountry area and establish a base camp from which you can explore the surrounding mountains, lakes, meadows and glaciers on day hikes. Base-camping permits flexibility in your trip; should illness or injury occur, you can quickly retreat to the car.

Hiking continuously through monotonous scenery will

dampen a child's enthusiasm. Hikes along ocean beaches, lakeshores, riverbanks and through meadows keep the mind occupied—they are also easier walking.

Choose a trail that has frequent interesting features, and plan time to stop and look at wildflowers, plants, meadows, trees, birds, waterfalls, rockslides and mountain vistas. Parents might want to study some nature lore so they can tell their children about the environment. If you're familiar with the area's history, you can point out interesting landmarks and relate interesting stories about the early settlers, surveyors, Natives or *coureurs de bois* fur traders who first travelled in the region. Interpretive trails explore natural or historic themes.

Show the older children how to use a map and compass and ask them to calculate the family's position by identifying landmarks on the map. Involve them in following the route on the map.

To maintain the child's energy level, stop often for drinks and snacks. Some parents have a 15-minute rest stop every hour. Try to schedule your stops at interesting places. Encourage them to observe and listen to birds and other wildlife.

Most children will enjoy the trip more if a friend of their own age comes along. Compatible families may wish to go together. Take care that the group is not too large.

It's important to make your children aware of hazards in the backcountry, but don't overwhelm them with horror stories so that they fear the outdoors. Tell young children to stay within sight of parents all the time. As children reach their teenage years, they want the independence to walk faster and discover the country by themselves. Let them get ahead of you on the trail, but tell them to wait for the whole group at junctions, road crossings and the top of mountains and passes. Some parents give each child a whistle and tell them that if they get lost to blow three blasts on the whistle (three of anything is the universal distress signal). Assure them that they will be found if they stay in one place and don't wander around.

Warn your children about poison ivy and poison oak; inform them that most berries and plants are not edible and that they should check with you before picking any.

In Camp

You're on an overnight hike and after the choruses of "Are we almost there?" you finally arrive at the campsite. Take a few minutes with the children to celebrate or just sit down and rest. If you insist on getting to work setting up camp right away the children may be very irritable. Set up camp boundaries that you want your children to stay within.

Every child should be given a job to do. Otherwise they may get into mischief. It's a good idea to assign jobs before reaching the campsite so there won't be any squabbling over who gets what job. It's important to involve children even though it may take longer to set up camp with them helping. By performing the tasks they are learning and growing.

Some of the chores that children can do are setting up tents, going for water, helping out in cooking dinner, gathering wood if you're going to have a fire, cleaning the food off dishes after dinner and looking for a good tree for hanging the food.

The skills and experiences that children acquire in the backcountry build self-confidence and help them learn to accept responsibility. A child who seems to avoid trying a certain task may fear he is not doing a good job. For example, a child who is self-conscious about being unable to get a fire going successfully should be taught how to collect the right wood and build a fire.

The body loses a lot of water while hiking; encourage children to drink often. Children often forget that they're thirsty and it's a good idea to plan hot soup as the first course for dinner. A full water bottle kept in the tent eliminates those midnight stumbles to the stream to get water for children who awake thirsty in the middle of the night.

Babies

Parents who wish to bring infants on a walking or hiking trip with them can use a child-carrier pack.

A baby carrier for hiking should protect the child and possibly have a pocket for carrying some of the baby's gear. It should be comfortable for both the baby and the parent. A carrier that will stand on its own when placed on the ground is handy. In one type of carrier the child faces forward always seeing the parent. This design puts the child's weight close to the parent's back making it more comfortable. Some parents prefer the child to face to the rear to keep baby's fingers out of their ears and hair, and to lessen the chance of the baby getting hit in the face by swinging branches. Facing rearward the baby gets lonesome unless the other parent is close behind, and in this design the weight rides lower and tends to pull the parent over backward. Adding a padded hip belt to a carrier makes the load easier to carry.

The baby carriers that carry the baby on your front offer the best protection for the child but tend to strain harder on the adult's neck and muscles. Carriers that put the child on your back are more comfortable but you must take extra caution that branches or twigs do not hit your child.

When carrying a child in a carrier, never bend forward from the waist as it can throw the child head-first out of the carrier. If you have to reach for something on the ground, bend from the knees. Watch for low-hanging branches that can brush against the baby's face. Someone should hold the branches while the parent and baby pass.

From Two to Four Years

Toddlers between two and four years old may be more difficult to take hiking than babies. At that age the child is too heavy to be carried for long distances and cannot yet walk very far himself. As trips usually involve the child walking part of the way and being carried the rest of the way, parents may find that trips with toddlers are shorter and slower than with infants. Always keep an eye on toddlers. They haven't yet learned what is dangerous and are curious about everything in the new world around them. If you're camping, choose a site near a small stream, away from lakes and rivers that the child can fall into.

7

Winter

IN WINTER the wilderness is a quiet world of clean, sparkling white snow, crisp air, glistening snow-covered trees and magnificent ice sculptures formed by frozen waterfalls. As you travel through the forest and across frozen lakes you feel the snow packing under each step. At the end of a day, feelings of accomplishment are deliciously warm.

Although keeping warm on a winter trip requires more equipment, being able to wander in the cold winter landscape and be comfortable relying on just what you're carrying on your back gives a greater feeling of freedom and self-reliance than a summer trip.

Winters in Canada can be long. The first snow and the accompanying cool, frosty weather generally arrive in November. Winter conditions usually last until early April. At high elevations snow cover remains until May. Exploring the outdoors on cross-country skis or snowshoes for a day-outing or on a winter backpacking trip is a welcome escape from the gray, slush-covered city. The backcountry trails are free of summer crowds and also gone are the maddening blackflies and mosquitoes.

Once there is more than a foot of snow on the ground it is too soft to support your weight unless there is a thick crust of ice that can be walked on. Travelling over deep powder snow requires snowshoes or cross-country skis to distribute your weight over a larger area than just your boot alone. Without

Ski-touring in Quebec's Jacques Cartier Provincial Park. A rucksack is preferred for ski-touring as its center of gravity is low and does not interfere with the skier's balance. (Quebec Tourist Branch)

something to support you on the top of the snow, almost every step will sink into the snow and you'll be quickly frustrated at your inability to cover any significant distance.

Snowshoes

For travelling over unbroken snow on steep slopes and through thickly wooded areas, snowshoes are superior to cross-country skis. The snowshoes' better traction provided by the rough webbing permits snowshoers to walk straight up a slope that a cross-country skier would have to traverse back and forth or side-step, exerting more energy. The snowshoes' greater stability is appreciated when carrying a heavy pack.

You can become proficient with showshoes in a very short time before your first trip. Just strap the snowshoes on and walk naturally with your feet the normal distance apart, letting the snowshoes glide over each other. To make a turn, take several short steps rather than changing direction in one step. When climbing or descending a steep hill, traverse the hill in a series of switchbacks.

The Algonquin, Cree, beaver-tail and bear-paw are the snowshoe designs most widely available and each is intended for different conditions. The bear paw, which is wider and shorter than the others, can be maneuvered in flat, open terrain, but because of its width is more difficult for climbing and descending hills through thickly wooded areas. The Algonquin and Cree snowshoes are suited for most terrains, the tail on these designs keeps the snowshoes straight while you are walking. Combining the advantages of the bearpaw and the Algonquin, the beaver-tail, which is also known as the modified bear-paw as it's narrower than the bearpaw, is lighter and easier to handle. The aluminum-framed snowshoes with neoprene webs are lighter and smaller than wooden snowshoes, a desirable advantage if you expect to carry your snowshoes for long distances.

Skis

Cross-country skis are ideal for trips over open rolling terrain. Several categories of touring skis are available; light touring, touring and mountaineering. For day excursions, use light touring or touring skis. For winter backpacking, touring skis are generally used as they are wider and heavier than racing and light touring skis, and provide the stability required for skiing off prepared tracks. Mountaineering skis are used by skiers who climb peaks and ridges and ski down the open runs.

Cross-country skiing technique is similar to ice skating, and the rhythm of striding should come naturally. If you can walk, you can ski.

Winter Backpacking

The best way to learn the intricacies of camping in winter is to accompany an experienced winter backpacker. If you don't know anyone who can help you, look for winter camping trips offered by community colleges, outfitters, outing clubs and other outdoor organizations.

Winter backpacking requires more advance planning than does a summer trip. The worn paths and many landmarks have disappeared under a blanket of snow. Extra care is required in planning food and shelter, keeping warm, travelling over the snow, and watching for the signs of frostbite and hypothermia. The fewer hours of daylight limit the travelling time per day, making the schedule on a winter camping trip less flexible than during the summer when you can make up for starting late by hiking later in the day.

Anyone undertaking a winter trip should be experienced with backpacking in summer and autumn. Before going on an overnight or longer trip, take several winter day excursions to get an idea of snow conditions and how far you can travel in one day. It's also a chance to explore possible routes to determine if they are suited for travel with cross-country skis or if snowshoes are preferable.

Keeping Warm

The most important difference between summer and winter trips is the effort required to maintain normal body temperature in winter. The main ways of keeping warm on a winter trip are wearing warm clothing, eating foods that will provide heat energy and getting enough rest.

Clothing

The layer system of dressing applies in winter in the same way as it does in summer. Wearing several layers of light breathable clothing rather than a single heavy layer enables you to shed layers while skiing or doing any other vigorous activity. Avoid perspiring by wearing just enough clothing necessary to retain your body warmth. Clothing that is damp from perspiration or melted snow will chill the body. Get into the habit of brushing snow off all your clothes before it has a chance to melt.

Wool is the only natural material that will keep you warm when it's wet or dirty. Cotton absorbs and retains moisture and is not good for winter trips, except for fishnet underwear which is very useful in many temperatures.

Your inner garments, such as pants, shirts and sweaters, should be made of wool. Outer clothing should comprise a down or synthetic-fill parka with a hood, preferably a snorkel hood which extends for several centimeters in front of your face and possibly trimmed with fur, a windproof nylon anorak shell, mittens and a wool hat or balaclava. During the day while travelling or involved in other vigorous activities you may be comfortable wearing just a sweater and pants. Soon after stopping, though, you'll reach for the parka and other warm clothing in your pack.

During winter excursions your feet will soon feel like blocks of ice if you don't wear proper boots. Summer hiking boots wih an extra pair of socks are not sufficient for Canadian winters. They do not provide enough insulation and the tight fit created by the extra socks constricts the blood flow resulting in cold feet and frostbite.

For extreme dry cold conditions mukluks, with rubber soles and canvas or nylon uppers and duffle or felt liners, will keep your feet snug and toasty warm. Mukluks are not suitable for spring thaws or other wet periods as the upper portion soaks quickly. For travelling in wet snow use insulated all-rubber boots. The trapper pac boots with rubber soles and leather uppers are suitable for general winter use when wet conditions are only occasionally encountered.

Food and Water

To continuously produce the large amount of heat energy needed to keep warm, the winter hiker's diet must be very nutritious and high in protein, carbohydrates and fat. One advantage of hiking in winter is that it's possible to bring fresh meat and vegetables as they will keep in a frozen state until cooked.

Nutritious food is the fuel that maintains your body heat and prevents premature fatigue. Eating a piece of chocolate or other sweet food before going to bed will help keep you warm while you sleep. (For more information on nutrition and planning a proper menu see Chapter 3 "Food and Cooking Gear.")

Though you may not feel as thirsty as on a hot summer day, it is important to drink as much liquid as possible while winter camping since the body is dehydrated by the dry cold air. Consume at least 1½ litres (about 1½ quarts) per day. It is all right to eat snow when you're thirsty, though let it melt in your mouth to prevent chilling your stomach. However snow has relatively little water and eating a lot of it will chill and tire your body.

Start your trip with a full water bottle and when it's half empty refill it with wet, dense snow, which will soon melt into water. Keep the canteen upside-down to prevent the cap from freezing.

When choosing a campsite try to find a spot near an open

Winter camping in La Mauricie National Park, Quebec. Cooking is done on a closed-cell foam pad to prevent the stove from melting snow and sinking. (La Mauricie National Park)

stream or other running water. If the snow is deep and the water difficult to reach, tie a pot or cup to the end of a ski pole or stick and scoop the water from a safe distance. Camping near open water will save fuel and time by eliminating the time-consuming process of melting snow with the stove. Many pots of snow are required to produce a pot of water and melted snow has a stale taste that has to be covered with coffee, tea or powdered juice crystals.

Sleeping bags

Equipment that can be relied on to keep you warm is essential on a winter trip. Most important is a good quality sleeping bag rated to the lowest temperature you expect to encounter. If you don't want to buy a winter bag because of the cost or want more versatility than a single winter bag provides, use a lightweight sleeping bag inside a medium-weight bag. This arrangement will keep you warm but tends to be heavier than a single winter bag. If you decide to shop around for a winter bag check the loft: a winter bag rated to minus 30°C (minus 20°F) should have at least 12 cm (4¾ inches) of loft.

In winter a sleeping pad is essential. The full-length closed cell pads 1 or 1¼ cm (⅜ or ½ inch) thick provide the needed insulation. The Therm-a-Rests pads provide more insulation and are more comfortable than closed-cell foam pads. They're also heavier and cost more.

Winter Tents

The winter campsite should be sheltered from the wind. Trees are a good windbreak. When you've chosen a good spot, pack down a platform for the tent and the area in front of it with snowshoes or skis.

A tent for winter backpacking, like a summer tent, should keep you dry, warm and comfortable. Also important in a winter tent is roominess, especially space for you to sit up.

During the winter you spend many more hours per day inside the tent than during the summer, and blizzards may keep you inside for several days. A tent that has room for you to sit up and stretch your arms and legs will keep you from going stir crazy. During blizzards a tent equipped with a cooking hole covered with a zippered flap is helpful.

The poles on a winter tent should attach to the floor as well the top of the tent. The self-supporting tents are an advantage in this respect. If the poles go directly on the ground, put it on a piece of wood to keep the pole from sinking into the snow.

The tents designed for winter expeditions have several special features. Snow flaps are edges of the tent floor extending 20 to 25 (8 to 10 inches) which can be banked with snow to prevent high winds from getting under the tent. A frostliner is a canopy hung inside the tent to absorb the moisture that might otherwise condense and freeze on the tent walls. In the morning the frostliner is detached, the frost shaken off of it outside and then rehung inside the tent. A vestibule is an extra sheltered space in front of the tent and is very useful for stowing gear and for keeping snow out of the main part of the tent. These features are not essential for a snow camping tent. If you plan to camp in forested areas sheltered from high winds, a three season tent is adequate.

Packs

For ski-touring, an internal frame or frameless alpine pack with a waist belt is preferred over an external frame pack. The internal frame pack's narrow cut doesn't protrude on top or at the sides. When travelling on skis try to keep the pack's center of gravity low to prevent the pack from putting you off balance. External frame packs keep the weight high on the back; though desirable and comfortable for summer hiking, for ski-touring they tend to overbalance skiers causing them to fall. If you only have an external pack, put the heavier items near the bottom, the opposite of what you would do in the summer.

Stoves

The best stoves for winter camping are those equipped with pumps and burn white gas or kerosene. Suitable models are manufactured by Optimus, Primus, MSR, Phoebus and Coleman. The butane and propane cartridge stoves don't function at below-freezing temperatures.

If you plan to melt snow for water, the extra fuel needed should be included when calculating your fuel requirements. When using your stove outside put a closed-cell foam pad under the stove to prevent the stove from melting the snow and sinking into it. If you use the stove inside a tent ensure that there is adequate circulation of air to prevent carbon monoxide poisoning. (For more information on types of stoves, and stove safety, see Chapter 3.) If you want to cook on a wood fire, build it on a platform of green limbs to prevent it from sinking and being extinguished by melting snow.

Frostbite and Hypothermia

Two of the serious consequences of not being equipped for cold on a winter backpacking trip are frostbite and hypothermia.

Frostbite is the freezing of body tissue and, if serious, can result in permanent disability. Caused by reduced circulation in the extremities of the body, frostbite usually affects the hands, toes, feet, nose and ears. Superficial frostbite is characterized by a general numbness in the affected part and the flesh appears white and waxy. To restore circulation in hands, toes, or feet, warm the part with body heat by placing it on a bare stomach, armpit or hand. If the nose, ears or cheeks are frostbitten, hold a warm hand on the affected area.

Deep frostbite is more serious, and has a hard and woody feeling. A person with deep frostbite should be moved inside as soon as possible, preferably to a sterilized setting such as a hospital. Thaw the frozen part by immersing it in warm water with a temperature of 42° to 44°C (108° to 112°F). Rewarming should take 20 to 30 minutes and is usually very painful. The patient might have to keep off his feet for several weeks.

Never walk on thawed feet or toes as very serious loss of tissue is almost certain to result. Don't try to rewarm deep frostbite outside. Wait till the patient is in a warm place where he won't have to walk.

Several obsolete ideas on treating frostbite that will actually increase the damage to the frozen part are still popular. Never rub a frozen part with snow, and never massage a frozen part before, during or after rewarming. Don't try to rewarm a frozen part by exercising it; this will most likely increase injury to the tissue. Don't use a gradual rewarming process by soaking the frozen part in cool water. It is just as painful as the correct rapid rewarming procedure but results in more tissue damage. Never try to rewarm a frozen part near a fire or with water hotter than 44°C (112°F) as the patient is not able to feel excessive heat and further damage can result.

Hypothermia, also known as exposure, is the lowering of the body temperature and can be fatal. Frostbite is a defense mechanism to maintain heat in the vital core, and if the body continues to lose heat faster than it produces it the core temperature will go down. Cold wet and windy conditions can chill the body if the person does not have proper clothing.

Protecting the head and the back of the neck is most important. At 4°C (40°F) up to one-half of the body's heat production can be lost from an uncovered head. There is an outdoors maxim: "When your feet are cold put a hat on." It is also important to keep your clothes dry. Wet clothing chills the body 240 times faster than does dry clothing. Woollen clothing is suited for winter outings as it keeps you warm even when wet.

When venturing outdoors always be alert for signs of hypothermia. The early symptoms are shivering and a general numb feeling. As the condition worsens the shivering becomes more intense, speech is slurred, judgment is impaired and there is a loss of coordination. If someone in your group shows signs of hypothermia, prevent further heat loss by immediately getting the person out of the cold. Remove all wet clothing and put him in a sleeping bag with another person who has also stripped. If you have a double sleeping bag huddle the victim between two people to transfer their body heat to him. Putting someone with hypothermia in a cold sleeping bag by himself is not sufficient as the body has lost its ability to generate heat by itself.

Warm him with warm drinks, candy and other sweetened foods that are high in carbohydrates and quickly transform into heat energy. Alcohol and tobacco should not be given to a hypothermia victim and in general should be avoided on winter outings. Alcohol has the effect of lowering the body's resistance to the cold as it can cause a sudden release of cold blood from the surface blood vessels to the core reducing the core temperature. Nicotine constricts the flow of blood through the blood vessels causing the extremities to become cold and can result in frostbite.

8

Preserving Our
Natural Environment

CANADA is fortunate to have a great diversity of natural environments preserved in its park systems for people to explore and enjoy. To preserve our outdoors in a natural state, we must be properly equipped to minimize our impact on the environment.

Many people see a trip into the backcountry as going back to their roots. Unfortunately they feel that, like their pioneer ancestors who uprooted trees and slashed underbrush to make farms and cities from wilderness, they too have to conquer a hostile environment. They cut down trees to make shelters and bough beds to carve a home in the forest for their weekend camp. The damage to the natural environment remains long after they have returned to the city. Hikers who follow lose the sense of discovery when they come upon a campsite with decrepit bivouacs, tattered sheets of plastic, and several blackened firepits. Surrounding the campsite are the scarred remains of trees from which boughs and branches were hacked off to build the now-decaying shelters.

The destruction caused by the conqueror type of camper can no longer be tolerated by the fragile wilderness environment. The increased use of the backcountry means hikers must follow practices that will not damage the environment. They must leave no trace of their visit so that those who follow them can also experience a place of solitude away from the destructive side of man and technology.

On the Trail

When following an established trail, always stay on the path. Steep sections of trails are often built with switchbacks to making hiking easier and reduce erosion. Cutting across switchbacks encourages run-off.

At the Campsite

Many of the early camping and woodcraft manuals inform hikers that they are fortunate if they are able to camp in virgin wilderness because they'll feel themselves akin to early pioneers hewing their homes out of the wilderness. These early camping books describe how to build shelters and lean-tos of sapling frames covered with boughs, and discuss the pleasures of sleeping on a bough bed. These practices are no longer acceptable or necessary. Lean-tos and shelters don't provide any protection from biting insects, and in cold weather don't keep the heat in as well as a closed tent. A sleeping pad provides better insulation and is more comfortable than a bough bed.

Modern equipment has eliminated the need for a campsite to provide wood and shelter. It is now more efficient and convenient to carry a lightweight stove and tent. A well-equipped hiker can set up camp in such bare spots as near a glacier or on treeless barrens, places where hikers with the pioneer attitude would have found it impossible.

On trails where the campsites are designated, camp only at these sites. This confines damage to the environment to particular spots and leaves the surrounding areas intact. Where there are no restrictions, camp at previously used campsites. When forced to use a virgin site, set up camp at least 30 meters (100 feet) away from the shores of lakes and streams.

Several parks now have quotas on the number of hikers permitted on a trail at one time and some also restrict the size of hiking groups allowed to camp at one site at the same time. Large groups occupy more space and have more impact on the environment than the same number of campers using the same site over an extended period of time. Limit the size of each group to ten participants. If your group is larger, divide it into two or more parties and have each party hike in a different area. Should a large number of hikers happen to be camping at the same site, everyone should make an effort to be extra courteous, especially after dark when many people want to listen to the night sounds of the forest. Nothing is more obnoxious than groups of loud, rowdy hikers who are inconsiderate of other hikers with whom they are sharing a campsite.

Clearing vegetation to make a site for your tent and putting ditches around the tent contributes to erosion. When setting up your tent choose a site that rain will drain away from. If heavy rains occur and ditches are necessary, make them only as deep as necessary to carry away the water, and fill them in before you leave.

Fires

The increase in the use of the backcountry has brought the traditional campfire into question. Campfires exude a cozy warmth that brings the members of a group together to sit around its flickering flames. However the supply of deadwood in many areas is being rapidly depleted. Many popular campsites have been devastated by excessive wood gathering and fire building. In some cases, unaware campers have cut green trees which do not burn.

Backpacking stoves are more efficient than fires, and leave no trace. If there is an adequate supply of wood and you want to have a fire, keep it small. (Building a campfire is described in Chapter 3, "Food and Cooking Gear.")

Keeping Animals out of Your Food

At many backcountry campsites lurk numerous animals just waiting for hikers to trudge in so that they can feast on their food. These scavengers, ranging from large bears, masked raccoons, unlovable porcupines all the way down to cute little mice, have learned that hikers mean easy food. With the increase in the number of people visiting their habitat, they are no longer afraid of humans or the noise they make. In the good old days when a bear came into your camp you banged two pots together and the noise would scare the beast away. Now many bears will let you smash away at your cookware until you're left with nothing more than a pile of crumpled tin, while they just continue filling their stomachs.

All food that is not canned should be placed in a sack and suspended between two trees. The sack should be at least 3 meters (10 feet) above the ground, 1.2 meters (4 feet) down from a branch and 3 meters (10 feet) out from the trunk. It's important that the sack be between two trees. Hanging it over one branch is virtually useless as black bears can climb trees and get at the sack of food.

Don't cook or eat in your tent as the lingering odors attract bears. Cooking should be done away from the tent. When preparing a meal take the required food out of the sack and put the remainder back up immediately. If you leave the food unattended on the ground for even a few minutes you may end up cutting your trip short and walking out hungry.

Hanging the food will take care of problems with bears, raccoons and mice. Porcupines are another matter. These unsociable creatures love salt and will eat anything that has absorbed perspiration, such as boots, hipbelts and the armpits of jackets. Keep these items inside the tent with you or hang them up if you're sleeping under a tarp that porkies can walk into. Lean-tos and cabins are favorite places for porcupines and you should always hang your pack, boots and food from the ceiling, preferably away from a wall.

Don't encourage problems with bears and other animals by leaving litter or burying trash around camp. Don't feed bears for any reason, even to snap that special picture to show the folks back home. Take photographs with a telephoto lens. Forget the Yogi-Bear and Winnie-the-Pooh storybook image of bears. Feeding bears is dangerous and unlawful; it encourages them to come around people, increasing the chances of a bear attacking a person. Remember, you are a visitor in the bear's country.

Garbage

The old practice of burying the garbage that doesn't burn is no longer ecologically sound. Many trails have too much traffic and cannot tolerate garbage, even material that will eventually decompose. Cans take up to 40 years to decompose, plastics take two centuries, aluminum takes half a millennium, and glass will still be around in one million years. Another problem is that often the garbage does not remain buried because animals smell the adhering food, dig it up and strew it around, making a mess and possibly injuring themselves.

"If you pack it in, pack it out," is the rule for litter in the backcountry. Empty food containers are much lighter than the full ones you carried in and there is absolutely no excuse for not packing them out.

When buying food for your trip try to select items that come in burnable packages, and avoid cans and bottles. Repackaging food in plastic bags will eliminate some of the non-burnable containers.

Empty cans should be washed along with the pots to remove food residues. Crush the cans with a rock or by stepping on them and pack them out in a plastic garbage bag. The wilderness environment can be preserved if all hikers are conscientious and pack out all their garbage, right down to the last chocolate bar wrapper.

Water pollution

Clean drinking water is essential and hikers should take precautions to safeguard water sources on the trail. As mentioned earlier, always camp at least 30 meters (100 feet) from lakes, rivers and streams. Washing near the water source can contaminate it and you should carry the water to wash yourself and your dishes at least 60 meters (200 feet) away. Use a bio-degradable soap, if you use any soap at all, and dump the soapy water where the ground can absorb it.

Sanitation

The proper disposal of human waste in the backcountry is important in preserving a healthy environment around campsites. On many trails privies have been provided and they should always be used.

On trails without privies, care must be taken not to pollute springs, ponds and streams. Choose a spot that is at least 60 meters (200 feet) from any water source and is not a potential campsite. An isolated spot in the woods high on a hill is a good place. Scoop a small hole about 10 to 15 cm (4 to 6 inches) deep. The bacteria at this depth will decompose the waste rapidly. After use, bury everything by covering it with loose dirt, stones and dead leaves.

Dogs

Dogs are prohibited in the backcountry of many parks as they can be a nuisance to other hikers and may disturb the wildlife. Hikers who have dogs they would like as hiking companions should check in advance with the park superintendent about regulations.

On trails where dogs are permitted, dog owners should use common sense and courtesy, and respect the rights of other hikers. Don't permit the dog to chase wildlife, and restrain it when approached by another dog, horses or hikers who appear nervous due to your dog's presence. Make sure the dog stays away from other hikers' food and out of the water source. Dog droppings on the trail or campsite should be buried. Loud yapping dogs are annoying to hikers and if you can't keep your dog quiet, leave it at home. Only responsible behavior by dog owners will insure that man's best friend is not banned from backcountry trails.

Now You're Ready

Part Two describes walking, day-hiking and backpacking opportunities in all ten provinces and two territories. Whether you want an easy walk for the family or a wilderness trek, the following chapters will help you choose where to go.

APPENDIX A
Safety

HERE is a summary of some of the more essential safety considerations to review before heading out. This list is by no means exhaustive. For more comprehensive information there are many books on first-aid and outdoor survival.

Blisters

—Make sure your hiking boots or shoes are well broken in before heading out on the trail.

—If you feel a hot spot on a foot, stop immediately and cover the chafed area with moleskin or molefoam.

—If a blister develops, immediate treatment is necessary. Cover a small blister with moleskin. If it's large and full of liquid, you may have to drain it to relieve the pressure and pain. Sterilize a needle in a match flame, apply antiseptic to the blistered area, and carefully puncture the blister on the edge, not on the top. Drain the liquid by pressing the blister gently, apply more antiseptic, and, if you must continue hiking, put some gauze on it and cover it with a piece of moleskin to prevent further irritation.

Hip belts

—When fording a stream, walking on logs and stretches of terrain with slippery footing, unbuckle the hip belt of your backpack so you can quickly jettison the pack in case you fall. If you fall while fording a swift flowing stream with the pack belt secured around your hips, the weight of the floating pack can hold your face down in the water.

Sleeping bags

—Make sure your sleeping bag is rated to the coldest temperatures you're likely to encounter.

Protect your head

—Always have a sunhat and a regular hat or cap to protect your head from cold, wind, sun and rain.

Cooking safety

—Avoid cooking or eating food in your tent as the lingering odors may attract bears and other animals.

—When priming a white gas stove, don't use an excessive amount of gas. Fill the tank away from all open flames and never when the stove is hot. If the stove runs out of gas in the middle of cooking a meal, let the stove cool before refilling it. If a small flame remains after you've turned the valve off, just blow it out. Don't open the fuel tank to release the pressure; it will allow gas vapor to escape and can ignite explosively.

—Use backpacking stoves outside whenever possible. If you have to use it inside a tent, leave a tent flap open to prevent carbon monoxide poisoning and asphyxiation.

Insects

—If you're hiking during bug season, bring light-colored clothing with long sleeves and full-length pants.

—Use insect repellant with a high percentage of active ingredient, most contain diethyl toluamide (abbreviated as DEET).

Cold Weather

—When hiking in winter, make sure your head and back of the neck are protected.

—If hands, toes or feet have superficial frostbite, warm them by placing on a bare stomach, armpit or hand. If the nose, ears or cheeks are frostbitten, hold a warm hand over the affected area.

—Never rub a frozen part with snow.

—Never massage a frozen part before, during or after rewarming.

—Don't try to rewarm a frozen part by exercising it: This will most likely increase injury to the tissue.

—Deep frostbite is serious, and the affected person should be moved inside as soon as possible, preferably to a hospital. Correct rewarming of a frozen part is by immersing it in warm water 42° to 44°C (108° to 112°F). Rewarming takes 20 to 30 minutes and is usually very painful. The patient might have to keep off thawed feet for several weeks.

—Never walk on thawed feet or toes as serious loss of tissue is almost certain to result.

—Don't use a gradual rewarming process by soaking the frozen part in cool water. It's just as painful as the correct rapid rewarming procedure, but results in more tissue damage.

—Never try to rewarm a frozen part near a fire or with water hotter than 44°C (112°F), as the patient will not be able to feel excessive heat and further damage may result.

—Be alert for the signs of hypothermia: The early symptoms are shivering and a general numb feeling. As the condition worsens the shivering becomes more intense, speech is slurred, judgment is impaired and there is a loss of coordination. If someone in your group shows signs of hypothermia, prevent further heat loss by immediately getting him out of the cold. Remove all wet clothing and put him in a sleeping bag with another person who has also stripped. If you have a double sleeping bag or can put two bags together, huddle the victim between two people to transfer their body heat to him. Putting someone with hypothermia in a cold sleeping bag by himself is not sufficient, as the body has lost its ability to generate heat by itself. Warm him with warm drinks, candies and other sweetened foods which are high in carbohydrates and quickly transform into heat energy.

—Avoid alcohol and tobacco on winter outings. Alcohol has the effect of lowering the body's resistance to the cold, as it can cause a sudden release of cold blood from the surface blood vessels to the core of the body, reducing the core temperature. Nicotine constricts the flow of blood through the blood vessels causing your extremities to become more susceptible to frostbite.

APPENDIX B
Checklist

When planning a trip prepare a checklist of the equipment you will need. Revise it as conditions change and you gain experience. Look at each piece of equipment and decide if you really need it. Avoid the temptation of filling your pack with unnecessary gadgets. When you're lugging the load up a steep climb on a hot windless day those extra grams soon feel like kilograms.

Below is a sample checklist; it is by no means the last word. Go through the list and select the items you think you will need on a trip. After the trip note what equipment wasn't used and decide if you should carry it on the next hike. Also note what equipment you lacked and want to take when you go out again.

Items that should be carried on all trips in the backcountry:

Map and compass
Waterproof matches
Fire starter (candle)
Flashlight
Whistle
Pocketknife
First-aid kit (see suggested reading)
Extra food, clothing and light
Plastic tarp
Sunburn protection and dark glasses

Transportation:
Hiking boots or shoes
Frame pack

Shelter:
Tent or tarp
Sleeping bag
Groundsheet
Sleeping pad

Cooking gear:
Water bottle
Water purification tablets
Stove and fuel
Cooking pots and utensils
Pot gripper
Cup
Spoon
Salt and pepper shaker
Sugar container
Food containers
Can opener
Scouring pad

Clothing:
Socks
Underwear
Long-sleeved shirt(s)
T-shirts
Wool sweater
Long pants
Belt or suspenders
Short pants
Nylon windbreaker or
    60/40 parka
Insulated vest
Wool tuque
Sunhat
Bandana
Swim suit
Sneakers or mocassins
Down booties
Gloves
Long underwear
Raingear
Gaiters

Toiletries:
Personal items
Insect repellant
Toothbrush and toothpaste
Bio-degradable soap
Washcloth
Toilet paper
Towel
Handkerchief
Comb
Suntan cream
Lip salve
Foot powder
Moleskin
Scissors

Miscellaneous items:
Nylon cord
Spare flashlight batteries and
    bulb
Candles
Binoculars
Camera and film
Notebook and pen or pencils
Plastic bags
Sewing kit
Safety pins
Fishing gear
Nature guides
Reading material
Watch
Thermometer
Pedometer
Signal flare
Quarters for emergency phone
    calls

Suggested Reading

First Aid

Medicine for Mountaineering, edited by James Wilkerson, M.D., (Seattle, Washington: The Mountaineers, 1977), covers 24 injuries and diseases that can occur on a hiking trip. The book contains more information than usual "first aid" books as it may be a long period of time until the patient is evacuated from the wilderness and arrives at a hospital. A list of the components of a complete medical kit is included.

Where to Walk, Hike and Backpack in Canada

How to Use
Part Two

CANADA abounds in the walking, dayhiking and backpacking opportunities and this comprehensive guide will help you select the trails most suited for your trips, to plan hikes well in advance and know what to expect when you reach the trail.

Each province and territory is covered in a separate chapter and is accompanied by a map.

The variety of paths are divided into three levels:

Walks: usually comprise interpretive nature trails where often a brochure or signs along the path explain the natural phenomena that can be observed. They also include short walks of up to two hours duration.

Hikes: describes trails that take anywhere from several hours to a full day, but are not meant as overnight backpacking treks.

Backpacking: includes routes that can be hiked for overnight or longer trips. These routes have backcountry campsites and some have cabins or shelters for backpackers' use. Parts of these trails are usually suitable for day-hikes.

Descriptions include information on the length of trails in kilometers (mileage is indicated in parentheses), the area of the park, the topography, wildlife, plantlife, what guidebooks are available (their cost and where to order them is included in the guidebook sources at the end of each chapter) and where to write or call for more information. The presence of shelters along the trails is indicated but hikers camping out should carry a tent or tarp since shelters may be full when you arrive. The availability of hiking supplies in the area is noted. Also included is information on reaching the backpacking areas that are not accessible by car, so that hikers must use other means of transportation such as train, airplane or ferry to reach them.

Most national and provincial parks require that backpackers register before going into the backcountry and notify them upon their return. Check with the park superintendent for local regulations. If you want to fish you'll need an angling license, and building fires in some areas requires a fire permit usually obtained when registering. Some parks have instituted a quota on the number of hikers allowed on a trail at one time. Usually a portion of the quota is given out by reservation and the rest on a first-come first-served basis. If you want to hike in one of these parks, make reservations as far in advance as possible, or if all reservations are taken, try to get to the park office early in the day for the remaining permits. A few parks have put a ban on bottles and cans in the backcountry and hikers interested in hiking in these areas will have to take this into account when planning a menu.

1

British Columbia

BRITISH Columbia's snow-capped mountain ranges were once a major obstacle to reaching the Pacific coast from the east. In 1793 Alexander Mackenzie was the first white man to journey overland across North America, 14 years before a comparable journey was made in the United States. In that year Mackenzie reached Bella Coola near present-day Tweedsmuir Provincial Park. In the park, part of the trail he followed has been restored for hikers. When British Columbia joined Canada in 1871, the construction of a railway from central Canada to the coast was promised. Over the next decade surveyors packed over mountain passes exploring possible routes for the railway. These mountain ranges now provide hikers with many exhilarating opportunities to hike through

Average daily minimum and maximum temperatures in British Columbia

		May		June		July		August		Sept.		Oct.	
		L	H	L	H	L	H	L	H	L	H	L	H
Vancouver	°C	8	18	11	21	13	23	12	23	10	19	7	14
	°F	47	65	52	70	55	74	54	74	50	67	45	58
Victoria	°C	8	16	10	18	11	20	11	20	10	18	8	14
	°F	47	61	50	65	52	68	52	68	50	65	46	57
Prince Rupert	°C	6	13	8	16	10	17	11	17	9	16	6	12
	°F	42	56	47	60	50	63	51	63	48	60	43	53

colorful alpine meadows, forests of towering Douglas fir and over rugged mountain passes.

British Columbia covers 1,048,234 km^2 (366,255 square miles) almost wholly in the Western Cordillera. In the west are the Coast Mountains, averaging 130 km (80 miles) wide and extending to the deeply indented coast. The highest peak in the lush rain forest and glacier-covered Coast Mountains is 3,978-meter (13,260-foot) Mount Waddington. On the eastern side of the province are the Rocky Mountains which average 80 km (50 miles) wide and form an almost continuous succession of ridges and peaks reaching 3,892 meters (12,972 feet) at Mount Robson, the highest peak in the Canadian Rockies. West of the Rockies are the Columbia Mountains consisting of the Purcell, Selkirk, Monashee and Cariboo ranges. In the south central portion of the province is the Interior Plateau. To the north are the Hazelton, Skeena, Omineca and Cassiar mountains.

The large number of hiking opportunities in British Columbia range from gentle rambles for families with young children to challenging wilderness treks. There are very scenic trails along unspoiled beaches where you can beachcomb for mussels and other shellfish in the tidal pools. Hiking routes in the far northern part of the province are generally primitive routes not as well developed as in the south.

British Columbia has many different climates due to the Pacific Ocean and the high mountain ranges. The warm Japanese current gives the coastal region a very moderate climate of mild, wet and foggy winters and moderate dry summers. The west coast of Vancouver Island is the wettest part of Canada with an average annual rainfall of 305 to 483 cm (120 to 190 inches). The Coast Mountains also receive a heavy rainfall as a result of the moisture-laden winds from the Pacific. East of the Coast Mountains, the Interior Plateau is dry. The higher air currents travel on to the lofty Selkirk Mountains where it rains frequently. The Rocky Mountains are protected by the Selkirks and receive much less precipitation.

Tourist Information: Tourism British Columbia, Parliament Buildings, Victoria, British Columbia V8V 1X4, or call toll-free

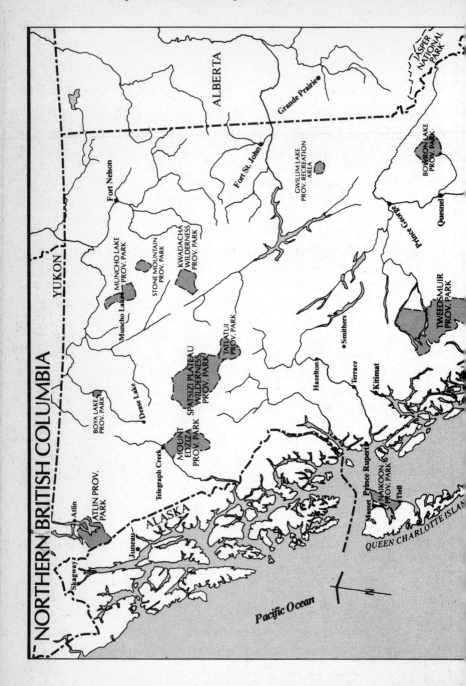

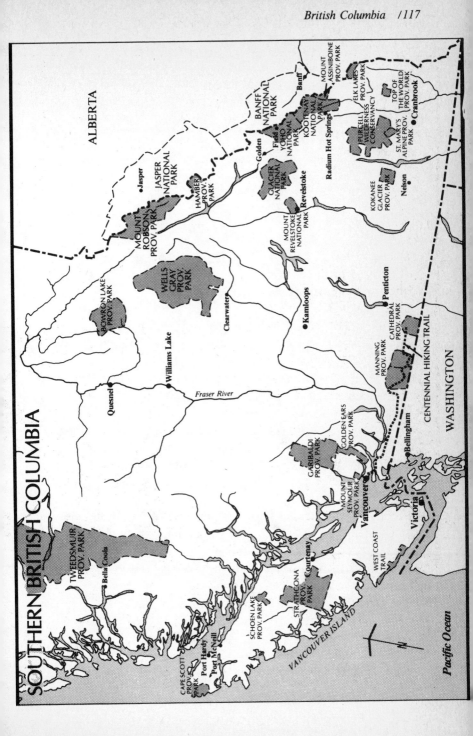

1-800-663-6000. Topographical maps are available from Maps-BC, Surveys and Resource Mapping Branch, Ministry of the Environment, Parliament Buildings, Victoria, British Columbia V8V 1X5. Hostels in British Columbia are operated by the Canadian Hostelling Association, British Columbia Region, 1515 Discovery Street, Vancouver, British Columbia V6R 4K5, (604) 224-7177.

Vancouver Island

Victoria Area Regional District Parks

Near Victoria, British Columbia's provincial capital, a variety of environments are preserved in 17 Capital Regional District Parks. Among them are:

East Sooke Regional Park covers 14 square km (5 square miles) of the rugged coast of the Strait of Juan de Fuca, rocky hills, rain forest and Coast Salish Indian rock carvings. Its 60 km (37 miles) of trails include the 10-km (6-mile) Coast trail along the shore with views of the Olympic Mountains. Other trails wind through the park's interior which has a variety of animal and plant life.

Galloping Goose Regional Park is a 46-km (28.5-mile) long park corridor, along a former railway right-of-way, linking View Royal, Colwood, Langford, Metchosin and Sooke. Part of it is along the coast. Hiking, cycling and horseriding are permitted on the trail.

Mount Work Regional Park encompasses 4 square km (1.5 square miles) on the Saanich Peninsula about 20 km (12 miles) northwest of Victoria. The park's 426-meter (1,400-foot) Mount Work is the peninsula's highest point. Trails lead to its summit and to the McKenzie Bight.

The trails in these parts are described in *Hiking Trails I: Victoria and Vicinity.*

More Information: Capital Regional District Parks, 400 Atkins Avenue, Victoria, British Columbia V9B 2Z8, (604) 478-3344 (or 604-474-PARK for recorded information).

Goldstream Provincial Park

Situated 19 km (11.8 miles) northwest of Victoria, Goldstream Provincial Park covers 3 square km (1.1 square miles) of south Vancouver Island forest land. The park is traversed by the Trans-Canada Highway and the Goldstream River. The discovery of gold in the area in 1885 spurred a brief gold rush. Though little gold was taken out, old shafts and tunnels dug by the early miners can be seen along some of the park's trails.

As the area was not logged, a variety of large trees including western yew, red alder, big leaf maple, western hemlock and black cottonwood still stand. Also found here are Douglas fir, western red cedar—some up to 600 years old, and the arbutus—Canada's only broad leaved evergreen. Salt marsh plants can be seen at the marsh where the Goldstream River empties into the sea at Finlayson Arm.

Walks: Among the park's short nature trails, ranging from 5 to 15 minutes in duration, are the Arbutus trail through forested upland, the Bridge trail along the Goldstream River, the Lower Falls trail along Niagara Creek to the base of the falls, and the Marsh trail to Finlayson Arm.

Hikes: The Gold Mine trail leading past gold rush remains to 30-meter (100-foot) high Niagara Falls takes about one and a half hours one-way. Along the Prospectors' trail, about two and a half hours one-way, are giant Douglas fir trees beside the Goldstream River.

A hike beginning in the Goldstream River Valley and leading outside the park to the summit of 415-meter (1,361-foot) Mount Finlayson takes about one and a half hours and offers good views of Victoria and the surrounding hills.

More Information: Ministry of Parks, 2930 Trans Canada Highway, RR 6, Victoria, British Columbia V8X 3X2, (604) 478-8341.

West Coast Trail, Pacific Rim National Park

On the night of January 22, 1906, the 253-foot (77-meter) passenger vessel *S.S. Valencia* ran aground north of the

Klanawa River on Vancouver Island's west coast. The lives of 126 passengers and crew were lost. This tragic event spurred the Canadian government to construct a lifesaving trail between the villages of Bamfield and Port Renfrew for shipwrecked sailors. This section of the coast had become known as the "Graveyard of the Pacific" as it has been the site of more than 60 shipwrecks since 1854. The 77-km (47-mile) West Coast Trail follows the route of the historic lifesaving trail along the unspoiled coast of the Juan de Fuca Strait and the Pacific Ocean.

Heavy rain, prolonged cloudiness and moderate temperatures have produced a dense forest of cedar, hemlock and amabalis fir, with sitka spruce on the fringe. The forest floor is hidden by a thick growth of salal, salmonberry and huckle-

Tsusiat Falls, West Coast Trail, Vancouver Island, B.C. (B.C. Government Photograph)

berry. During the summer Pacific gray whales and sea lions can be seen offshore. Harbor seals inhabit the sheltered coves.

At low tide mussels, barnacles, hermit crabs, starfish, limpets, sponges and sea anemones can be found in the tidal pools. Many hikers supplement their meals with fresh mussels. Razor clams, beach hoppers and colorful sea worms are found on the beaches. Many of the streams crossed by the West Coast Trail contain trout.

As the park is on the Pacific Flyway, thousands of migrating ducks and geese stop to feed and rest on the lakes and estuaries during the spring and fall. Birds that inhabit the park include forest species such as woodpeckers, Steller's jays, brown creepers, red crossbills and chickadees. Shoreline birds that can be seen include redthroated loons, great blue herons, bald eagles and oystercatchers. There are also a small number of red squirrels, mink, marten, racoons, black-tailed deer, black bears and cougars.

The 47-km (29-mile) section, from the trail's northern

Carmanah Lighthouse on the West Coast Trail, Vancouver Island. (B.C. Governmnent Photograph)

terminus at Pachena Bay near Bamfield to Carmanah Point, is a wide and clear path. A large part of it can be covered on the very scenic sandy beaches and sandstone shelves. A highlight of the trail is Tsusiat Falls which cascade 15 meters (50 feet) down to the beach. The 29-km (18-mile) section, from Carmanah to Port Renfrew, requires hikers to cross gullies on fallen trees, wade fast-moving streams, climb numerous vertical ladders and walk on logs laid end to end. This section should be attempted by experienced backpackers only.

There are two major river crossings on the trail. The Gordon River at the southern end of the trail and the Nitinat Narrows near the mid-point. They cannot be forded, members of the local Indian bands ferry hikers across.

Hiking the entire West Coast Trail takes between six and ten days. To avoid the difficult southern section you can start from Bamfield and hike as far as Tsusiat Falls, the Nitinat Narrows or Carmanah Point and turn back. Hikers should expect and be prepared for rainy weather. Average annual rainfall in Bamfield is 269 cm (106 inches), with moderate summer temperatures between 10° and 24°C (50° and 75°F). The Tofino tide tables in Volume 6 of the *Canadian Tide and Current Tables*, published by the Canadian Hydrographic Service, should be carried when hiking the West Coast Trail.

Access to Port Renfrew is by highway from Victoria, or logging road from Shawinigan Lake and Lake Cowichan. Bamfield can be reached by logging road from Port Alberni, or on the foot passenger boat *M.V. Lady Rose* which sails from Port Alberni. The ferry service is operated by Alberni Marine Transportation Ltd., P.O. Box 188, Port Alberni, British Columbia V9Y 7M7, (604) 723-8313.

Backpackers should arrive self-sufficient, as supplies cannot be acquired near the trail. Register for a free permit before beginning the hike. *The West Coast Trail and Nitinat Lakes, The Pacific Rim Explorer* and *Blisters and Bliss* describe the route. The recommended map for hiking the trail is "West Coast Trail, Port Renfrew-Bamfield," which should be purchased before arriving at the trailhead. They can be ordered from Map Production, Surveys and Mapping Branch, Ministry of the Environment, 553 Superior Street, Victoria B.C. V8V 1X4, (604) 387-1441.

More Information: The Superintendent, Pacific Rim National Park, Box 280, Ucluelet, British Columbia V0R 3A0, (604) 726-7721.

Long Beach, Pacific Rim National Park

Stretching along the Pacific coast of Vancouver Island between the tiny fishing villages of Tofino and Ucluelet, Long Beach is 11 km (7 miles) of surf-swept sandy beaches and rocky headlands, backed by almost impenetrable rain forests and snow-capped 1,200-meter (4,000-feet) mountains. The most easily accessible unit of Pacific Rim Park, Long Beach offers easy walking, less rigorous than the West Coast Trail.

Walks: After absorbing the ocean scenery and exploring Long Beach's tidal pools and rocky shoreline, you can walk some of the nature trails, which range in length from 0.5 to 2.5 km (0.3 to 1.5 miles). Several of the trails follow parts of the overland path used to pack supplies from Ucluelet to Tofino until 1942 when the road was completed.

On the 1.2-km (0.7-mile) Rain Forest Trail you pass cuts made through the trunks of fallen trees that were saplings before the first European set foot in North America. The 2.1-km Willowbrae Trail leads to the seacoast at the south end of Florencia Bay. The 2-km (1.2-mile) Gold Mine trail explores the remains of placer mining at the mouth of Lost Shoe Creek from the early 1900s.

More Information: The Superintendent, Pacific Rim National Park, Box 280, Ucluelet, British Columbia V0R 3A0, (604) 726-7721.

Strathcona Provincial Park

Dominated by rugged snowcovered mountain peaks, lakes, alpine tarns and rivers, Strathcona Provincial Park is a

2270-km^2 (877-square-mile) mountain wilderness almost at the center of Vancouver Island. The park includes 2,200-meter (7,216-foot) Golden Hinde Mountain, the highest point on Vancouver Island. Strathcona also contains the highest waterfall in Canada, Della Falls, which drops 440 meters (1,443 feet) in three cascades.

Strathcona Park was created in 1911 and is the oldest provincial park in British Columbia. The history of the area dates to 1778 when Captain James Cook of the Royal Navy landed at Nootka Sound on Vancouver Island's west coast, a few kilometers from the present western park boundary.

The park is a wildlife sanctuary and contains some of the last remaining Roosevelt elk on Vancouver Island, as well as deer, black bear, cougar, wolves and wolverines. Birds are not numerous, but grouse, jays and the occasional eagle can be sighted. The forest cover in the valley and lower mountain slopes comprises western red cedar, Douglas fir, grand fir, amabilis fir and western hemlock of the Coast Forest. In the subalpine areas are alpine fir, mountain hemlock, lodgepole pine and creeping juniper. Wildflowers, giving some areas of the park a spectacular display of flora, grow at elevations between 1,200 and 1,800 meters (4,000 and 5,900 feet). The park's lakes and rivers provide good fishing for cutthroat trout, rainbow trout and Dolly Varden.

Walks: Among Strathcona's variety of nature walks are the five-minute Auger Point loop showing how nature is reclaiming an area burned in a forest fire, the 0.9-km (0.5-mile) Lady Falls trail, and the 2-km (1.2-mile) Karst Creek trail exploring limestone features including sinkholes, disappearing streams and waterfalls. The 1-km (0.6-mile) Paradise Meadows-Battleship Lake trail is a popular access to the Forbidden Plateau area.

Hikes: The park offers more than 100 km (60 miles) of marked hiking trails in the Buttle Lake, Forbidden Lake and Kwai Lake areas. Hikes from Buttle Lake include the 10-km (6-mile) Elk River trail to Landslide Lake, the 5-km (3-mile) Crest Mountain trail offering views of the surrounding valleys, and the 6-km (3.7-mile) Flower Ridge trail through an alpine area.

In the Forbidden Plateau area, trails include the 4.5-km (2.7-mile) Mount Belcher trail which offers a panoramic view of the Coast Mountains on the British Columbia mainland, and the 15-km (9.3-mile) trail to Kwai Lake from where short trails lead to surrounding lakes.

Backpacking: With the exception of the areas around Buttle Lake and Forbidden Plateau, Strathcona Park is largely undeveloped and its primary appeal is to backpackers. A unique feature of the park is the interconnecting high alpine ridges that form spectacular hiking circuits. Many of the park's trails are access routes to these high ridge routes.

From Buttle Lake there are four routes; each takes about a week to hike. The easiest and most popular begins and ends at Phillips Creek. The route follows the entire Phillips Creek watershed along the high divide and crosses Marble Meadows. Reaching the access trail to this route involves crossing Buttle Lake by boat. The other high ridge routes follow the Ralph River watershed, the Shepherd Creek watershed and the Henshaw Creek watershed which includes the Flower Ridge Trail.

A three-week-long trip on the Buttle Lake watershed is almost entirely in alpine parkland or high alpine terrain and includes the highest sections of the four routes described above. From Mount Becher near the Forbidden Plateau the route follows the ridges south to Comox Glacier, west to Septimus and Big Interior, then north to Mount Thelwood and Burman Lake, skirting south of Golden Hinde Mountain and going north down to the Elk River Valley.

Strathcona's high-ridge routes are not marked and should be attempted only by experienced, well-equipped hikers. The routes and access trails are described in *Hiking Trails III: Central and Northern Vancouver Island.*

More Information: Zone Manager, Ministry of Parks, R.R. 1, Site 11, C - 1, Black Creek, British Columbia V0R 1C0, (604) 337-5121.

Cape Scott Provincial Park

At the isolated northwestern tip of Vancouver Island, Cape Scott Park is a rugged coastal wilderness of 149 km^2 (57 square miles). The 64 km (40 miles) of scenic ocean frontage includes 23 km (14 miles) of shoreline spread over nine beaches. The wide sandy beaches from Nissen Bight in the north to San Josef Bay in the south are divided by rocky headlands and promontories. Nels Bight, a fine white sand beach 2.4 km (1.5 miles) long and 210 meters (689 feet) wide is the most impressive of these.

The highest point in the park is Mount St. Patrick at 415 meters (1,361 feet) above sea level. Forest cover is composed of red cedar, yellow cedar, lodgepole pine, hemlock and true fir in the upland areas. Undergrowth is mainly salal, salmonberry, evergreen huckleberry and fern. Canada geese and other waterfowl travelling the Pacific Flyway stop at Hansen Lagoon. Sea birds can be seen on the shoreline. Deer, elk, bear, otter, cougar and wolves inhabit the forests and open upland areas. Seals and sea lions can be observed on the offshore islands.

In 1897 and again in 1910 Danish pioneers attempted to settle the area but were unsuccessful due to weather conditions, the distance from markets and lack of suitable access routes. A few frame buildings and rusting farm implements are all that remain.

Hikes/Backpacking: Cape Scott Park can only be entered by foot and has 50 km (30 miles) of hiking trails. The 24-km (15-mile) Cape Scott Trail begins at the parking area near the southeastern park boundary and follows the old telephone line from Holberg Inlet northwest to Cape Scott Lighthouse, Fisherman Bay and Hansen Lagoon. The trail also provides access to the beaches at Nissen Bight, Nels Bight, Experiment Bight and Guise Bay. From the wildlife marshes and wide sandy beaches at San Josef Bay a 10-km (6-mile) trail leads to the summit of Mount St. Patrick and then to the beach at Sea Otter Cove. From there a 2-km (1.2-mile) trail goes to another beach at Lowrie Bay. Exploring all of Cape Scott Park takes about one week.

Hiking on the coastline off designated trails should not be attempted as many of the headlands are impassable. Any other coastal travel should be attempted at low tide. Backpackers planning to use the beaches should carry a tide table. Tide listings for Cape Scott are in Volume 6 of the *Canadian Tide and Current Tables* available from the Canadian Hydrographic Service.

Hikers in Cape Scott Park should be prepared for adverse weather conditions. Annual precipitation in the area, almost all in the form of rain, is between 375 and 500 cm (146 and 195 inches). Prolonged sunny periods are rare, even during the summer. Trails can be very muddy; bring high rubber boots in addition to hiking boots.

Located 448 km (278 miles) from Victoria, access to Cape Scott Park is by logging roads from Port Hardy, 64 km (40 miles) east of the park. Port Hardy can be reached by highway or B.C. Ferry from Prince Rupert.

Cape Scott is a wilderness area; bring complete supplies with you. *Hiking Trails III: Central and Northern Vancouver Island* describes the park's trails.

More Information: Zone Manager, Ministry of Parks, R.R. 1, Site 11, C - 1, Black Creek, British Columbia V0R 1C0, (604) 337-5121.

Queen Charlotte Islands

Naikoon Provincial Park

The Queen Charlotte Islands lie in the Pacific Ocean about 100 km (62 miles) west of Prince Rupert on the British Columbia coast. Naikoon Park covers 718 km² (277 square miles) of the northeastern tip of Graham Island, the largest of the islands.

A 32-km (20-mile) fine sandy beach stretches from the park's northwest boundary at the mouth of the Sangan River to Rose Point where the 5-km (3-mile) long Rose Spit separates the waters of Dixon Entrance and Hecate Strait. Naikoon is a Haida Indian word meaning "long nose" and is the old Haida name for Rose Point.

South of Rose Point to the park boundary at the Tlell River is 80 km (50 miles) of beaches backed by sand bluffs ranging from 5 to 60 meters (16 to 20 feet) above the surf. The northern inland section of the park consists of the Argonaut Plain, a wildland of muskeg, stunted pine, meandering streams, meadows and low flat-topped hills that reach 120 to 150 meters (400 to 500 feet).

Black bear, marten and blacktail deer inhabit the northern area. Trout can be found in Mayer Lake in the southern section of the park and in some of the other lakes and streams. Bald eagles, sea birds and migrating waterfowl travelling the Pacific Flyway can be seen. Fur seals and whales can be sighted from the beach. Beachcombers can find numerous types of shellfish in the tidal pools.

Walks: The 5-km (3.1-mile) Tlell River trail winds along the rivershore to the beach, and the half-hour Tow Hill trail leads to a Blow Hole on the beach and the summit of Tow Hill.

Hikes: The Cape Fife trail leads 10 km (6 miles) to Fife Point.

Backpacking: Naikoon's main backpacking resource is the scenic 95-km (59-mile) hike along the sandy beaches from the park headquarters at Tlell to Tow Hill. The route can be covered in six or seven days, but some hikers take ten days walking at a very leisurely pace. The route has three major river crossings; the Oeanda, Cape Ball and Mayer rivers. All rivers in Naikoon are tidal. Hikers should carry tide tables and plan their crossings for low tide. Volume 6 of the tide tables published by the Canadian Hydrographic Service of Environment Canada includes the Queen Charlotte Islands.

Weather conditions in the area change rapidly and storms lasting up to three or four days can occur. Precipitation, mostly in the form of rain, averages 140 cm (55 inches) annually.

The Queen Charlotte Islands may be reached by air from Vancouver and Prince Rupert and by ferry from Prince Rupert to Queen Charlotte City. Local transportation by road from Masset to Tlell is easily arranged. Food supplies can be purchased at most towns on the islands but it's recommended that hikers bring complete supplies with them to insure fulfilling their needs.

More Information: Zone Manager, Ministry of Parks, Bag 5000, Smithers, British Columbia V0J 2N0, (604) 847-7320.

Southwestern British Columbia

Vancouver Area Regional District Parks

Greater Vancouver Regional District Parks offer diverse walking and hiking trails close to the city. Among the 16 district parks offering hiking opportunities are:

Lynn Headwaters Regional Park in North Vancouver is a 47 square km (18 square mile) wilderness mountain park. During the 1880s giant fir, hemlock and cedar trees from the Lynn Valley were used for beams and spars. The park's 20 km (12 miles) of trails include the 5.4 km (3.3 mile) Lynn Loop Trail, an interpretive path that leads to an abandoned cabin with a view of the Lynn Valley. The 15-km round trip Headwaters Trail starts at the top of the switchback of the Lynn Loop Trail and leads to Norvan Falls. From the top of the nearby Grouse Mountain Skyride, a 4.5-km (2.7-mile) hike leads to a panoramic view from Goat Ridge. (Information: 604-985-1690).

The Seymour Demonstration Forest, covering 56 square km (22 square miles) between Lynn Headwaters Park and Mount Seymour Provincial Park, offers over 40 km (25 miles) of trails including the 1.5-km (0.9-mile) Integrated Forest Resource Management Loop Trail and the 0.4-km (0.2-mile) Forest Ecology Loop interpretive trail. Among the park's other routes are the 2.2-km (1.3-mile) Twin Bridges trail, the 5.5-km (3.4-mile) Fisherman's Trail and the 1-km (0.6-mile) Homestead trail. (Information: 604-432-6286).

Pacific Spirit Regional Park encompasses upland forest of trembling aspen, old-growth fir and cedar, ocean beaches of rock and sand, and river frontage beside the University of British Columbia, near downtown Vancouver. The park's over 50 km (31 miles) of trails follow the ocean shore (including a clothing optional beach) and traverse the interior. Most of the trails are multi-purpose routes used for hiking, cycling and horseback riding. (Information: 604-432-6352).

Belcarra Regional Park covers 6 square km (2.5 square miles) at Burrard Inlet's entrance to Indian Arm, a 19-km (11-mile) fjord. The 9 km (5.5-miles) of marine shoreline is accessible by trail. Sunflower stars, moon jellyfish and beds of eelgrass can be seen. At the park's Sasmat Lake is swimming and a trail along its shore. (Information: mid-May to August 604-420-3031, September to mid-May 604-432-6350).

More Information: Greater Vancouver Regional District Parks, 4330 Kingsway, Burnaby, British Columbia V5H 4G8, (604) 432-6350.

Centennial Trail

Crossing the varied terrain of southwestern British Columbia, the Centennial Trail extends for 258 km (160 miles) from Simon Fraser University in Burnaby near Vancouver, to Cathedral Provincial Park. Although intended as a hiking trail, the 72-km (45-mile) section from Simon Fraser University to Sumas Mountain near Chilliwack is, due to private property holdings, mostly on secondary roads and is more suited to bicycling.

From Sumas Mountain the trail follows rivers and creeks and goes over several mountains including 2,587-meter (8,622-foot) Lakeview Mountain, and passes close to the 2,239- and 2,246-meter (7,464- and 7,486-foot) peaks of the Twin Buttes. In Manning Park, 192 km (119 miles) east of Simon Fraser University, the trail utilizes the park's very scenic Skyline Trail. Between the Ashnola River and Lakeview Creek in Cathedral Provincial Park, 24 km (15 miles) east of Manning Park, there is an 8-km (5-mile) stretch through high open country. From Monument 83 in Manning Park to Cathedral Park, the trail is in poor condition due to a fire that burned the area. The eastern terminus of the trail is at the junction of Ewart Creek and the Ashnola River Road near the town of Keremeos.

Campsites are located on the trail. A hostel operated by the Canadian Hostelling Association is situated near Chilliwack Lake. From Vedder Crossing to Cathedral Park the route is entirely through wilderness and supplies are not available.

More Information: Canadian Hostelling Association, British Columbia Region, 1515 Discovery Street, Vancouver, British Columbia V6R 4K5, (604) 224-7177.

Garibaldi Provincial Park

Garibaldi Provincial Park is a 1,920-km^2 (741-square-mile) alpine wilderness in the Coast Range, 64 km (40 miles) north

Garibaldi Lake, Garibaldi Provincial Park. (B.C. Government Photograph)

of Vancouver. The park is named after and encompasses 2,678-meter (8,784-foot) Mount Garibaldi. Many of the peaks in the park, particularly those in the area around Garibaldi Lake, including Price Mountain, the Table, Mount Garibaldi, the Cinder Cone and the Glacier Pikes, are the result of recent volcanic action. The Black Tusk has been intensely eroded and is the most interesting of the peaks formed by volcanoes.

Forest cover at lower levels comprises a dense growth of Douglas fir, western red cedar and western hemlock. Birch and alder grow along the waterways. Mountain hemlock, yellow cedar, alpine fir and white bark pine are at higher elevations. The alpine areas are carpeted with many varieties of colorful wild flowers including western anemone, lupine, arnica, Indian paint brush and snow lily. Deer, mountain goat, grizzly bear and black bear inhabit the park but are seldom seen. Birds that can be observed include the Canada jay, golden eagle and ptarmigan.

The park's main hiking areas are Diamond Head in the southwest section, and Black Tusk/Garibaldi Lake in the central area.

Hikes/Backpacking: In the Diamond Head area an 11.2-km (7-mile) trail begins at the parking lot 16 km (10 miles) off Highway 99, and goes along Paul Ridge to the Elfin Shelter and primitive campsites near Elfin Lakes and Red Heather Meadows. An A-frame shelter providing accommodation for up to 30 people is also located near Elfin Lakes. Hikers can establish a base camp and explore the area on day hikes. From Elfin Lakes an 11-km (7-mile) trail to Mamquam Lake passes Diamond Head, the Gargoyles which are strange visages formed in eroding lava, and the Opal Cone, a disintegrating volcanic mound.

In the Black Tusk area a 9-km (5.6-mile) trail leads to a campsite on the edge of the Black Tusk Meadows on the shore of Garibaldi Lake where a base camp can be set up. Some of the scenic features that hikers can explore in this area are Panorama Ridge, Mimulus Lake, Black Tusk Lake and Helm Lake. You can also pass near Helm Glacier and the volcanic

Cinder Cone. From Black Tusk Meadows a 14.4-km (9-mile) trail leads to Cheakamus Lake, a glacier-fed lake at 914 meters (2,998 feet) elevation surrounded by towering mountains rising up to 1,500 meters (5,000 feet) from the shore. This lake, which has fishing for rainbow trout and Dolly Varden, can also be reached by a 3.2-km (2-mile) trail whose trailhead is 8 km (5 miles) along a logging road from Highway 99.

Garibaldi Park is a wilderness area, and hikers should arrive with complete supplies, which can be acquired in Vancouver, Squamish and Whistler.

More Information: Zone Manager, Ministry of Parks, Box 220, Brackendale, British Columbia V0N 1H0, (604) 898-3678.

Golden Ears Provincial Park

Situated in the rugged Coast Mountains north of the Fraser River 48 km (30 miles) east of Vancouver, this 550-km^2 (212-square-mile) park is named for prominent twin-peaked 1,706-meter (5,598-foot) Golden Ears Mountain. Garibaldi Park is on the northern park boundary but an almost impenetrable mountain barrier in the region of Mount Glendinning makes travel between the two parks almost impossible.

Vegetation in the area is typical of the Coast Mountains. Douglas fir, hemlock, western red cedar and balsam grow at lower elevation. Cottonwood and alder are found along creek and river banks. The park's lakes and rivers contain coastal cutthroat, kokanee and Dolly Varden.

Walks: The Spirea Bog interpretive trail is a 45-minute walk that explores a bog from a series of boardwalks. The Viewpoint trail is a 1.5-km (0.9-mile) walk to Lake Viewpoint offering good views and during wet season a waterfall. The 2.7-km (1.6-mile) Lower Falls trail is a popular walk along Gold Creek to the 10-meter (33-foot) high falls.

Hikes: The park's network of more than 50 km (30 miles) of hiking trails includes 4.2-km (2.6-mile) Mike Lake trail which links with the 1.2-km (0.7-mile) Incline trail which in turn joins with the 10-km (6-mile) Alouette Mountain hiking trail to panoramic views of Alouette Mountain.

Backpacking: The Golden Ears trail is a strenuous 12 km (7.5 mile) each way hike through second growth, first growth and subalpine forest to alpine terrain on Panorama Ridge, from which, as its name infers, there are magnificent views in all directions. A mountain shelter is located near the ridge.

More Information: Zone Manager, Ministry of Parks, Box 7000, Maple Ridge, British Columbia V2X 7G3, (604) 463-3513.

Cypress Provincial Park

The North Shore Mountains, which form a backdrop to Vancouver, offer hiking close to the city. Situated north of West Vancouver, 30-square-km (11-square-mile) Cypress Provincial Park is just 12 km (7 miles) from downtown Vancouver via the Lions Gate Bridge.

Cypress Park is bounded on the west by Howe Sound, and on the northeast by 1,454-meter (4,770-foot) Mount Strachan and 1,325-meter (4,347-foot) Hollyburn Mountain which along with 1,217-meter (3,992-foot) Black Mountain are the park's highest peaks. A Coastal Douglas fir forest is found at lower elevations, while near ridge tops are mountain hemlock, 40-meter (130-foot) high amabalis fir and yellow cypress.

Animal life in the park includes deer, black bears, coyotes, squirrels, hares and weasels. A variety of birds including ravens, gray jays, chickadees, warblers and woodpeckers can be seen.

Walk: The Yew Lake interpretive trail is a 1.4-km (0.8-mile) loop skirting Yew Lake and exploring the role of water, snow and ice in the development of plants and animals.

Hikes/Backpacking: The 6-km (3.7-mile) Hollyburn Mountain Trail leads from the Hollyburn Ridge parking area to the mountain's peak.

The Howe Sound Crest Trail with good views of Howe Sound and the Coastal Mountain Range, is a 29 km (18 mile) route along mountain ridges from Cypress Bowl in Cypress Park to Highway 99 just south of Porteau Cove Provincial Park on Howe Sound.

The Baden Powell Centennial Trail extends for 42 km (26 miles) from Eagle Ridge near Horseshoe Bay to Deep Cove along the North Shore Mountains. Two sections traverse Cypress Park, an 8.5-km (5.2-mile) section from Horseshoe Bay up Eagle Ridge, over Black Mountain to Cypress Bowl ski area, and a 9.5-km (5.9-mile) section from the Cypress Bowl ski area to Hollyburn Lodge, along Blue Gentian Lake and Lawson Creek to the British Properties.

More Information: Ministry of Parks, Regional Director, 1610 Mount Seymour Road, North Vancouver, British Columbia V7G 1L3, (604) 929-1291.

Mount Seymour Provincial Park

Located just 15 km (9 miles) from downtown Vancouver, this 35-km^2 (13.5-square-mile) park encompasses most of 1453-meter (4,766-foot) Mount Seymour and is bounded on the north by the Coast Mountain Range. The forest is typical of the Coastal Range and comprises Douglas fir and western red cedar at lower elevations, alpine fir and pine at higher elevations, and some areas above the treeline are carpeted with alpine flowers. Wildlife includes blackbear, deer, coyote and a large variety of birds.

The park is mainly a day-use area for the Vancouver and Lower Mainland area, but overnight trips are permitted.

Walks: The Goldie Lake interpretive trail is a 2-km (1.2-mile) loop through a mountain hemlock forest. The Dinky Peak trail leads almost 1-km (0.6-mile) to a view of the Vancouver area.

Hikes: The 4-km (2.4-mile) Mount Seymour trail climbs to the summit. Several trails lead off from this trail.

Backpacking: The 42-km (26-mile) Baden Powell trail which connects Deep Cove with Eagle Ridge near Horseshoe Bay passes through the park.

More Information: Zone Manager, Mount Seymour Provincial Park, 1610 Mount Seymour Road, North Vancouver, British Columbia V7G 1L3, (604) 929-4818.

Manning Provincial Park

Situated in the Cascade Mountains, 224 km (139 miles) east of Vancouver, Manning Park is 665 km² (256 square miles) of mountains, deep valleys, alpine meadows, lakes and rivers. Within the park are the sources of two major rivers: the Skagit which flows west and south to the Pacific Ocean; and the Similkameen, a major tributary of the Columbia River flowing east into the Okanagan.

The mountain slopes are covered with conifers including Douglas fir, western red cedar, hemlock, white spruce and lodgepole pine. Wild flowers carpet the alpine meadows including the spectacular meadows covering an area of 24 km (15 miles) in length and up to 4.8 km (3 miles) in width stretching from Blackwall Mountain to Nicomen Ridge. The Heather Trail traverses this subalpine meadow. Indigenous wildlife includes mule deer, coyote, moose and black bear. Over 190 bird species have been observed in the park.

Walks: Among the park's self-guiding nature trails are the 0.5-km (0.3-mile) Beaver Pond trail which offers excellent bird watching in May and June, the 1-km (0.6-mile) Paintbrush trail which leads through subalpine meadows, and the 0.5-km (0.3-mile) Rein Orchid walk where orchids and other bog flora can be seen.

Hikes: The Three Falls trail is a 9-km (5.5-mile) hike to Shadow, Nepopekum and Derek falls. The Windy Joe Mountain trail is a 14-km (8.6-mile) return hike offering scenic views and a fire lookout interpretive display. The 17-km (10.5-mile) Whatcom trail leads through forest and meadows to Whatcom Pass.

Backpacking: Manning Park is laced with 270 km (167 miles) of trails. By linking trails there are several 50-km (30-mile) trips. The 21-km (13-mile) Heather Trail through alpine meadows to Three Brothers Mountain connects with the 22-km

(14-mile) Bonnevier Trail at Big Buck Mountain and continues to Nicomen Ridge, where the trail links with the 17-km (11-mile) Granger Creek trail.

Manning Park contains part of two major long-distance hiking trails in western North America. In the southern section of the park is the northern terminus of the 3,864-km (2,400-mile) Pacific Crest Trail, a high mountain wilderness route along the crests of the Cascade Range of Washington and Oregon, and the Sierra Nevada and other mountains in California. Manning Park contains 12.5 km (7.5 miles) of the trail from the park headquarters to Monument 78 on the United States border. Hikers crossing the border must comply with all customs regulations. Information on the Pacific Crest Trail can be obtained from Pacific Crest Trail Conference, 365 West 29th Avenue, Eugene, Oregon 97405, USA.

The 258-km (160-mile) Centennial Trail which extends from Simon Fraser University near Vancouver to Cathedral Provincial Park traverses Manning Park on the 18-km (11-mile) Skyline II Trail over Lone Goat and Snow Camp mountains. From Monuments 83 in Manning Park it is about 66 km (40 miles) east along the Centennial Trail, (described separately in this chapter) to Cathedral Park.

Hikers should bring supplies with them as there are no large stores near the park.

More Information: District Superintendent, Manning Provincial Park, Box 123, Manning Park, British Columbia V0X 1R0, (604) 840-8836.

Cathedral Provincial Park

Azure lakes, alpine meadows and the jagged peaks of the Okanagan Mountains form Cathedral Provincial Park, a 300-km^2 (127-square-mile) wilderness area 30 km (19 miles) southwest of the town of Keremeos. The park is bounded on the south by the United States border, on the east by Ewart Creek and on the west and north by the Ashnola River, a tributary of the Similkameen.

The plant and wildlife is typical of the transition zone

between the rain forests of the Cascade Mountains and the drier Okanagan Valley. Forest cover is mainly Douglas fir at lower levels, with cottonwood and aspen along creeks and rivers. At higher elevations are lodgepole pine and Engelmann spruce which give way to subalpine fir and alpine fir near the timberline. Wildlife includes mule deer, mountain goat and California bighorn sheep. Most of the lakes contain Kamloops trout and cutthroat trout.

The five turquoise-colored Cathedral Lakes, the Haystack Lakes and Stone City, a wind eroded quartzite formation looking like a city of a future age, are some of the scenic highlights. The highest peak in the park is 2,628-meter (8,620-foot) Lakeview Mountain.

Hikes/Backpacking: Cathedral Park has about 90 km (56 miles) of trails, including 24 km (15 miles) of the Centennial Trail along Wall Creek, the Ashnola River, Easygoing Creek to the Paysayten River and extending to Monument 83 in Manning Park. Following the Centennial Trail it's about 32 km (20 miles) from Cathedral Park to Manning Park. The entire Centennial Trail is described earlier in this chapter.

A network of 46 km (29 miles) of trails radiates from Quiniscoe Lake to the other scenic lakes, Lakeview Mountain, Bomford Mountain, Pyramid Mountain and Stone City. The Cathedral Lakes can also be reached by a 20-km (12-mile) trail that follows Wall Creek from the Ashnola River.

Access to Cathedral Park is via a secondary road and the Ashnola Forest Development Road for a total distance of 22 km (14 miles) from Highway 3. It's about 16 km (10 miles) along a trail and jeep road from the park entrance to the Cathedral Lakes area.

Cathedral Park is a wilderness area; supplies are not available at the park and hikers should arrive self-sufficient. Topographical maps for the park can be obtained locally at the Government Agent's Office, Penticton, British Columbia.

More Information: Zone Manager, Ministry of Parks, Box 318, Summerland, British Columbia V0H 1Z0, (604) 494-0321.

West-Central British Columbia

Tweedsmuir Provincial Park

A vast unspoiled wilderness, Tweedsmuir Park covers over 9,600 km² (3,700 square miles) in British Columbia's west central region and is the largest provincial park in the province. It is bounded on the west and southwest by the Coast Mountains which average 2,100 meters (6,900 feet), on the east by the Interior Plateau and on the north and northwest by the Ootsa-Whitesail Lakes reservoir. Monarch Mountain in the Coast Range, at 3,533 meters (11,588 feet), is the park's highest peak. Glaciers cling to many of the mountain slopes. The Rainbow Mountains, a range of brightly colored peaks of glistening reds, yellows, greys, lavenders and violets, are in the east central area of the park.

The park's vegetation is as varied as the terrain. Douglas fir, cedar, hemlock and balsam cover the lower slopes of the Coast Mountains. Pine and spruce grow in the northern and central areas. Along the eastern boundary are the rolling grasslands of the Cariboo Plateau. Indigenous wildlife includes moose, mule deer, mountain caribou, black bear and grizzly bear. Bald eagles, golden eagles, ospreys, hummingbirds, horned owls, grouse, ptarmigan, whisky-jacks, ravens, trumpeter swans and loons can be seen. The lakes contain steelhead, kokanee, rainbow trout, cutthroat trout, Dolly Varden, Rocky Mountain whitefish and salmon.

Walks: Among the park's walks is the two-hour Kettle Ponds trail loop leading to a kettle pond and a bog, and the two-hour Burnt Bridge trail loop to a viewpoint overlooking the Bella Coola Valley.

Hikes: The Rainbow trail leads 8 km (4.9 miles) to an unnamed alpine lake from where hikers can explore surrounding terrain. The Octopus trail leads 18 km (11 miles) through the Rainbow Mountains where it connects with the 20-km (12-mile) Capoose trail which follows a network of lakes and waterfalls through the Capoose Valley.

Backpacking: Tweedsmuir Park's most popular trail is the

32-km (20-mile) route along the Atnarko River from Highway 20 to the 260-meter (853-foot) Hunlen Falls and then onto Turner and Lonesome lakes.

The Alexander Mackenzie Heritage trail stretches 300 km (186 miles) from Blackwater River near Quesnel to Bella Coola. The 80-km (50-mile) section within Tweedsmuir Park, considered the most scenic part of the route, takes about 5 to 7 days to hike.

The trail was originally used by Indians for packing oolichan oil (a food rendered from the oolichan fish and highly valued for its tonic qualities) to the interior for trade. In 1793, Alexander Mackenzie, the fur trader, travelled the route on his journey to the Pacific coast, the first overland crossing of North America. For more information of this trail, contact the Alexander Mackenzie Trail Association, P.O. Box 425, Station A, Kelowna, British Columbia V1Y 7P1.

Supplies are not available locally and hikers should arrive self-sufficient.

More Information: District Manager, Tweedsmuir Provincial Park, Ministry of Lands, Bag 5000, Smithers British Columbia V0J 2N0, (604) 847-7320; or 540 Borland Street, Williams Lake, British Columbia V2G 1R8, (604) 398-4414.

Kitimat-Smithers Area

In this region of west central British Columbia the Coast Mountains rise from sea level to an average of 1,800 to 2,100 meters (6,000 to 6,900 feet). Some peaks reach over 2,700 meters (9,000 feet). The snowfield-and glacier-covered Coast Mountains are characterized by densely wooded valleys. The climate is affected by the moist Pacific air. The weather changes rapidly and is very difficult to predict. During the summer there are long hours of daylight.

The area where Highway 16 angles northwest from Smithers to Hazelton, then southwest to Terrace and Kitimat, includes the Nass Range, Rocher Deboule Range, Babine Range, Bulkley Ranges, Hudson Bay Mountain and the Telkwa Range of the Coast Mountains. The region has numerous trails built for mineral exploration which remain in good condition and are now used for hiking. Many trails lead to alpine meadows and some have cabins. *Trails to Timberline* by Elinar Blix is a guide to exploring the hiking trails in this area of the Coast Mountains.

Columbia Mountains

Glacier National Park

In the heart of the Columbia Mountain system, Glacier Park covers 1,350 km² (521 square miles) of the jagged Purcell and

Asulkan Valley, Glacier National Park. (Stewart Guy, Parks Canada)

Selkirk ranges. The mountains are characterized by narrow valleys and uniformly massive bedrock which contrasts with the broad valleys and sedimentary bedrock of the Rocky Mountains to the east. Over 400 glaciers cling to the park's mountain slopes which rise to 3,000 meters (10,000 feet). Half of the land is above 1,800 meters (6,000 feet) and about 12 per cent of the park is covered with snow and ice the year round.

During the summer one can expect some rain about every second day. The moist air from the Pacific rises and condenses when it hits the Selkirk Mountains, resulting in heavy rainfall. The wet valley bottoms are covered with a thick rainforest of huge cedar and hemlock. Spruce and fir are found on the mountain slopes below the timberline. Grizzly and black bear inhabit the park, but other large animals such as deer and moose are not common. A small number of birds such as ravens, Steller's jays, gray jays and Clark's nutcrackers can be seen year-round in the park.

Walks: The 1.2-km (0.7-mile) Abandoned Rails trail explores the history of Rogers Pass, and is wheelchair accessible for most of its route. The 1.6-km (1-mile) Loop Brook trail also highlights railway history.

Hikes: Among the variety of day-hikes in Glacier Park is the 10.4-km (6.4-mile) Flat Creek trail through a valley travelled by prospectors and surveyors during the early days of exploration in this area. The Bostock Creek trail leads 9 km (5.5 miles) to views of the Selkirk Ranges. The 4.2-km (2.6-mile) one-way Avalanche Crest trail leads to views of Rogers Pass, the Hermit Range and the Illecillewaet River Valley.

Backpacking: Glacier Park has more than 160 km (100 miles) of hiking trails. The best overnight trip in the park is the 16-km (10-mile) Copperstain Trail which traverses the extensive alpine meadows on Bald Mountain and has a view of the eastern side of the Sir Donald Range. The 9-km (5-mile) Bostock Creek Trail combined with the 16-km (10-mile) Casualty Creek Trail makes an interesting two- or three-day trip through a series of subalpine meadows. The 42-km

(26-mile) route up the Beaver River, which divides the Purcell and Selkirk ranges, to the southern park boundary takes about three days to hike each way.

Revelstoke and Golden are the closest towns for supplies. Topographical maps can be obtained at the Rogers Pass Communication Building.

More Information: The Superintendent, Glacier National Park, Box 350, Revelstoke, British Columbia V0E 2S0, (604) 837-7500.

Mount Revelstoke National Park

The massive, steep-walled mountains and narrow valleys of the Columbia Mountains distinguish the Mount Revelstoke area from the broad valleys and sedimentary bedrock of the Rocky Mountains to the east. Mount Revelstoke Park occupies 260 km² (100 square miles) between the Columbia and Illecillewaet rivers and includes the Clachnacudainn Range of the Columbia Mountain system.

The Columbia Mountains are one of Canada's wettest areas. Precipitation, produced by moist Pacific air, hits the mountains and is forced to rise. As it rises, the air cools and the moisture condenses and falls as rain. Valleys are covered by a thick rainforest of huge western red cedar, western hemlock, western white pine and devil's club. The subalpine forest between 1,300 and 2,000 meters (4,200 and 6,500 feet) comprises subalpine fir and Engelmann spruce. Above the treeline the alpine meadows are ablaze in late July and August with scarlet Indian paintbrush, blue lupin, yellow arnica and white valerian. Black bears, mountain goats and deer inhabit the park. Bird species include Steller's jays, gray jays and blue grouse.

Walks: The Giant Cedars trail is a 0.5-km (0.3-mile) walk along a boardwalk through a stand of 800-year-old cedars. The 1.2-km (0.7-mile) Skunk Cabbage trail leads through a swamp inhabited by muskrats, beaver, skunk cabbages and many birds. Meadows in the Sky trail is a 1-km (0.6-mile) paved trail through a sub-alpine meadow.

Hikes: The Summit trail leads 10 km (6 miles) one way to the summit of 1,938-meter (6,350-foot) Mount Revelstoke. The Inspiration Woods trail is a 3-km (1.8-mile) hike through a typical Columbia forest. The 8-km (4.9-mile) Lindmark trail leads to meadows just below the summit of Mount Revelstoke.

Backpacking: The park's overnight routes include the 6-km (3.7-mile) Eva Lake trail across gently rolling country and subalpine meadows to a small cabin. Hikers on the 9-km (5.5-mile) Jade Lakes trail reach the jade-green waters of the Upper and Lower Jade Lakes.

Topographical maps can be purchased at the park office. Supplies can be obtained in the town of Revelstoke which borders the park.

More Information: The Superintendent, Mount Revelstoke National Park, Box 350, Revelstoke, British Columbia V0E 2S0, (604) 837-7500.

Earl Grey Pass Trail, Purcell Wilderness Conservancy

The Purcell Wilderness Conservancy preserves 1,315 km^2 (508 square miles) of the craggy Purcell Mountains, the most easterly of the three southern ranges of the Columbia Mountain system. Mount Toby at 3,212 meters (10,537 feet) is the highest peak in the area.

Backpacking: The wilderness conservancy is known for the Earl Grey Pass Trail, named for the Canadian governor-general who travelled the pass in 1908. The 61-km (38-mile) trail straddles the summit of Kootenay Divide and extends from the town of Argenta on the east side of Kootenay Lake in the West Kootenay to Invermere in the East Kootenay.

From the old mining community of Argenta, the trail follows Hamill Creek and climbs 1,341 meters (4,398 feet) over a distance of 45 km (28 miles) reaching an elevation of 2,256 meters (7,400 feet) at Earl Grey Pass. Suggested hiking time from Argenta to the pass is five days. The eastern side of the trail from Invermere follows Toby Creek for a distance of 16 km

(10 miles) with an elevation gain of 1,070 meters (3,510 feet) to the pass, and takes about three days to hike. The Earl Grey Pass Trail is a rigorous hike and should only be attempted by experienced, well-equipped backpackers.

Different forest types are encountered as the trail gains elevation. At lower levels are young alder, hemlock and Douglas fir. Above this zone is an area of hemlock and cedar where some of the trees are almost a thousand years old. Just below the timberline are Engelmann spruce and subalpine fir, and above it are alpine meadows and tarns. Mountain goats may be seen near Toby Glacier and the pass.

Toby Creek is reached by travelling on 32 km (20 miles) of logging roads from the town of Invermere. Argenta is accessible by a secondary road from Highway 31 north of the town of Lardeau.

More Information: Zone Manager, Ministry of Parks, Box 118, Wasa, British Columbia V0B 2K0, (604) 422-3212.

Kokanee Glacier Provincial Park

Glaciers, glacial and freshwater lakes, alpine meadows and steep rocky canyons make up this 320-km^2 (123-square-mile) mountain wilderness in the rugged Slocan Range of the Selkirk Mountains in the West Kootenay region. Named for the glacier that clings to the easterly slopes of 2,774-meter (9,099-foot) Kokanee Peak, most of the park is at an elevation of over 1,800 meters (5,900 feet) and half of it is above 2,100 meters (6,900 feet). The more than 30 gem-colored alpine lakes are nestled at elevations ranging from 1,700 to 2,100 meters (5,575 to 6,900 feet).

The deep valleys are covered with hemlock, western red cedar, lodgepole pine, larch and Engelmann spruce. Dwarf huckleberry, white rhododendron and alpine flowers carpet the alpine meadows. Wildlife is not abundant, but includes mountain goat, deer, black bear, grizzly bear, hoary marmot, pika and rockrabbit. Blue grouse, Franklin grouse and golden eagles can be seen. Several lakes are stocked with cutthroat trout, and the streams contain cutthroat trout.

Walk: A 2-km (1.2-mile) self-guiding nature trail loops around Gibson Lake.

Hikes/Backpacking: Most of the more than 80 km (50 miles) of trails follow creeks to scenic lakes and provide the only access to the park's main area.

From the park access road at Gibson Lake in the south a 10-km (6-mile) trail parallels Kokanee Creek past Kokanee Lake and Kaslo Lake where a trail leads to Slocan Chief Cabin which accommodates 12 people. A 10-km (6-mile) trail from the access roads on the western park boundary follows Enterprise Creek to Enterprise Pass. From the southwestern boundary a 10-km (6-mile) trail parallels Lemon Creek to the Sapphire Lakes. The 9-km (5.5-mile) trail along Silver Spray Creek from Woodbury Creek at the eastern park boundary leads to Silver Spray Cabin which provides accommodation for four people. Another trail starting at Woodbury Creek leads 9 km (5.5 miles) to Woodbury Cabin which holds 8 people.

Kokanee Glacier Park is 29 km (18 miles) northeast of the town of Nelson. Two primary roads and four secondary roads provide access to trailheads. The closest sources of supplies are Nelson, Kaslo, Balfour, New Denver and Slocan City.

More Information: Zone Manager, Kokanee Creek Provincial Park, R.R. 3, Nelson, British Columbia V1L 5P6, (604) 825-4421.

Wells Gray Provincial Park

A vast primitive area in the Cariboo Mountains, Wells Gray Park encompasses a wide variety of scenery including glaciers, alpine meadows carpeted with colorful flowers, numerous waterfalls, extinct volcanoes, lava beds and mineral springs. Helmcken Falls, 135-meters (450-feet) is the highest waterfall. The 5,200 km² (2,008-square-mile) wilderness area is bordered by mountains on the east and north, the upland plateau on the west and encompasses the greater part of the Clearwater River watershed.

On lower mountain slopes grows a dense forest of Douglas fir, western red cedar and hemlock. Above 1,200 meters (3,900 feet) are alpine fir and white spruce, and above the timberline is alpine tundra. Wildlife is plentiful and includes mule deer, caribou, moose, mountain goat, black bear, grizzly bear, weasel, fisher, marten, mink, wolverine, beaver, squirrel, coyote, timber wolf, pika and marmot. Lakes, rivers and streams contain rainbow trout, lake trout and Dolly Varden.

Walks: The Trophy Mountain trail allows walkers to experience an alpine meadow within 45 minutes of the trailhead. Other walks ranging from one-half to four hours explore a variety of sites including the rim of Helmcken Falls and a pioneer farm.

Hikes/Backpacking: The network of over 150 km (95 miles) of trails provide access to the highlights of the park's varied scenery. The 25-km (15-mile) trail to Battle Mountain traverses alpine meadows and links with a 16-km (10-mile) trail to Stevens Lake, a 5-km (3-km) route to Mount Philip and an 8-km (5-mile) hike to Table Mountain.

Murtle Lake, reserved for canoeing only, offers an opportunity to combine backpacking and canoeing. Six trails, ranging from 1 to 12 km in length, lead from the lakeshore to panoramic views, alpine meadows or productive fishing.

Exploring Wells Gray Park by Roland Neave includes descriptions of a number of trails in the park. Limited camping supplies are available in the town of Clearwater, 40 km (25 miles) south of the park.

More Information: Zone Manager, Wells Gray Provincial Park, Box 70, Clearwater, British Columbia V0E 1N0, (604) 587-6150.

Rocky Mountains

Yoho National Park

The action of glaciers, wind and water have produced the erosion pillars known as hoodoos, deep river valleys, cirques, glacial lakes and waterfalls in 1,313-km² (507-square-miles) Yoho National Park. Lying on the western slopes of the Rocky Mountains, Yoho includes 28 peaks over 3,000 meters (10,000

Yoho National Park. (Interpretative Service, Yoho National Park)

feet) and the Kicking Horse River which begins at the Continental Divide and crosses the park from east to west. Banff and Kootenay national parks are on the eastern and southern borders.

The montane zone plant life comprises grassy meadows and forests of Douglas fir, white spruce, trembling aspen and lodgepole pine. Moose, deer, elk, black bear, cougar and mountain goat live at lower elevations, while marmot, pika, and grizzly bear inhabit the alpine areas above 2,100 meters (6,900 feet). The varied birdlife includes Canada geese, ducks, pine siskin, red-breasted nuthatch and golden-crowned kinglet. The golden eagle, white-tailed ptarmigan and gray-crowned rosy finch are seen at higher elevations. The park's lakes and streams contain Dolly Varden, cutthroat trout, brook trout, lake trout and splake trout.

Walks: Among Yoho Park's variety of walks is the Takakkaw Falls trail, a 1-km (0.6-mile) return interpretive walk beside the falls. The 5.2-km (3.2-mile) Emerald Lake circuit goes around the blue-green lake and offers views of Mount Burgess. The 4-km (2.4-mile) return Walk in the Past is a self guiding trail leading to the wreck of an old steam locomotive. The 5.4-km (3.3-mile) Point Lace Falls and Angel Staircase trail is a walk along the Yoho Valley trail from the Takakkaw Falls campground.

Hikes/Backpacking: The park's 400 km (250 miles) of trails reach nearly every part of the park. The extensive trail networks in the Yoho Valley and at Lake O'Hara are popular for day-hiking and overnight trips. In the Yoho Valley five backcountry campsites enable backpackers to hike circuit routes or establish base camps from which to explore the surrounding area. Among the trails is the 16.6-km (10.3-mile) Iceline trail through an avalanche path offering excellent views.

The Lake O'Hara area can be reached only by hiking the 12.8-km (7.9-mile) Cataract Brook or by reserving a seat on the bus (call Lake O'Hara reservation line at 604-343-6433). Trails in the Lake O'Hara area include the 5-km (3-mile) Opabin Pass loop which crosses the Opabin Plateau, the 3-km (2-mile) trail past Seven Sisters Falls to Lake Oesa in a high alpine region and the 3.5-km (2-mile) McArthur Lake Trail. For longer trips there is the 27-km (17-mile) McArthur Pass trail. Due to the popularity of the Lake O'Hara and Yoho Valley backcountry camping areas reservations are necessary.

Longer backpacking trips can be undertaken on the less-used trails in other areas of Yoho Park. Some of these trails are the 40-km (24-mile) Amiskwi fireroad, the 23-km (14-mile) Ice River fireroad, and the 14-km (9-mile) Ottertail River fireroad which links the Lake O'Hara region with the trail system in Kootenay National Park to the south.

Hikers should be equipped with a backpacking stove as fires are not permitted in the backcountry. Trail maps are available at the park office in Field. *The Canadian Rockies Trail Guide* and *The Wonder of Yoho* describe the park's trails. Limited supplies are available in Field and full supplies are best obtained in the larger centers of Banff, Lake Louise or Golden.

More Information: The Superintendent, Yoho National Park, Box 99, Field, British Columbia V0A 1G0, (604) 343-6324.

Kootenay National Park

Kootenay National Park is situated in the Vermillion, Mitchell and Brisco ranges of the western Rocky Mountains, and is bounded on the north by Yoho National Park and on the east by Banff National Park and Mount Assiniboine Provincial Park. The 1,383-km² (534-square-mile) park extends for about 8 km (5 miles) on both sides of the Banff-Radium Highway, and is cut by the Vermillion River Valley and sections of the Sinclair and Kootenay river valleys.

Douglas fir and spruce are found in the Columbia and Kootenay valleys, which have hot and dry summers. The Vermillion Valley to the north has moderate summers and is predominated by Engelmann spruce at lower elevations and alpine fir higher up. Above the timberline at 2,100 meters (6,900 feet) the alpine meadows are covered with red and white mountain heather, dwarf willow and bog laurel. Elk, mule deer, bighorn sheep, mountain goats, black bears and grizzly bears inhabit the park. Among the 160 bird species seen in Kootenay Park are the western tanager, pine siskin, Audubon warbler, olive-sided flycatcher, northern three toed woodpecker, Canada jay and nuthatch. The park's rivers contain Dolly Varden, brook trout, cutthroat trout, rainbow trout and whitefish. The park is known for the mineral waters at the Radium Hot Springs which backpackers with trail-tired muscles may wish to investigate.

Walks: The 0.8-km (0.5-mile) Paint Pots nature trail explores ochre beds where Indians obtained vermillion paint used to decorate their skin and tipis. The Marble Canyon self-guiding trail leads 0.8 km (0.5 mile) along the rim of this narrow chasm to waterfalls. The 0.8-km (0.5-mile) Fireweed trail explores the renewal of a forest burned in a fire in 1968.

Hikes: Kootenay Park's hikes include the 2.7-km (1.6-mile) Dog Lake trail, and the 2.7-km (1.6-mile) Cobb Lake trail. The 4.2-km (2.6-mile) Stanley Glacier trail leads up the Vermillion Valley to the Stanley Glacier basin. The 7.2-km Sinclair Creek trail leads through alpine meadows and links with 9.3-km (5.7-mile) Kindersley Pass trail to form a circuit.

Backpacking: Kootenay has over 200 km (125 miles) of trails in the park. For extended trips, several trails from the Banff-Radium Highway to the spectacular Rockwall region in the northwest corner of the park can be linked or combined with trails in Yoho Park. The Rockwall, the eastern escarpment of the Vermillion Range, has a sheer vertical rise of 700 meters (2,300 feet). The main routes to this area are the 17-km (11-mile) trail along Helmet Creek and the 15-km (9-mile) route along Tumbling Creek. Among the options open to hikers who wish to explore the area is the 55-km (34-mile) Rockwall Highline route.

In the eastern section of the park is the 32-km (20-mile) route to Mount Assiniboine via the Simpson River, Surprise Creek and Ferro Pass.

The Canadian Rockies Trail Guide describes the trails in Kootenay Park. Topographical maps are available at the park information center. A limited selection of hiking supplies is available in the town of Radium, but it's best to do your shopping in Banff.

More Information: The Superintendent, Kootenay National Park, Box 220, Radium Hot Springs, British Columbia V0A 1M0, (604) 347-9615.

Mount Robson Provincial Park

Lofty and usually cloud-topped Mount Robson reaches 3,954 meters (12,972 feet) and is the highest peak in the Canadian Rockies. Bounded on the east by the Continental Divide and Jasper National Park, Mount Robson Park is 2,172 km² (839 square miles) of rugged snow-capped mountains, broad valleys, steep canyons and glacier-fed lakes, rivers and streams. Forest cover comprises spruce, fir, cedar, balsam, alder, lodgepole pine and birch.

Walks: The 2-km (1.2-mile) Fraser River nature walk explores plantlife, wildlife and the Fraser River. The 1-km (0.6-mile) Robson River walk follows gravel flats along the river. The 0.5-km (0.3-mile) Portal Lake Walk goes along the shore of Portal Lake.

Hikes: The 7-km (4.3-mile) each way Kinney Lake trail is a popular hike. Other routes include the 5-km (3.1-mile) Overlander Falls trail and the Mount Fitzwilliam trail which climbs 7.2 km (4.4 miles) to good views.

Backpacking: Of the park's 100 km (60 miles) of backpacking trails, the most popular by far is the 22-km (14-mile) trail to Berg Lake from which Mount Robson rises 2,400 meters (7,872 feet). Elevation gain on the trail is 725 meters (2,380 feet) including a rigorous 450-meter (1,475 feet) climb over a distance of 3.5 km (2 miles) in the spectacular Valley of the Thousand Falls. From Berg Lake the trail continues 2 km (1.2 miles) to Robson Pass where it links with the North Boundary Trail in Jasper Park. The Berg Lake and North Boundary trails are described in *The Canadian Rockies Trail Guide*.

Complete supplies can be obtained in the Jasper townsite.

More Information: Zone Manager, Mount Robson Provincial Park, Box 579, Valemount, British Columbia V0E 2Z0, (604) 566-4325.

Mount Assiniboine Provincial Park

Resembling the Matterhorn of Switzerland, 3,561-meter (11,680-foot) Mount Assiniboine is the highest peak in the Rocky Mountains between the United States border and the Trans Canada Highway. Mount Assiniboine Park occupies 386 km^2 (149 square miles) bounded on the east by Banff National Park and on the west by Kootenay National Park. The only access is by hiking from Banff and Kootenay parks, and from the Spray Reservoir Road from Canmore.

The entire park lies at an elevation of more than 1,500 meters (5,000 feet). The lower areas of the park have a boreal forest of spruce, alpine fir and lodgepole pine. At higher levels are alpine larch and Engelmann spruce. Above the timberline the colorful alpine meadows are carpeted with western anemone, alpine arnica, columbine, Indian paintbrush, spring beauty, alpine fleabane and mountain daisies. Elk, mule deer, mountain goats and bighorn sheet inhabit the area. Among the 63 species of birds observed in the park are the Canada jay, Clark's nutcracker, white-tailed ptarmigan, golden eagle, broadwinged hawk, sparrow, nuthatch, robin, sapsucker and chickadee.

Hikes/Backpacking: Lake Magog at the base of Mount Assiniboine is the goal of most hikers in the park, and there are four main routes there. The 27-km (17-mile) route from Sunshine Ski Village goes over Citadel Pass and through Golden Valley and Valley of the Rocks. From the Spray Reservoir south of the town of Canmore there are two routes: a 24-km (15-mile) route along Bryant Creek and over Assiniboine Pass; and a 25-km (15-mile) route via Wonder Pass. Beginning in Kootenay National Park is the 32-km (20-mile) route along the Simpson River and Surprise Creek, and over Ferro Pass. At Lake Magog there are the four Naiset Cabins that are open to hikers at a cost of $8 per person, in addition to camping sites. *The Canadian Rockies Trail Guide* describes the trails into the park.

From the park's core area there are a variety of trails to explore the surrounding area on day-hikes. Among them is the

5.6-km (3.4-mile) Og Lake trail, the 4.8-km (2.9-mile) Mount
Cautley trail, the 5.6-km (3.4-mile) Wonder Pass Viewpoint
trail and the 5.7-km (3.5-mile) Windy Ridge trail.

More Information: Zone Manager, Ministry of Parks, Box
118, Wasa, British Columbia V0B 2K0, (604) 422-3212.

Top of the World Provincial Park

Most of 80-km^2 (31-square-mile) Top of the World Park is a
magnificent alpine plateau at an elevation of more than 1,800
meters (6,000 feet) enclosed by 2,700-meter (9,000-foot) peaks
in the Rocky Mountains of southeastern British Columbia.
West of the plateau are the jagged peaks of the Hughes Range
and to the east is the Van Nostrand Range dominated by
2,912-meter (9,551-foot) Mount Morro, the highest peak in the
park.

Forest cover consists of alpine fir and Engelmann spruce in
the subalpine area. The plateau is carpeted with colorful alpine
flowers including mountain meadow cinquefoil, mountain
forget-me-nots and white dryas. The park has a small number
of moose, elk, white-tailed deer, wolverine, porcupine, Rocky
Mountain bighorn sheep and mountain goats. The abundant
birdlife includes Clark's nutcrackers, Steller's jays, whiskey
jacks, spotted sandpipers and white-winged crossbills. There is
excellent fishing for cutthroat trout and Dolly Varden in Fish
and Blue lakes.

Hikes/Backpacking: Top of the World Park has about 40 km
(25 miles) of hiking trails. The 6-km (3.7-mile) Fish Lake trail is
an easy hike through dense forest and past rock slides to open
meadows. In addition to 28 primitive campsites there is a cabin
at Fish Lake with room for about 24 people.

From Fish Lake there are several scenic hiking trails
including the 7-km (4.3-mile) trail to the Sugarloaf, the 4-km
(2.4-mile) route to Summer Pass, the 3.2-km (2-mile) hike to
Wildhorse Ridge, and the 2.8-km (1.7-mile) trail to Sparkle
Lake. At the end of most trails are wilderness routes that can be
explored by hikers experienced in route finding.

More Information: Zone Manager, Ministry of Parks, Box 118, Wasa, British Columbia V0B 2K0, (604) 422-3212.

Elk Lakes Provincial Park

Lying in an isolated area of the Front Ranges of the Rocky Mountains on the Alberta boundary, much of this 56-km^2 (22-square-mile) wilderness is above the treeline and is bounded by towering glaciated peaks.

Lower Elk Lake, Elk Lakes Provincial Park. (B.C. Government Photograph)

Among the park's scenic highlights are Upper and Lower Elk lakes. Upper Elk Lake, at an elevation of 1,800 meters (5,900 feet) is fed by the Petain, Elk and Castelneau glaciers. Lower Elk Lake is 100 meters (328 feet) lower and about 800 meters (2,600 feet) southwest of Upper Elk Lake. Engelmann spruce, lodgepole pine and alpine fir grow below the timberline. Scrub birch, cinquefoil, saskatoon, gooseberry and a variety of colorful alpine flowers carpet the alpine meadows. Small numbers of elk, moose, mountain goats, Rocky Mountain bighorn sheep, grizzly bears and black bears are indigenous to the park. Spruce grouse, several members of the jay family and a variety of waterfowl can be seen. The park's lakes contain Rocky Mountain whitefish, cutthroat trout and Dolly Varden.

Hikes/Backpacking: Elk Lakes Park shares a common boundary along the Continental Divide with Peter Lougheed Park in Alberta's Kananaskis Country. Among Elk Lakes Park's 20 km (12.4 miles) of trails is a 4-km (2.4-mile) trail from the Park entrance to Peter Lougheed Park via West Elk Pass. Another route from Peter Lougheed Park leads 7 km (4.3 miles) to Upper Elk Lake.

Within Elk Lakes Park is a 1.6-km (1-mile) trail from Lower Elk Lake to Upper Elk Lake, a 2.4-km (1.5-mile) trail along Upper Elk Lake, and a 4-km (2.4-mile) route from Upper Elk Lake to Petain Creek Waterfall.

Elk Lakes Park is 104 km (65 miles) north along a gravel road from the town of Elkford. Complete supplies should be carried.

More Information: Zone Manager, Ministry of Parks, Box 118, Wasa, British Columbia V0B 2K0, (604) 422-3212.

Hamber Provincial Park

One of the least accessible of the Rocky Mountain parks, this 245-km^2 (95-sqare-mile) wilderness area of spectacular beauty can only be reached by hiking a very difficult trail. The park adjoins Jasper National Park on three sides and encompasses several peaks over 3,000 meters (10,000 feet) including

3,058-meter (10,032-foot) Chisel Peak, 26-km² (10-square-mile) subalpine Fortress Lake, the South Alnus and Serenity glaciers on the western part of the park and part of the Chaba Icefield in the southeast corner. Fortress Lake has good fishing for brook trout.

The only access to Hamber Park is over a 23-km (14-mile) trail that starts at Sunwapta Canyon in Jasper Park, and goes along the Athabasca River and the Chaba River to Fortress Lake. The route is relatively level but has one river ford. Although murky, the Chaba River is usually shallow and has a sandy bottom. It can be treacherous depending on changing seasonal daily run-off. The best time to wade across the river is early September prior to fall freeze-up when the glacier fed Chaba River is at its lowest level.

The trek should be attempted by experienced backpackers only. The Fortress Lake trail is described in *The Canadian Rockies Trail Guide*.

More Information: Zone Manager, Hamber Provincial Park, Box 579, Valemount, British Columbia V0E 2Z0, (604) 566-4325.

Northern British Columbia

Stone Mountain Provincial Park

Named after the 2,041-meter (73-foot) mountain situated north of the park, Stone Mountain Park covers 256 km² (99 square miles) of the northern Rocky Mountains characterized by many barren and imposing peaks. Mount St. George at 2,261 meters (7,419 feet) in the southern section is the park's highest. The northern section of the park is dominated by Mount St. Paul which reaches 2,127 meters (6,979 feet). Glacial green Summit Lake, 2,000 meters (6,560 feet) long and 400 meters (1,312 feet) across at its widest point, is the park's largest lake. There are small populations of moose, mountain goats, stone sheep and Osborne caribou. Grizzly bears are occasionally sighted. Fishing opportunities are poor.

The Alaska Highway traverses the park for 13 km (8 miles) from the eastern entrance at Km 619 (Mile 385) which is 159 km (99 miles) northwest of Fort Nelson, to the western boundary at Km 634 (Mile 394). Summit Pass, situated in the park, is the highest point on the Alaska Highway.

Walk: The Erosion Pillars are a 0.5-km (0.3-mile) walk across from Rocky Crest picnic area.

Hikes: Summit Peak is a 5-km (3-mile) round trip offering an alpine view. The Flower Springs trail is a 5.7-km (3.5-mile) hike to alpine lakes and waterfalls.

Backpacking: MacDonald Creek Valley offers a one- to three-day trip where caribou, sheep and moose can be seen. A two-day hike up the Churchill Mine Road leads to the Wokkpash Valley where there are hoodoos. The Wokkpash and MacDonald Creek hikes can be combined for a 70-km (43-mile) trip.

Hikers should bring complete supplies with them. The few stores on the Alaska Highway have limited selections and high prices.

More Information: Zone Manager, Ministry of Parks, 9512 - 100th Street, Fort St. John, British Columbia V1J 3X6, (604) 787-3407.

Muncho Lake Provincial Park

Muncho Lake Park covers 885 km² (342 square miles) of rugged wilderness in the Terminal and Sentinel Ranges of the northern Rocky Mountains which rise to 2,134 meters (7,000 feet) surrounding Muncho Lake. The Alaska Highway bisects the park with the eastern boundary at Km 683 (Mile 424 which is 223 km (139 miles) northwest of Fort Nelson, and the western boundary at Km 771 (Mile 479).

Muncho Lake, a glacial jade lake whose name is an Indian word for "big water," and the surrounding area are considered to be the most scenic on the British Columbia section of the Alaska Highway. The valley bottoms in the park are covered with white spruce and lodgepole pine. The heavy growth at low elevations thins to scrubby alpine spruce and ends abruptly at the treeline. Dwarf alpine plants are scattered on the higher slopes.

Moose, mountain goat, stone sheep, Osborne caribou, elk, coyote, fox, marten, grizzly bear and black bear inhabit the park. Golden eagles, hawks, spruce grouse, willow ptarmigan and Canada jays are among the birds that have been observed. Fishermen may catch Dolly Varden, Arctic grayling and Rocky Mountain whitefish in Muncho Lake, the Todd River and the Trout River.

Walk: A 45-minute loop trail explores natural mineral lick formations near the banks of the Trout River.

Hikes/Backpacking: Trails parallel to the Trout River give access to a variety of remote areas suitable for wilderness backpacking. Cross-country travel is also possible. Problems with grizzly and black bears in the park have increased in recent years and hikers should not travel alone. Package all food in sealed containers and ensure that your clothing does not have any food odors on it.

Complete supplies should be acquired before travelling to the park.

More Information: Zone Manager, Ministry of Parks, 9512 - 100th Street, Fort St. John, British Columbia V1J 3X6, (604) 787-3407.

Tatlatui Provincial Park

Situated on the remote Stikine Plateau and the Tatlatui Range of the Skeena Mountains, this 1,058-km^2 (408-square-mile park has many peaks over 2,000 meters (6,500 feet) of which Melanistic Peak at 2,350 meters (7,710 feet) is the highest. The park is 182 km (113 miles) north of Hazelton, 443 km (275 miles) northwest of Prince George, and borders on the northwest with Spatsizi Plateau Wilderness Provincial Park.

Wildlife includes moose, mountain goats, sheep, elk, wolves, grizzly bears and black bears. Anglers can fish for rainbow trout, Dolly Varden, lake char and Arctic grayling.

Backpacking: Trails may be followed into interesting areas of the park with primitive camping on lakes and streams. The trails are not marked or regularly maintained. It may be difficult to locate the starting point of some trails.

There are no roads into the park. Access is by float plane. The nearest charters are at Smithers and Eddontenajon Lake. The park does not have any facilities and backpackers should be self-sufficient. Those wishing to travel into this remote area may wish to avail themselves of the services of one of the outfitters that operate in the park.

More Information: Zone Manager, Ministry of Parks, Bag 5000, Smithers, British Columbia V0J 2N0, (604) 847-7320.

Spatsizi Plateau Wilderness Provincial Park

Spectacular alpine plateau scenery and a top-quality wildlife habitat is preserved in this 6,753-km^2 (2,608-square-mile) wilderness park east of the British Columbia Railway and 320 km (200 miles) north of Smithers. The diverse terrain ranges from bogs to alpine and glacial areas.

The area supports a large population of stone sheep, Osborne caribou, mountain goat, moose, grizzly bear and wolf. The Gladys Lake Ecological Reserve, occupying 332 km^2 (128 square miles) within the park, is designated for the long-term study of stone sheep and mountain goats, and their environment.

Backpacking: A variety of trails in Spatsizi Park lead to alpine areas, many with extensive plateaus offering excellent terrain for hiking.

Access into the park by trail is along McEwan Creek or Eaglenest Creek from the B.C. Rail grade south of the Ealue Lake Road. The McEwan Creek trail leads through the Stikine River Provincial Recreation Area to Cullivan Creek which it follows to Cold Fish Lake. The Eaglenest Creek trail traverses the Gladys Lake Ecological Reserve, where stone sheep and mountain goats may be seen, to Cold Fish Lake.

From Cold Fish Lake, trails lead to Black Fox Creek,

Caribou Mountain, Ice Box Canyon and Bates Mountain. Most of the park's trails, which were originally game trails and later horse trails, are blazed and usually cleared. Many have water crossing and should be attempted on foot only in late summer when water levels are lower.

Spatsizi Park can also be reached by float plane. Aircraft can be chartered at Dease Lake, Eddontenajon Lake, Terrace and Smithers. Backpackers should carry complete supplies with them. Individuals or groups may wish to use the services of a licensed outfitter.

More Information: Zone Manager, Ministry of Parks, Bag 5000, Smithers, British Columbia V0J 2N0, (604) 847-7320.

Atlin Provincial Park

Atlin Provincial Park lies in the remote northwest corner of British Columbia east of the Alaska border and 48 km (30 miles) south of the Yukon. The 2,330-km^2 (900-square-mile) wilderness area is situated on the Tagish Highlands, a transition zone between the Interior Plateau and the Coast Mountains. Atlin Lake, whose name is derived from the Tagish Indian word meaning "big water," is one of the largest bodies of fresh water in the province. The spectacular Liewillyn Glacier covering 710 km^2 (275 square miles) and the 100-km^2 (39-square-mile) Willison Glacier dominate nearly one-third of the park's area.

The forest cover consists of open stands of aspen, white spruce and lodgepole pine at lower elevations, and the alpine areas are covered with heather, dwarf willow, juniper, mosses, lichens and grasses. Blacktail deer, moose, cinnamon bear and grizzly bear live at lower elevations; and stone sheep, mountain goat and Osborne sheep inhabit the higher areas. Birds that are indigenous to the area or migrate through include Bonaparte gulls, Arctic terns, common loons, several species of ducks, snipe, plower, bald eagle and ptarmigan.

Backpacking: Atlin Park has no maintained trails. From the head of Skoko Inlet overgrown trails lead to Skoko Lake and to

Llewellyn Glacier. A short trail goes from the head of Llewellyn Inlet to a viewpoint overlooking the glacier. There is access to alpine areas from the southeast slopes of Birch Mountain and Mount McCallum. The historic Telegraph Trail is now virtually impassable and fording the O'Donnel River impossible except in low water conditions.

Access to the park is by boat from the community of Atlin, or charter aircraft. The town of Atlin is on Highway 7, 98 km (59 miles) from Jake's Corner in the Yukon. Supplies cannot be obtained locally and hikers should arrive self-sufficient. Backpackers may wish to join organized treks to the Atlin area.

More Information: Zone Manager, Ministry of Parks, Bag 5000, Smithers, British Columbia V0J 2N0, (604) 847-7320.

Guidebook Sources

The Best of B.C.'s Hiking Trails, by Bob Harris, describes 20 hikes including Earl Grey Pass, Chilkoot Trail, Tweedsmuir Park, Great Divide Trail, and Kokanee Glacier Park. Available from: Lone Pine Publishing, 414, 10357 - 109 Street, Edmonton, Alberta T5J 1N3; $9.95.

Blisters and Bliss: A Trekker's Guide to Vancouver Island's West Coast Trail, by David Foster and Wayne Aitken. Available from: Cloudcap, Box 27344, Seattle, Washington 98125, USA; $11.95.

The Canadian Rockies Trail Guide, by Brian Patton and Bart Robinson, is a guide to many of the trails in the Rocky Mountains of British Columbia and Alberta. Available from Summerthought Ltd., P.O. Box 1420, Banff, Alberta T0L 0C0; $14.95 (plus $3 for postage and handling).

Easy Hiking Around Vancouver, by Jean Cousins and Heather Robinson, contains 36 hikes on wilderness trails around Vancouver. Available from Douglas and McIntyre, 1615 Venables Street, Vancouver, British Columbia V5L 2H1; $8.95 (for mail orders include postage of $1 plus 50 cents per book).

Exploring Manning Park, by Robert Cyca and Andrew Harcombe, is a guide to the park's trails. Available from Douglas and McIntyre; $1.95.

Exploring Wells Gray Park, by Roland Neave, is a guide to the park's trails. Available from The Friends of Wells Gray Park, Box 1386, Kamloops, British Columbia V2C 6L7; $9.95.

51 Hikes on Vancouver's North Shore Mountains, by Trevor Summers. Available from: Gordon Soules Books Publishers Ltd., 1352A Marine Drive, West Vancouver, British Columbia V7T 1B5; $9.95.

A Guide to Climbing and Hiking in Southwestern British Columbia, by Bruce Fairley. Available from: Gordon Soules Book Publishers Ltd.; $24.95.

Hiking Trails I: Victoria and Vicinity describes more than 20 hiking areas including several beach hikes. Most are day hikes. Available from Outdoor Club of Victoria Trails Information Society, P.O. Box 1875, Victoria, British Columbia V8W 2Y3; $7.50 (plus $1 for postage and handling, which is sufficient for orders of up to three).

Hiking Trials II: Southeastern Vancouver Island covers the area from the Kiksilah River to Mount Arrowsmith, and includes several overnight trips. Available from Outdoor Club of Victoria Trails Information Society; $8.

Hiking Trails III: Central and Northern Vancouver Island includes trails and high ridge routes in Strathcona Park, and trails in Cape Scott Park. Available from Outdoor Club of Victoria Trails Information Society; $8.

Island Adventures: An outdoors guide to Vancouver Island, by Richard K. Blier, includes a variety of hiking on the island. Available from: Orca Book Publishers, P.O. Box 5626, Station B, Victoria, British Columbia V8R 6S4; $12.95 (plus postage and handling $1 in Canada, $1.50 for U.S. and overseas.)

Islands for Discovery: An outdoors guide to B.C.'s Queen Charlotte Islands, by Denis Horwood and Tom Parkin, includes Naikoon Provincial Park. Available from: Orca Book Publishers; $14.95.

103 Hikes in Southwestern British Columbia, by David Macaree, details hiking trails on the North Shore, Vancouver Island, the islands on the Strait of Georgia, the Garibaldi area, the Fraser Valley and the Manning Park area. Most are day hikes. Available from Douglas and McIntyre; $12.95.

109 Walks in B.C.'s Lower Mainland, by David and Mary Macaree, includes hikes in the Vancouver, North Shore, Fraser Valley, Chilliwack River, Hope Canyon, Fraser Canyon and Howe Sound areas. Available from Douglas and McIntyre; $12.95.

The Pacific Rim Explorer, by Bruce Obee, describes the West Coast Trail and Long Beach. Available from Whitecap Books, 1086 West 3rd Street, Vancouver, British Columbia V7P 3J6; $12.95.

Sunshine and Salt Air: A recreation guide to the Sunshine Coast, by Karen Southern. Available from Harbour Publishing, Box 219, Madeira Park, British Columbia V0N 2H0; $8.95.

Trails to Timberline, by Einar Blix, is a guide to trails in the Kitimat-Smithers area of west-central British Columbia. Available from Fjelltur Books, Box 2604, Smithers, British Columbia V0J 2N0; $12.95.

The West Coast Trail and Nitinat Lakes: A Trail Guide, by the Sierra Club of British Columbia. Available from Douglas and McIntyre; $9.95.

The Wonder of Yoho, by Don Beers, describes trails in Yoho National Park. Available from Rocky Mountain Books, 106 Wimbledon Crescent S.W., Calgary, Alberta T3C 3J1; (write for current price).

2

Yukon

THE THREE men stared in awe at the flecks of yellow in the cold waters of Rabbit Creek. The year was 1896, and George Carmack and his two Indian companions had found gold in this lonely tributary of the Klondike River. Soon it was lonely no more as thousands of excited "sourdoughs" tore up the streams and valleys in the great Klondike Gold Rush of 1898. They came by sea and then packed hundreds of pounds of food and gear, climbing in an endless file up the towering Chilkoot Pass. Their trail is still marked, and is an exhilarating adventure for hikers.

The Yukon is 536,326 km² (207,087 square miles) of high mountains and hills, fast-flowing streams and broad valleys cut by great rivers. The Yukon Plateau is a basin-like area 600 to 900 meters (2,000 to 3,000 feet) high of rolling hills, deep valleys and isolated mountain ranges, drained by the Yukon River and its tributaries. West of the plateau are the St. Elias and Coast Mountain Ranges, to the north is the Ogilvie Range and the Mackenzie Mountains are to the east.

Most of the Yukon's marked and maintained hiking trails are in Kluane National Park in the St. Elias Range, and through the Coast Range. For hikers skilled with map and compass there are opportunities to follow abandoned trapping trails and mining roads throughout the Yukon. These routes are marked on topographical maps but they are not maintained.

Whitehorse is the capital of the Yukon and the territory's

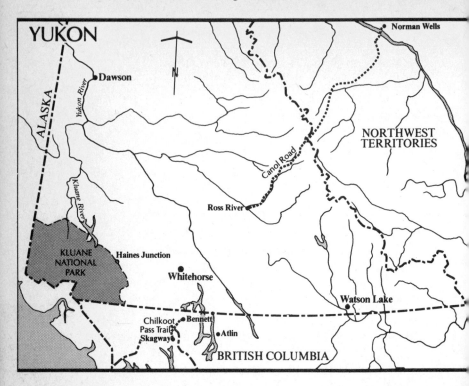

largest city. Hiking supplies can be acquired there. Prices in the Yukon are higher than in southern Canada and if you are travelling north you may wish to stock up on supplies beforehand.

In the south, lying at a higher elevation, there is an average of 45 days without frost, while the area around Dawson City has an average of 75 frost-free days. The interior is dry, as the moisture carried by the prevailing easterly winds from the Pacific strikes the Coast Mountains, cools, condenses and falls as rain or snow. The average annual precipitation in the Yukon ranges from 23 to 33 cm (9 to 13 inches) with about half of it falling during the four summer months.

The best time of year for hiking is from the middle of June to the end of August. Conditions for hiking during September and October depend on weather conditions; snow storms can occur at high elevations in September. During the summer the Yukon has long hours of daylight.

More Information: Yukon Department of Tourism, Box 2703, Whitehorse, Yukon, Y1A 2C6 (403) 667-5340. Hostels in the Yukon are operated by the Yukon Hostelling Association, Box 4762, Whitehorse, Yukon Y1A 4N6, (403) 667-4471.

Chilkoot Pass Trail

Between the summers of 1897 and 1898 about 40,000 men and women challenged the Chilkoot Pass through the Coast Mountains on their way to the Klondike gold fields. The

Chilkoot Pass Trail. (Alaska Division of Tourism)

North-West Mounted Police required that anyone travelling to the Yukon have one year's provisions, which weighed about 900 kg (2,000 pounds). The grueling trek relaying supplies over the Chilkoot Pass has remained a symbol of the Gold Rush stampede.

The 53-km (33-mile) trail which runs between Dyea, 14 km (9 miles) from Skagway, Alaska to Bennett, British Columbia, is maintained for hikers and has several shelters and campsites. Hikers can see many Gold Rush artifacts remaining along the trail. Wildlife that can be observed includes bald eagles, hummingbirds, bears and an occasional lynx. Blueberries, salmon-berries, currants, high-bush and low-bush cranberries and goose-berries grow along many parts of the trail.

The route has an elevation gain of over 600 meters (2,000 feet) and is considered difficult. It usually takes five days to hike. Weather is variable and hikers should be prepared for cool temperatures with rain, fog, snow and high winds.

More Information: Parks Canada, 119-204 Range Road, Whitehorse, Yukon Y1A 3Y1 (403) 668-2116

Kluane National Park

The lofty peaks of the St. Elias Mountains including 5,950-meter (19,520-foot) Mount Logan, Canada's highest peak, and some of the world's largest nonpolar icefields are embraced in 22,014-km² (8,500-square-mile) Kluane Park. Covering the southwest corner of the Yukon, Kluane is Canada's second largest national park and is characterized by rugged mountains, wide valleys, mountain lakes, valley glaciers, alpine meadows and tundra.

There are two major mountain ranges in the park. The Kluane Range is a chain of 2,500-meter (8,200-foot) summits interrupted by several large valleys and cut by rivers, three of them glacier-fed. The Icefield Range includes Mount Logan and a number of other high peaks of 4,500 to 5,400 meters (15,000 and 18,000 feet). Separating the Kluane and Icefield ranges is a narrow trough known as the Duke Depression

Kluane National Park. (Parks Canada)

consisting of several large plateaus and a series of valleys where the tongues of glaciers protrude.

Below the timberline at 1,050 to 1,200 meters (3,500 to 4,000 feet) is a montane forest of white spruce, trembling aspen and poplar. Willow, shrub birch, alder and many small plants and flowers are found above the timberline. Wildlife that inhabits Kluane includes moose, Dall sheep, mountain goats and caribou. Grizzly bears are found throughout the park, and black bears in the forested areas. Over 170 species of birds have been observed including the upland sandpiper, Arctic tern, peregrine, flacon, bald eagle, golden eagle, mountain bluebird and sharptailed grouse. Large lake trout, pike, grayling and kokanee can be found in the park's lakes and streams.

Walks: The Williscroft Canyon trail is a 1.5 km (1 mile) route through a gorge near Kluane Lake's western shore. Dall sheep and golden eagles can be seen in this area. The 5.5-km (3.4-mile) Wetland Interpretive Trail goes along the Dezadeash River with views of wildflowers, waterfowl and views of the Kluane Ranges. The Rock Glacier Trail is a self-guiding route leading 0.8 km (0.5 mile) to a rock glacier. The St. Elias Lake trail leads 4 km (2.4 miles) to an alpine lake.

Hikes: The 7.5-km (4.6-mile) Mt. Decoeli route leads to the mountain's summit with views of the Shakwak Valley. The 11.5 (7-mile) Sheep Mountain Ridge hike is mostly above the timberline. Along the 11.4 km (7-mile) one way Bullion Creek route, gold found in 1903 brought a rush of thousands of fortune-seekers. The 19-km (11.8-mile) round trip Auriol Trail goes through the Auriol Range.

Backpacking: The Alsek Trail leads 29 km (18 miles) through the only major river flowing from the Yukon to the Pacific. The 16-km (10-mile) Sheep-Bullion Plateau hike is an overnight route through alpine tundra. The 48.5-km (30-mile) Nines Creek trail is a five- to six-day hike across alpine tundra. The 85-km (53-mile) Cottonwood Trail is a four- to five-day trip through a variety of alpine scenery. *Kluane National Park Hiking Guide* details the park's trails.

More Information: The Superintendent, Kluane National Park, Haines Junction, Yukon Y0B 1L0, (403) 634-2251.

Other Alpine Hikes

Several spectacular hiking areas are accessible from Yukon highways. Some of these are North Fork Pass in the Tombstone Mountains reached off the Dempster Highway; the Macmillan Pass region at the end of the North Canol Road near the Northwest Territories border; and Lapie Lake on the South Canol Road south of the community of Ross River.

Canol Heritage Trail

The Canol Heritage Trail from Ross River in the Yukon through the Mackenzie Mountains to Norman Wells in the

Northwest Territories is accessible to hikers in the Yukon. Consult the chapter on the Northwest Territories for more information.

Guidebook Sources

Kluane National Park Hiking Guide by Darryl Bray, is a guide to the park's trails. Available from Travel Vision, 79 - 100 Lewes Blvd., Whitehorse, Yukon Y1A 3W1; $12.95 (plus $1 for postage and handling).

3

Alberta

THE MAJESTIC Rocky Mountains are Alberta's most widely known outdoor resource. The province's three Rocky Mountain national parks—Jasper, Banff and Waterton Lakes—have between them over two thousand kilometers of trails through spectacular alpine scenery for walking several hours, day hikes and backpacking trips from overnight or extended trips of several weeks duration. Less well known are Kananaskis country and the wilderness areas which border the national parks.

The Rocky Mountains comprise only a part of Alberta's 660,933 km² (255,200 square miles). To the east are the Foothills and the Alberta Plateau, the third prairie level, which

Average daily minimum and maximum temperatures in Alberta

		May		June		July		August		Sept.		Oct.	
		L	H	L	H	L	H	L	H	L	H	L	H
Banff	°C	1	15	4	18	6	23	5	22	2	16	−2	10
	°F	33	59	39	65	43	73	41	71	35	61	29	50
Jasper	°C	1	16	5	20	7	23	6	22	3	17	−1	11
	°F	34	61	41	68	45	74	43	71	37	63	30	51
Calgary	°C	3	17	7	20	9	24	8	23	4	18	−1	12
	°F	37	63	44	68	49	76	46	74	39	64	30	54
Edmonton	°C	4	18	8	21	11	24	8	22	4	17	−1	11
	°F	39	64	46	70	51	75	47	72	39	63	30	52

is rolling prairie in the south, and forest, lake and river country in the north.

Weather

Alberta receives the most sunshine in Canada; in Banff the July average is 255 hours. Summers are hot and winters are cold since the Rocky Mountains block the moderating influence of the Pacific Ocean.

Snow is usually gone from trails in valleys below 1,500 meters (5,000 feet) by the beginning of May. Trails at elevations between 1,500 and 2,100 meters (5,000 to 6,900 feet) are free of snow by June, and routes above 2,100 meters (6,900 feet) are clear by late June or early July.

Tourist Information: Alberta Tourism, City Centre, 10155 - 102 Street, Edmonton, Alberta T5J 4L6, (403) 427-4321, toll-free throughout Canada and the United States 1-800-661-8888, from within Alberta 1-800-222-6501.

Maps: Topographical maps can be purchased from Maps Alberta, 2nd Floor, North Tower, Petroleum Plaza, 9945 - 108 Street, Edmonton, Alberta T5J 3Z3, (403) 427-3520.

Hostels in Alberta are operated by Canadian Hostelling Association—Mountain Region, 1414 Kensington Road, N.W., Calgary, Alberta, T2N 3P9, (403) 283-5551, and the Alberta Hostelling Association, 10926-88th Avenue, Edmonton, Alberta T6G 0Z1, (403) 432-7798.

Rocky Mountains

Jasper National Park

Offering spectacular alpine scenery, Jasper Park covers 10,878 km^2 (4,200 square miles) on the eastern side of the Continental Divide and is the largest of the national parks in the Canadian Rocky Mountains. To the west is British Columbia's Mount Robson Provincial Park, and Banff National Park is on its southern boundary. Jasper's peaks and broad flat valleys were carved by glaciers of the last Ice Age. The Columbia Icefield, a remnant of the glacial age, straddles the Continental Divide at

the south end of the park, and waters from its glaciers feed
rivers that flow west to the Pacific Ocean, north to the Arctic
Ocean and northeast to Hudson Bay. The Athabasca River, the
major drainage system in Jasper Park, flows north through the
park's mountain ranges to the Arctic Ocean.

Lodgepole pine, poplar, aspen, white spruce and grassy
meadows are found on lower mountain slopes. Just below the
timberline at 2,100 meters (6,900 feet) are continuous bands of
Engelmann spruce and alpine fir. Stunted alpine vegetation

Mount Edith Cavell, Jasper National Park, Alberta. (Parks Canada) produced by a subarctic climate is found above the treeline.

Native wildlife includes mule deer, elk, moose, coyote, marten and black bear at the lower elevations, and grizzly bear, mountain goats, bighorn sheep, marmot and pika in the remote upper regions. The bird population, which is smaller than on the wetter western side of the Rockies, includes eagles, pipits and ptarmigans at higher elevations, and gray jays, ravens and black and white magpies at lower elevations.

Jasper Park is known for its very well developed system of trails. More than 960 km (595 miles) of hiking trails wind through the mountains, and some go through areas that were important to the fur trade of the early 1800s.

Walks: Jasper Park offers a large variety of walks. Among the paths near Jasper townsite is the 6.4-km (4-mile) Old Fort Point Trail offering views of the Athabasca Valley, the 3.5-km (2.1-mile) Lac Beauvert loop, the 2.4-km (1.5-mile) Lake Annette loop and a variety of walks along the Athabasca River.

The Maligne Canyon's walks range from the 0.8-km (0.5-mile) Maligne Canyon loop, to the 3.2-km (2-mile) Maligne Lakeside loop. Walks from the Icefield Parkway in Jasper Park include the 2-km (1.2-mile) Athabasca Glacier Trail, the 1.4-km (0.9-miles) Athabasca Falls Trail and the 6-km (3.7-mile) Valley of the Five Lakes Trail.

Hikes: Longer day-hikes in Jasper Park include the 12-km (7.4-mile) return Wilcox Pass route, the 8-km (5-mile) Angel Glacier-Cavell Meadows loop, the 7.2-km (4.5-mile) Jasper-Pyramid Lake trail, the 9.6-km (6-mile) Maligne Lake Road to Summit Lake route, and the 10-km (6-mile) Bald Hills Lookout hike.

Backpacking: For trips of three to four days there are the 48-km (30-mile) Jonas Pass Trail, the 50-km (31-mile) Maligne Pass Trail and the 45-km (28-mile) high alpine Skyline Trail. These three trails connect at different points making longer trips possible.

The Tonquin Valley Trail, a 42-km (26-mile) loop traversing alpine and subalpine terrain and the 19-km (12-mile) route to

Fryatt Creek offer hikers opportunities to establish a base camp in the backcountry and explore the area on day hikes. The Pobotan-Brazeau-Nigel Loop is a 72-km (45-mile) route that crosses two major passes and extensive alpine meadows.

The 193-km (120-mile) North Boundary Trail and the 185-km (115-mile) South Boundary Trail are for extended wilderness hikes of ten days to two weeks duration. Access trails from the North Boundary Trail reach into Willmore Wilderness Park.

Topographical maps can be purchased at the park information center. *The Canadian Rockies Access Guide* details the park's walks and hikes. *The Canadian Rockies Trail Guide* describes shorter and longer trails.

Jasper Park has a quota on the number of hikers permitted on a trail at one time. Reservations are accepted on up to one-third of the trail's capacity and can be made by writing to or telephoning the park superintendent. The remaining two thirds of the quota is on a first come, first served basis. Topographical maps can be purchased at the park information centre.

More information on Jasper Park, contact: The Superintendent, Jasper National Park, P.O. Box 10, Jasper, Alberta T0E 1E0, (403) 852-6177.

Banff National Park

Established in 1885 as a 26-km^2 (10-square-mile) reserve around hot sulphur springs, Banff National Park is Canada's oldest national park and now occupies 6,641 km^2 (2,564 square miles) of spectacular glaciated scenery in the Rocky Mountains. The park stretches for 240 km (150 miles) along the eastern slope of the Continental Divide. To the west are Yoho and Kootenay national parks and the Columbia Icefields are at the northern boundary with Jasper Park.

The U-shaped valleys and steep peaks, characteristic of the Rocky Mountains, were carved by glaciers during the last Ice Age. The park's forest cover consists of dense stands of lodgepole pine, white spruce and Douglas fir on the lower slopes, and sub-alpine fir and Engelmann spruce at higher elevations. Above the treeline at 2,100 meters (6,900 feet) a semi-arctic climate has produced stunted, windswept vegetation. Alpine meadows are carpeted with colorful alpine flowers for a few weeks during the summer.

Moose, elk, deer and black bear can be seen at lower elevations. The grizzly bear, mountain goat and bighorn sheep inhabit the high alpine areas though grizzly bears are found at low elevations as well. The park's evergreen forests do not support a large number of bird species. Chickadees, nutcrackers, gray jays and magpies can be seen the year round. During the summer, golden eagles, warblers and many types of waterfowl can be observed.

Banff National Park has more than 1,500 km (900 miles) of hiking trails reaching into all parts of the park.

Walks: Self-guiding interpretive trails near the town of Banff include the 2-km (1.2-mile) Fenland Trail which traverses an area of marsh and forest. The Tunnel Mountain Hoodoos path leads to the Hoodoo formations (pillars of silt, gravel and rocks) and views of the Bow Valley and Mount Rundle. The 1.1-km (0.6-mile) Bankhead Trail explores the ruins of the coal mine located here in 1911.

At the Cave and Basin hot springs are two boardwalk trails which are wheelchair accessible. The 0.4-km (0.2-mile) Discovery Trail explains the Cave and Basin's geology and human history, the 0.5-km (0.3-mile) Marsh Trail goes through the lush vegetation that thrives on the hot mineral waters flowing out of the hillside.

Short walking trails near the town of Banff include the 2.3-km (1.4-mile) trail to the summit of Tunnel Mountain, the 3.7-km (2.3-mile) Sundance Trail past swamps made by beavers and wetlands home to a variety of birds and animals, and the 1.6-km (1-mile) Middle Springs Trail to a small cave with hot springs in their natural setting.

In the Lake Louise area the most popular trails are the 3-km (1.8-mile) Louise Lakeshore Trail leading along the level northwest shore of Lake Louise and links with the Plain of Six Glaciers Trail, the 1.5-km (0.9-mile) Moraine Lakeshore Trail

Moraine Lake, Banff National Park, Alberta. (Travel Alberta)

along Moraine Lake's northwest shore, and the 0.8-km (0.5-mile) Moraine Lake Rockpile Trail offering the view of the Valley of the Ten Peaks pictured on the back of the $20 bill.

Self-guiding interpretive trails along the Icefields Parkway include the 2.1-km (1.3-mile) round trip Bow Summit Trail overlooking Peyto Lake, Peyto Glacier and Mistaya Valley, the 0.3-km (0.2-mile) Mistaya Canyon path, and the 5-km (3-mile) Parker Ridge Trail through a tundra-like environment.

Hikes: Some of the day-hikes near the town of Banff include the 5.3-km (3.2-mile) each way Spray River loop, the 7.7-km (4.7-mile) Cascade Amphitheatre Trail leads through an alpine meadow to a cirque (the depression gouged by glacier in the mountainside) on Cascade Mountain, and the 3.9-km (2.4-mile) each way C-Level Cirque Trail past ventilation shafts of the old Bankhead mine and views of Lake Minnewanka.

Day-hikes in the Lake Louise area include the 6.8-km (4.2-mile) each way Plain of Six Glaciers Trails which begins at the end of the Louise Lakeshore Trail and continues up the valley to the Victoria Glacier, a teahouse serving light lunches and refreshments, and viewpoints of Abbot Pass and the Death Trap, the glacier-filled gorge between Mount Victoria and Mount Lefroy.

From Moraine Lake, the Larch Valley Trail climbs 3 km (1.8 miles) to wide encompassing views and joins with a 2.8-km (1.7-mile) trail to Sentinel Pass, one of the highest passes in Banff Park. The 8.8-km (5.4-mile) Boulder Pass Trail leads from the Lake Louise ski area to an open alpine pass with magnificent views.

Hikes from the Icefields Parkway include the 6.8-km (4.2-mile) Bow Lake Trail along the lakeshore to a huge water-fall, the 10-km (6-mile) Cirque Lake Trail to a subalpine lake, and the 10-km (6-mile) Sunset Lookout Trail to a lookout.

Backpacking: Trips of overnight to several weeks duration are possible. Trails include the 37-km (23-mile) trip from Mount Norquay to Johnston's Canyon via Mystic Pass, the 21-km (13-mile) Palliser Pass route, the 26-km (16-mile) route from Johnston's Canyon to Pulsatilla Pass via Luellen Lake and networks of trails in the Egypt Lake, Skoki Valley and Boulder Pass areas. Trails can be linked for trips of one or two weeks or longer. An interesting 66-km (41-mile) trip can be made by connecting the Dolomite Pass-Isabella Lake trail with the Fish Lakes-North Molar Pass trail via Pipestone Pass. *The Canadian Rockies Trail Guide* describes the park's trails. *The Canadian Rockies Access Guide* details walks and hikes, and *Hiking Lake Louise* focuses on trails in that area.

Topographical maps can be obtained by mail or in person from the park's headquarters. Complete backpacking supplies can be acquired in the town of Banff.

More Information: The Superintendent, Banff National Park, P.O. Box 900, Banff, Alberta T0L 0C0 (403) 762-3324.

Waterton Lakes National Park

Waterton Lakes National Park covers 525 km² (203 square miles) of the Rocky Mountains in the southwestern corner of Alberta. On the western boundary is the Continental Divide, the United States border is on the south and the rolling prairie grassland is on the northeastern boundary. With Glacier National Park in Montana the two parks form the Waterton-Glacier International Peace Park.

The transition zone between prairie and mountain has bands of trembling aspen, cottonwood, Douglas maple and other deciduous trees. On the mountain slopes the forest cover below the treeline at 2,100 meters (6,900 feet) is made up of Douglas fir, lodgepole pine, limber pine and white spruce. Engelmann spruce, whitebark pine and alpine fir are found at higher elevations.

Wildlife at middle elevations includes moose, red squirrel, black bear and grizzly bear. At higher levels are bighorn sheep, mountain goats, mule deer, elk, golden-mantled ground squirrels, marmot and pikas. Swans, herons, gulls, waders and shore and marsh birds inhabit the park. During spring and autumn migrations ducks and geese rest in Waterton Lakes. The park's lakes contain pike, whitefish and several species of trout.

Walks: Among the variety of walks in Waterton Park are the 5.8-km (3.6-mile) Lower Bertha Falls Trail with good views down Waterton Lake and the prairies, the Bear's Hump Trail which climbs 2 km (1.2 miles) to a summit with a panoramic view, and the 0.7-km (0.3-mile) Red Rock Canyon Loop Trail explores a red-hued canyon.

Hikes: The Rowe Lakes Trail is a 6.4-km (3.9-mile) each way route to sub-alpine meadows. The 8.7-km (5.4-mile) each way Crypt Lake Trail involves reaching the trailhead by boat across Waterton Lake and includes going through a natural tunnel. The 8-km (5-mile) each way trail from Summit Lake leads to the secluded Carthew Lakes.

Backpacking: The Crypt Lake Trail (described above) is a suitable overnight trip. The 36-km (22-mile) Tamarack Trail in the western section of the park is on the Great Divide. From the Waterton Park townsite, a trail runs along Upper Wateron Lake and provides access to the 1,120 km (695 miles) of trails in 4,100-km^2 (1,584-square-mile) Glacier National Park in Montana. Backpackers hiking into Glacier Park from Waterton Park should register with rangers at Goat Haunt Ranger Station. Information on Glacier Park is available from the Superintendent, Glacier National Park, West Glacier, Montana, U.S.A. 59936, (406) 888-5441.

The Canadian Rockies Access Guide and *Waterton and Northern Glacier Trails for Hikers and Riders* describe the Waterton Park's trails. *The Canadian Rockies Access Guide* details the park's walks and day-hikes.

More Information: The Superintendent, Waterton Lakes National Park, Waterton Park, Alberta T0K 2M0, (403) 859-2224.

Great Divide Trail

The Great Divide Trail is a proposed long-distance route running south to north through the Rocky Mountain parks joining existing trails with segments that will be constructed.

From Palliser Pass at the southern tip of Banff Park the trail passes near Mount Assiniboine, through Kootenay National Park and north into Yoho Park passing the Lake O'Hara area. North of Yoho the trail goes out of the national parks to Howse Pass and then re-enters Banff Park. Reaching the Banff-Jasper Highway near the Saskatchewan River crossing, the trail continues at the road's junction with Norman Creek, and leads to Maligne Lake near the Jasper townsite. From Jasper there is a choice of routes to Mount Robson.

The proposed trail between Waterton Lakes Park and Banff Park is divided into five sections: Red Rock, Flathead, Hanging Valley, High Rock and Wapiti.

The trails that make up the route from Palliser Pass to Mount Robson are described in *The Canadian Rockies Trail Guide.* An extension of the trail connecting Banff Park with Waterton Lakes National Park has been partly completed.

More Information: Great Divide Trail Association, Box 5322, Station A, Calgary, Alberta T2H 1X6.

Kananaskis Country

Forests and meadows of the Rocky Mountain Foothills – the montane mix of prairie and mountain plants and animals and alpine meadows, glaciers and snowfields – are compressed in this 4,000-km² (1,600-square-mile) wilderness area southwest of Calgary. Within the alpine area are 17 peaks over 3,000 meters (10,000 feet), including 3,400-meter (11,300-foot) Mount Joffre, the most southerly glaciers in Alberta's Rocky Mountains, and blue alpine lakes. Three Isles, Maude and Lawson lakes contain cutthroat trout. Among the wildlife that may be seen in Kananaskis Country are sheep, elk, moose, weasel, coyote, hares, pikas, marmots, squirrels, warblers, chickadees, Spruce grouse and Canada jay. Kananaskis Country features a network of over 1,500 km (900 miles) of hiking trails.

Walks: Kananaskis Country's over 15 interpretive trails include the 2.2-km (1.3-mile) Montane trail loop through the montane forest, the 1-km (0.6-mile) Sibbald Flat loop offering a view to a Sundance site, the 2-km (1.2-mile) one way Heart Creek Trail up a narrow creek canyon to a waterfall, and the 0.5-km (0.3-mile) Barrier Lake trail loop to a view overlooking Barrier Lake and the Kananaskis Valley. The 1-km (0.6-mile) Spruce Road Trail and the Marl Lake Trail with 1.6-km (1-mile) and 3.6-km (2.2-mile) sections are wheelchair accessible.

Hikes: The many day-hikes in Kananaskis Country include the 6.6-km (4.1-mile) return Lower Lake trail along Lower Kananaskis Lake, the 10-km (6-mile) Elk Pass Trail which leads to Elk Pass and the 15.6-km (9.6-mile) Upper Lake Trail loop along Upper Kananaskis Lake.

Backpacking: Overnight and Longer Trips. The 32-km (20-mile) Maude Lawson trail along the Upper Kananaskis River to Lawson and Maude lakes and the North Kananaskis Pass. The 23-km (14-mile) Three Isle Lake trail follows along Three Isle Creek to Three Isle Lake and the South Kananaskis Pass. A circuit into British Columbia from North Kananaskis Pass to South Kananaskis Pass is also possible. Campfires are permitted at only some of the campsites, so it is necessary to carry a backpacking stove.

Kananaskis Country Trail Guide by Tony and Gillian Daffern is a hiking guide to the area. *The Complete Guide to Kananaskis Country* includes several hikes.

More Information: Kananaskis Country, 1011 Glenmore Trail S.W., Suite #412, Calgary, Alberta T2V 4R6, (403) 297-3362.

Willmore Wilderness Park

Situated north of Jasper National Park and east of the British Columbia boundary, Willmore Wilderness Park occupies 4,593 km² (1,774 square miles) of the Front Ranges, Main Ranges and Foothills of the Rocky Mountains. Forest cover is dominated by Engelmann spruce, lodgepole pine and alpine fir. Above the treeline between 1,860 and 1,950 meters (6,100 and 6,400 feet) are shrubs including dwarf willows, gooseberry and white, yellow and purple heathers. Elk, woodland caribou, Rocky Mountain sheep, Rocky Mountain goats, black bears and grizzly bears and numerous birds including ruffed grouse, spruce and blue grouse, sparrows, robins and white-tailed ptarmigan inhabit the area. Anglers can fish for Dolly Varden, Rocky Mountain whitefish, Arctic grayling and rainbow trout.

Backpacking: Willmore Wilderness Park's 750 km (460 miles) of trails are situated in most of the valley systems and over most of the passes in the eastern portion of the park. Willmore Park is linked with the North Boundary Trail in Jasper Park by trails along Rock Creek, Blue Creek, Smoky River, and a route along Chown Creek, over Bess Pass and Jackpine Pass. There are interesting cross-country travel routes along the high ridges and over many of the saddles and unnamed passes. It is also possible to hike along the Continental Divide on the park's western boundary.

Willmore Wilderness Park by the Alberta Wilderness Association describe the park's hiking routes.

More Information: Willmore Wilderness Park, Alberta Forestry, Lands and Wildlife, Box 239, Grande Cache, Alberta T0E 0Y0, (403) 827-3626.

White Goat Wilderness Area

The 443-km^2 (171-square-mile) White Goat Wilderness Area lies in the Front Ranges and Main Ranges of the Rocky Mountains adjacent to the southern boundary of Jasper National Park and the eastern boundary of Banff National Park. The 3,000-meter (10,000-foot) mountain ranges containing alpine lakes and several major streams are separated by wide valleys. The subalpine forest is dominated by white spruce, subalpine fir and lodgepole pine. Above the treeline at 2,100 meters (6,900 feet) are alpine meadows carpeted with grasses, sedges and brightly colored flowers. Crutose lichen occurs on the rocks. Bighorn sheep, mountain goats, mountain caribou, wolves, mountain lions, coyote, elk, grizzly bears, black bears and a few wolverines and martens inhabit the wilderness area. Among the 100 to 120 species of birds observed in the area are Canada jay, ptarmigan, spruce grouse and Clarke's crow.

Hikes/Backpacking: Travel within the White Goat Wilderness Area is by foot only. The wilderness area's 112 km (70 miles) of trails generally follow rivers and include the

61-km (38-mile) Cline River Trail, the 21-km (13-mile) Cataract Creek Trail and the 30-km (19-mile) McDonald Creek Trail. From the Banff-Jasper Highway the area can be reached via the Norman Creek trail, over Sunset Pass to Pinto Lake connecting with the Cline River Trail, or by the Nigel Pass Trail and over Cataract Pass. These two access routes are described in *The Canadian Rockies Trail Guide*. Another access route is by the trail along the north side of the Cline River from the David Thompson Highway. *Hiking Alberta's David Thompson Country* describes the area's trails.

More Information: White Goat Wilderness Area, Box 920, Rimbey, Alberta T0C 2J0, (403) 843-2237.

Siffleur Wilderness Area

The 412-km^2 (159-square-mile) Siffleur Wilderness Area is situated in the Front Ranges and Main Ranges on the northeastern boundary of Banff National Park. Elk, mountain goats and a few grizzly bears inhabit the area.

Hiking trails are generally situated along rivers. The most popular route through the Siffleur Wilderness Area is the 28-km (17-mile) Siffleur River Valley Trail leading from the David Thompson Highway to Dolomite Pass in Banff Park.

Hikes: The Siffleur Falls route leads 3.7 km (2.3 miles) from the Siffleur Falls Parking lot off the David Thompson Highway to the falls. An 11-km (6.5-mile) route goes to Landslide Lake which offers good fishing opportunities.

Backpacking: Among the backpacking opportunities in the Siffleur area are a 54-km (32-mile) route along Whiterabbit Creek and Ram River and a 30-km (18-mile) route along the Siffleur River to the Escarpment Lakes.

Travel in the area is by foot only. The area's trails are described in *Hiking Alberta's David Thompson Country*. Access from Banff Park is by Dolomite Pass which is described in *The Canadian Rockies Trail Guide*.

More Information: Siffleur Wilderness Area, Box 920, Rimbey, Alberta T0C 2J0, (403) 843-2237.

Ghost River Wilderness Area

Surrounded by the 2,900-meters (9,500-foot) Palliser Range, the 153-km^2 (59-square-mile) Ghost River Wilderness Area is almost a complete ecological unit. The subalpine coniferous forest contains white spruce, Engelmannn spruce, subalpine fir and lodgepole pine. Above the treeline at 2,100 meters (6,900 feet) the alpine tundra comprises grasses, sedges, lichens and colorful alpine flowers. Wildlife includes bighorn sheep, mountain goats, mountain caribou, wolves, mountain lions, coyote, elk, black bears and grizzly bears. A small number of wolverine and marten also inhabit the area. Among the more than 100 species of birds observed in the area are Canada jay, ptarmigan, spruce grouse and Clarke's crow. Travel within the wilderness area is by foot only.

Hikes: The 2.7-km (1.6-mile) hike to Mockingbird Hill Lookout leads to views of the limestone cliffs of the Palliser Range. An 8-km (5-mile) route leads to the Ghost Lakes, and a 4.5-km (2.8-mile) steep hike goes to the summit Black Rock Mountain.

Backpacking: There are over 50 km (31 miles) of backpacking routes. The 21-km (13-mile) Ghost River trail connects with several trails along Ghost River tributaries and also with the 18-km (11-mile) Aylmer Pass Trail into Banff National Park.

Hiking Alberta's David Thompson Country describes the area's trails.

Access is by foot only on two routes. Aylmer Pass provides access from Banff Park and is described in *The Canadian Rockies Trail Guide*. From the east the wilderness area is reached by hiking about 10 km (6 miles) along the Ghost River from a secondary road, 19 km (12 miles) west from the Forestry Trunk Road in the Bow-Crow Forest Reserve.

More Information: Ghost River Wilderness Area, Box 920, Rimbey, Alberta T0C 2J0, (403) 843-2237.

Foothills

Bighorn Wildland Recreation Area

Covering 3,966 square km (1,532 square miles) on the eastern slopes of the Rocky Mountains, the Bighorn Wildland Recreation Area is a wilderness encompassing the Bighorn, Front, Continental and Ram ranges of the Foothills. The area features rugged topography and dense forest cover. Indigenous wildlife is abundant and includes bighorn sheep, elk, mountain goat, black bear, grizzly bear and wolf.

Hiking routes include the Onion Lake Trail, Hummingbird Creek Trail, South Ram River Trail, Ranger Creek Trail, Lost Guide Canyon Trail, Forbidden Creek Trail and Skeleton Creek Trail. Some of the area's trails are described in *Hiking Alberta's David Thompson Country*.

More Information: Rocky/Clearwater Forest Headquarters, Alberta Forestry, Lands and Wildlife, Box 1720, Rocky Mountain House, Alberta T0M 1T0 (403) 845-8250.

Bow-Crow Forest

The Bow-Crow Forest covers the large area between Banff National Park, Waterton Lakes National Park and the British Columbia boundary.

While there are no designated hiking trails within the forest, several hiking opportunities through the white spruce and lodgepole pine forest exist, but topographic maps are needed.

More Information: Forest Superintendent, Bow-Crow Forest, Alberta Forest Service, Box 3310, Postal Station B, Calgary, Alberta T2M 4L8, (403) 297-8800.

Rocky-Clearwater Forest

The Rocky-Clearwater Forest is situated in the Rocky Mountain Foothills north of the Bow-Crow Forest and is

Bow-Crow Forest. (Travel Alberta)

bounded on the west by Banff and Jasper national parks. There are numerous trails through the river valleys of the forest and some of these trails lead into the national parks. Detailed trail descriptions prepared by the Rocky-Clearwater office outline 22 trails totalling 600 km (373 miles).

More Information: Rocky-Clearwater Forest, Alberta Forest Service, Box 1720, Rocky Mountain House, Alberta T0M 1T0, (403) 845-3003.

Alberta Plateau

Waskahegan Trail

The Waskahegan Trail is a loop trail that begins and ends in Edmonton, and connects Wetaskiwin, Camrose, Fort Saskatchewan and St. Albert. When completed it will be 352 km (220 miles) in length. About 224 km (140 miles) of the route have been completed.

Southward from Edmonton the trail follows Blackmud Creek through old Gwynne Outlet to glacial Lake Edmonton. The trail then goes along Saunders Lake and Coal Lake and south to Gwynne, via the Battle River Valley which the trail follows into the town of Camrose. From Miquelon Provincial Park the trail goes north to the Ministik Waterfowl Sanctuary,

Waskahegan Trail. (Stan Peters, Waskahegan Trail Association)

Wanisai Lake and Elk Island National Park. From Elk Island Park the trail turns west to Fort Saskatchewan and Lamoureux. North of Lamoureux the trail is planned to go through the Sturgeon Valley to St. Albert and then west to the trail's starting point in Edmonton.

Most of the Waskahegan Trail crosses private farm land with some forested areas. Campsites and shelters are situated along the route. Water is not always available and should be carried. Food and fuel supplies can be acquired in Edmonton, Camrose and Fort Saskatchewan. There are also small stores where food can be obtained in Gwynne and north of Miquelon Lake.

Elk Island National Park offers short dayhiking trails. More information on this 194-km^2 (75-square-mile) park can be obtained from: The Superintendent, Elk Island National Park, Site 4, R.R. No. 1, Fort Saskatchewan, Alberta, T8L 2N7, (403) 992-6380.

A Waskahegan Trail guidebook is available to members from the Waskahegan Trail Association, P.O. Box 131, Edmonton, Alberta T5J 2G9.

Cypress Hills Provincial Park

Rising more than 750 meters (2,500 feet) above the surrounding prairie, the Cypress Hills in eastern Alberta reach an elevation of 1,450 meters (4,800 feet). Alberta's 202-km^2 (78-square-mile) Cypress Hill Provincial Park is located on the Saskatchewan boundary and borders on the provincial park of the same name in Saskatchewan.

The green forests and grasslands of the Cypress Hills plateau contrast markedly with the dusty brown flatland prairie. Lodgepole pine, a tree native to the Rockies, is found in the rocky soil at higher elevations of the plateau. White spruce and aspen poplar grow at lower elevations and 14 species of mountain and woodland orchids can be seen. Elk, moose, white-tailed deer, mule deer, coyote, muskrat, mink and beaver make the Cypress Hills their home. Among the birds that can be seen are ruffed grouse, horned owls, hawks and many types of shoreline birds and waterfowl. Rainbow trout, brook trout, northern pike and yellow perch are found in the park's lakes and streams.

Walks/Hikes: Among the park's trails are the 1-km (0.6-mile) Soggy Bottom trail, a wheelchair accessible route through a field, forest and marsh, the 3-km (1.8-mile) Shoreline Trail which follows the south shoreline of Elkwater Lake, and the 5-km (3.1-mile) Streamside Trail loop which follows a stream through a spruce forest.

Backpacking: The 11-km (7-mile) trail from Elkwater to Spruce Coulee has a backcountry campsite located at the east end of Spruce Coulee. The 8 km (5 mile) Beaver Creek-Horsehoe Canyon loop has an overnight stop at Nichol Springs campground. Open fires are not permitted.

Supplies are available in the town of Elkwater.

More Information: Cypress Hills Provincial Park, Elkwater, Alberta T0J 1C0, (403) 893-3777

Guidebook Sources

Alberta's Eastern Slope: Wildlands for Recreation, by the Alberta Wilderness Association, describes the proposed wildland recreation areas. Available from Alberta Wilderness Association, Box 6398, Station D, Calgary, Alberta T2P 2E1; (write for current price).

The Canadian Rockies Access Guide, by John Dodd and Gail Helgason, includes 115 day hikes in Banff, Jasper, Waterton Lakes, Kootenay and Yoho national parks and Kananaskis Country. Available from Lone Pine Publishing, Suite 206, 10426 - 81 Avenue, Edmonton, Alberta T6E 1X5; $12.95 (plus $1.50 for postage and handling).

The Canadian Rockies Trail Guide, by Brain Patton and Bart Robinson, is a trail guide to the major trails in the Rocky Mountains of Alberta and British Columbia. Available from Summerthought Ltd., P.O. Box 1420, Banff, Alberta T0L 0C0; $14.95 (plus $3 postage and handling).

The Complete Guide to Kananaskis Country, by Norma Ramage and Jim Wilson, describes some hikes. Available from Lone Pine Publishing; $8.95.

Hiking Alberta's David Thompson Country, by Patricia Kariel, is a guide to trails in the Ghost River, Red Deer Valley, Siffleur Wilderness, Ram Range and White Goat Wilderness. Available from Lone Pine Publishing; $9.95.

Hiking Alberta's Southwest, by Joey Ambrosi, details trails in the Castle River, Carbondale River, Crowsnest River, Oldman River, Porcupine Hills and Highwood River areas. Available from Douglas and McIntyre, 1615 Venables Street, Vancouver, British Columbia V5L 2H1; $4.99 (for mail orders include postage of $1 plus 50 cents per book).

Kananaskis Country Trail Guide, by Tony and Gillian Daffern, is a hiking guide to the area. Available from Rocky Mountain Books, 106 Wimbledon Cr. S.W., Calgary, Alberta T3C 3J1; $12.50.

Waterton and Northern Glacier Trails, describes the trails in Waterton National Park and Montana's Glacier National Park. Available from: Waterton Natural History Association, P.O. Box 145, Waterton Park, Alberta T0K 2M0; (write for current price).

Willmore Wilderness Park, by the Alberta Wilderness Association, includes information on hiking routes. Available from Alberta Wilderness Association, P.O. Box 6398, Station D, Calgary, Alberta T2P 2E1; (write for current price).

4

Northwest Territories

THE Northwest Territories cover more than 3,367,000 km² (1,300,000 square miles) between the sixtieth parallel and the North Pole. The territories contain exciting opportunities for hikers to experience the remote wilderness.

Food and other hiking supplies in the North are more expensive than in southern Canada and choice is limited. If you are travelling to the Northwest Territories it is best to bring your supplies with you.

More Information: TravelArctic, Yellowknife, N.W.T. X1A 2L9, toll free 1-800-661-0788. Topographical maps should be ordered from the Canada Map Office, 615 Booth Street, Ottawa, Ontario K1A 0E9, (613) 952-7000.

Mean temperatures in the Northwest Territories

		June	*July*	*August*	*September*
Norman Wells	°C	13.7	16.0	13.2	5.8
	°F	56.6	60.9	55.7	42.8
Fort Simpson	°C	14.4	16.7	14.4	7.8
	°F	58	62	58	46
Fort Smith	°C	13.3	16.1	14.4	7.8
	°F	56	61	58	46
Frobisher Bay	°C	3.3	7.8	7.2	2.2
	°F	38	46	45	36
Yellowknife	°C	12.2	16.1	13.9	6.7
	°F	54	61	57	44

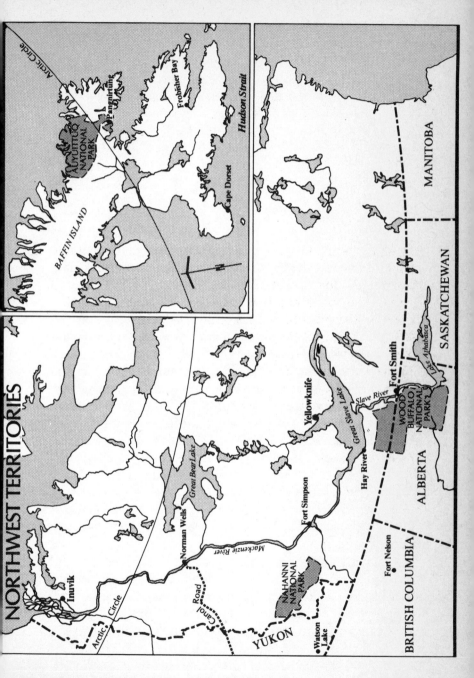

Southern Baffin Island experiences short, cool summers. July is the warmest month with a mean high of 10°C (50°F) and a mean low of 2°C (35°F). During June, July and August there is only 12 to 25 cm (5 to 10 inches) of rain. Summers in the southern Mackenzie Valley are similar to those in the prairie provinces but with slightly lower temperatures. The mean maximum for July is about 21°C (69°F) and the mean minimum is 10°C (50°F). During the month of June there are about 20 hours of daylight.

Auyuittuq National Park

Auyuittuq is an Inuit word meaning "the place which does not melt." Located on the Cumberland Peninsula of Baffin Island, Auyuittuq National Park lies on the Arctic Circle and is Canada's northernmost park. From May through July Auyuittuq has 24 hours of daylight. A large part of the 21,470-km^2 (8,290-square-mile) park is on the Penny Highlands, the extreme northern part of the Precambrian Canadian Shield. Peaks in the area reach 2,100 meters (6,900 feet) in height. The Penny Ice Cap covers 6,000 km^2 (2,300 square miles) and is a remnant of the last Ice Age. Coronation Glacier, a river of ice 32 km (20 miles) long, is the largest of the glaciers spawned by the ice cap. Pangnirtung Pass is an example of the U-shaped valleys carved by glaciers over hundreds of thousands of years. The pass forms a 97-km (60-mile) long, ice-free trough through the mountains joining Cumberland Sound with Davis Strait. Along the park's coast the glaciers have carved spectacular fjords with sheer cliffs up to 900 meters (3,000 feet) high.

Only hardy lichens, mosses and Arctic heather are found on the park's barren highlands. Cotton grass, Labrador tea, sedges and the dwarf willow grow on the valley floors. Arctic flowers such as white mountain avens, yellow Arctic poppy and purple saxiflage are in bloom during June and July, and the barren, rocky terrain is ablaze with color.

Owl Valley, Pangnirtung Pass Trail, Auyuittuq National Park.
(Parks Canada)

The sparse tundra vegetation supports a small number of mammals. Wildlife includes the lemming, weasel, Arctic fox, polar bear, and the barren ground caribou. Marine animals that can be seen off the coast include ringed, harp and bearded seals, narwhals and white whales and Atlantic walruses. Among the 40 species of birds that may be observed are Canada geese, ptarmigan, snowy owls, eider ducks, ravens, and glaucous gulls. The peregrine falcon and gyr falcon are two rare birds found in the park.

Backpacking: Pangnirtung Pass Trail begins at Overlord, the park entrance on the Pangnirtung Fjord, and follows the east bank of the Weasel River and goes around Glacier Lake and Summit Lake. At 400 meters (1,300 feet) above sea level, Summit Lake is the highest point in the pass. The trail returns to Overlord on the west side of the river. The route traverses sandy slopes, gravel fans, mossy and wet tundra and crosses moraine and glacial creeks. The 103-km (64-mile) round trip averages about 47 hours of hiking. Some hikers begin at Broughton Island and hike the full length of the pass from north to south. The main trail is also the starting point of unmarked routes to the glaciers on both sides of the pass. Nine emergency shelters equipped with first-aid supplies and two-way radios are located in Pangnirtung Pass.

Backpackers in Auyuittuq should be experienced and have equipment designed for arctic conditions. Trips also require careful planning because though some supplies can be obtained in Pangnirtung, it is best to arrive self-sufficient.

Auyuittuq Park is located 2,400 km (1,500 miles) northeast of Montreal. Reaching the park involves flying from Montreal to Iqaluit and then onto Pangnirtung or Broughton Island.

More Information: The Superintendent, Auyuittuq National Park, Pangnirtung, N.W.T. X0A 0R0, (819) 473-8828.

Ellesmere National Park Reserve

Covering 37,775 square km (14,590 square miles) of northern Ellesmere Island, this park is situated in the eastern high arctic. Icefields 900 meters (3,000 feet) cloak the Grant Land Mountains that cover the northern part of the park. The ice is a remnant of the last continental glacier that covered North America ten thousand years ago. Several peaks of the Grant Land Range are over 2,500 meters (8,250 feet). Mount Barbeau at 2,616 meters (8,633 feet) is the highest mountain in eastern North America. Glacial valleys and fiords cut into the park's ocean coastline.

Hikes/Backpacking: Most hikers undertake the long-distance trek from Tanquary Fiord to Lake Hazen via the Very and MacDonald river valleys. There are also possibilities for shorter overnight hikes and day hikes from base camps in the Rollrock and Redrock valleys near Tanquary Fiord, or Glacier and Blister Creek valley near Hazen Camp.

Reaching the park involves flying to Resolute Bay, N.W.T.,

and continuing by charter aircraft to Lake Hazen or Tanquary Fiord. Information on charter companies and outfitters offering organized trips is available from the park superintendent.

More Information: Superintendent, Ellesmere Island National Park Reserve, Pangnirtung, N.W.T. X0A 0R0, (819) 473-8828.

Wood Buffalo National Park

Straddling the boundary between the Northwest Territories and the province of Alberta, this 44,807-km^2 (17,300-square-mile) park was created in 1922 to protect the last remaining herd of wood bison. There are now 4,000 bison in the

Wood Buffalo National Park. (Parks Canada)

park, the world's largest free roaming herd. The major part of this wilderness area is the flat, glacial-outwash plain known as the Alberta Plateau. The Birch Mountains in the southwest of the park and the Caribou Mountains in the west are erosion plateaus left by glaciers. The park has several sinkholes characteristic of karst topography. Some parts of the salt plains located in the area drained by the Salt River contain no plant life due to the high salt content of the ground.

The park's forest is typical of the boreal forest zone and is dominated by white and black spruce, jack pine and tamarack. Moose, woodland caribou and black bears inhabit the area. Wood Buffalo Park is the only known nesting ground of the endangered whooping crane. Hawks, eagles, owls and ravens are present throughout the park. Anglers can fish for pike, pickerel, goldeye and trout in the park's lakes and streams.

Walks: The Salt River Trail features a 7.5-km (4.6-mile) North Loop and a 9-km (5.5-mile) South Loop through the gypsum karst terrain of caves, sinkholes and underground streams. The 16-km (10-mile) Lane Lake Trail explores a chain of sinkhole lakes.

Hikes/Backpacking: Trail development in Wood Buffalo Park is in its infancy. At present there are three hiking trails totalling about 40 km (25 miles). Hiking can also be done cross-country using a map and compass. It is also possible to follow bison trails.

The park may be reached via the Mackenzie Highway to Hay River and Highway 5 to Fort Smith, or by air to Fort Smith 36 km (22 miles) from the park. Topographical maps should be obtained from the Canada Map Office in Ottawa.

More Information: The Superintendent, Wood Buffalo National Park, Box 750, Fort Smith, N.W.T. X0E 0P0, (403) 872-2349.

Nahanni National Park

Created in 1971, Nahanni Park is a 4,764-km^2 (1,840-square-mile) wilderness area in the southwest corner of the

Northwest Territories. The South Nahanni River flows over 320 km (200 miles) through the park from the Ragged Range of the Selwyn Mountains to the Franklin Mountains near the southeast park boundary at the Splits, a 48-km (30-mile) stretch of river up to 3 km (2 miles) wide and divided into many shallow channels. At Virginia Falls the South Nahanni River plummets 90 meters (300 feet).

The park features sulphur hotsprings at the lower mouth of the First Canyon, the Wild Mint Mineral Springs near Flat River and Rabbitkettle Hotsprings in the northwest portion of the park. Alpine tundra is found above the timberline which is between 1,050 and 1,200 meters (3,500 to 4,000 feet). Dense growth of white spruce and balsam poplar are found in the valley bottoms. The general lowland forest contains open stands of white spruce and trembling aspen. Moose, beaver, woodland caribou, Dall sheep, black bear, white deer and mule deer inhabit the park.

Hiking/Backpacking: There are no constructed hiking trails except for portages. Most hiking is done on creek beds. The Deadman Valley region has three hiking areas which contain a number of routes that lead to alpine plateaus. There are also hiking routes near Virginia Falls, Rabbitkettle Lake, Flat River and Yohin Lake. The trips range in length from a few hours to several days duration.

Nahanni Park is accessible only by air or water. The park is 145 km (90 miles) west of Fort Simpson, N.W.T., and 1,046 km (650 miles) northwest of Edmonton. Fort Simpson, and Watson Lake, Yukon, are the major jumping-off and supply points for Nahanni and have facilities for chartering aircraft. Both centers can be reached by all-weather highways and by air. Hikers should bring their supplies with them. A list of aircraft charter companies and river outfitters can be obtained from the park office. Topographical maps should be ordered from the Canada Map Office in Ottawa.

More Information: The Superintendent, Nahanni National Park, Bag 300, Fort Simpson N.W.T. X0E 0N0, (403) 695-3151.

Canol Heritage Trail

The Canol Heritage Trail extends 372 km (232 miles) through the Mackenzie Mountains from Norman Wells on the Mackenzie River to Ross River in the Yukon. The Backbone Range to the west averages 2,100 meters (6,900 feet), with some peaks over 2,400 meters (8,000 feet). The Canyon Range in the eastern Mackenzie Mountains is characterized by many canyons carved by streams.

The Canol Road and pipeline were started in 1942 to move oil from the fields at Norman Wells to Whitehorse and the Alaska Highway as part of the American war effort to protect Alaska from attack. The project was completed in 1945, before the end of war but too late to be of any use. The pipeline was scrapped and the road abandoned. In recent years backpackers have walked the route.

Many parts of the road are eroded and overgrown but most of it is good for hiking, particularly the sections in higher country. The highest point on the route is 1,650 meters (5,500 feet) at the Plains of Abraham. The bridges have been washed away and heavy rainfall can result in delays at river crossings or detours upstream.

Norman Wells is accessible by air from Edmonton and Yellowknife. Ross River can be reached by summer road from Whitehorse.

Hiking the Canol Heritage Trail requires extra care in planning and should only be attempted by experienced backpackers. Supplies should be acquired beforehand. Local outfitters offer guided trips. Maps should be obtained from the Canada Map Office in Ottawa.

More Information: Department of Economic Development, and Tourism, Yellowknife, N.W.T. X1A 2L9, toll-free 1-800-661-0788.

5

Saskatchewan

ONE usually thinks of Saskatchewan as a province of rolling wheatfields, and so it is. But it is also a province of forest and lake and muskeg, rich in wildlife and exciting for hikers. Most of the northern third of the province, an area of 233,010 km² (90,000 square miles) of Saskatchewan's total area of 651,651 km² (251,700 square miles), lies on the Canadian Shield underlain with Precambrian rock and covered with a northern coniferous forest of black spruce, jack pine, larch and poplar. The area has many lakes and rivers, wide areas of muskeg and swamp, forest and outcroppings of rock.

Most of the southern two thirds of the province is a great plain sloping gradually from an elevation of 900 meters (3,000 feet) in the southwest to 450 meters (1,500 feet) in the northeast.

Average daily minimum and maximum temperatures in Saskatchewan

		May		June		July		August		Sept.		Oct.	
		L	H	L	H	L	H	L	H	L	H	L	H
Prince Albert	°C	3	18	8	22	12	25	10	23	4	17	−1	10
	°F	38	64	47	71	53	77	50	74	40	63	30	50
Regina	°C	3	19	8	23	11	27	9	26	4	19	−2	12
	°F	38	66	47	73	52	81	49	78	39	67	29	53

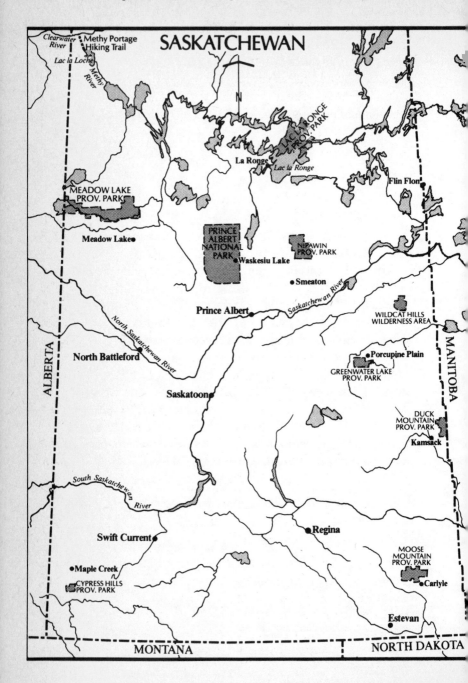

SASKATCHEWAN

Clearwater River
Methy Portage Hiking Trail
Lac la Loche
Methy River

LAC LA RONGE PROV. PARK
La Ronge
Lac la Ronge

Flin Flon

MEADOW LAKE PROV. PARK

Meadow Lake

PRINCE ALBERT NATIONAL PARK
Waskesiu Lake

NIPAWIN PROV. PARK

Smeaton

Saskatchewan River

Prince Albert

North Saskatchewan River

WILDCAT HILLS WILDERNESS AREA

North Battleford

Porcupine Plain
GREENWATER LAKE PROV. PARK

Saskatoon

DUCK MOUNTAIN PROV. PARK
Kamsack

South Saskatchewan River

Swift Current

Regina

MOOSE MOUNTAIN PROV. PARK

Maple Creek
CYPRESS HILLS PROV. PARK

Carlyle

Estevan

ALBERTA

MANITOBA

MONTANA   NORTH DAKOTA

Exceptions are the Cypress Hills in the southwest corner of the province, and the Missouri Coteau, the long narrow escarpment extending from south-central Saskatchewan into northeastern Alberta and separating the Saskatchewan Plain and the Alberta Plateau. The moraine-covered Missouri Coteau consists of rolling hills rising 60 to 150 meters (200 to 500 feet) above the Saskatchewan Plain.

The transition zone between the prairie of the south and the northern forest region is known as the park belt, and contains many lakes and rivers, and a forest consisting of white poplar, white spruce, black spruce and jack pine.

Most of Saskatchewan's hiking opportunities are located in the park belt, though hiking routes exist in all parts of the province.

Saskatchewan has a continental climate with short, hot summers and long, cold winters. During the summer the average temperature varies from 10°C (50°F) at sunrise to 24°C (75°F) in the afternoon. Average annual precipitation is 28 to 51 cm (11 to 20 inches) with half occurring during June, July and August.

More Information: Tourism Saskatchewan, 1919 Saskatchewan Drive, Regina, Saskatchewan S4P 3V7, or call toll-free in Saskatchewan, 1-800-667-7538, elsewhere in Canada and the United States, 1-800-667-7191.

Hostels in Saskatchewan are operated by the Saskatchewan Hostelling Association – Saskatchewan Sport and Recreation Center, 2205 Victoria Avenue, Regina, Saskatchewan S4P 0S4, (306) 522-3651.

Prince Albert National Park

Prince Albert Park is situated in the transition zone between the boreal forest, aspen parkland and prairie grasslands, and has plantlife characteristic of these three floral zones. The boreal forest which covers more than half the park consists of white spruce, black spruce and jack pine, and has several lakes and numerous streams. Among the animal life inhabiting the park is

Prince Albert National Park. (Parks Canada)

the badger in the prairie area, elk in the aspen parkland and wolf in the boreal forest. White-tailed deer, mule deer, moose, black bear and woodland caribou are also found. The park is home to a colony of white pelicans and a herd of free-roaming bison. Great blue herons inhabit the marshes, pileated woodpeckers live in the forest and waterfowl are found on the lakes. Other birds that can be seen are the common loon, gray jay, black-billed magpie and common raven.

Walks: Among the park's walking trails are the 2-km (1.2-mile) Mud Creek self-guiding nature trail loop along the south shore of Waskesiu Lake, the 2-km (1.2-mile) Boundary Bog loop on a boardwalk through bog lowlands, and the 1.5-km (0.9-mile) one-way Kingsmere River Trail to the shores of Kingsmere Lake.

Hikes: The King Fisher Trail is a 13-km (8-mile) loop where a variety of animal tracks can be seen. The 27-km (16-mile) Freight Trail follows the historic route used to transport furs and supplies between Prince Albert and Waskesiu. The Spruce River Highlands trail is a 8.5-km (5-mile) loop through hilly terrain.

Backpacking: The Grey Owl Trail is a 20-km (12.4-mile) each way route along Kingsmere Lake and across rolling terrain to Ajawaan Lake and the cabin of Grey Owl, a famous conservationist who lived here in the 1930s. The Fish, Hunters and Elk trail circuit is a 41-km (25-mile) route suitable for a three day backpacking trip. There are also extensive hiking possibilities on sections of the 240 km (150 miles) of trails in the southern half of the park.

Prince Albert National Park Trail Guide describes the park's trails. Topographical maps are available at the park office.

More Information: The Superintendent, Prince Albert, National Park, Box 100, Waskesiu Lake, Saskatchewan S0J 2Y0, (306) 663-5322.

Cypress Hills Provincial Park

Situated in the southwestern corner of the province, the Cypress Hills are a dissected flat-topped plateau rising 2,000 meters (6,100 feet) above the surrounding prairie and extending in an east-west direction for about 130 km (80 miles) and 24 to 40 km (15 to 25 miles) wide. The hills reach 1,370 meters (4,500 feet), the highest point in Saskatchewan, and offer a panoramic view of the surrounding prairie.

The plant life is a mixture of the prairie vegetation of the surrounding plains, and montane vegetation characteristic of the Rocky Mountain Foothills 320 km (200 miles) to the west. Elk, moose, mule deer and white-tailed deer are common. Among the 207 bird species that can be observed are Audubon warbler, yellow-shafted flicker and western red-shafted flicker.

The 144-km^2 (55-square-mile) park is divided into two sections; the Centre Block which is the core area, and the West Block, 24 km (15 miles) to the west.

Walks: The park's Centre Block offers the 1-km (0.6-mile) Valley of the Windfalls nature trail, the 1.5-km (0.9-mile) Valley of the Rippling Waters nature trail and the 2-km (1.2-mile) Valley of the Beavers interpretive trail.

Hikes/Backpacking: The Western Block offers 31 km (19 miles) of hiking trails in addition to fireguard trails.

Topographical maps are needed. The development of extensive hiking-trail networks in the Centre Block and in the West Block, where they will connect with trails in Alberta's Cypress Hills Park is planned.

More Information: Cypress Hills Provincial Park, Box 850, Maple Creek, Saskatchewan S0W 1N0, (306) 662-4411.

Methy Portage Trail, Clearwater Provincial Park

Situated on northern Saskatchewan's longest portage trail; this 20.5-km (13-mile) hiking trail traverses the watershed between the Churchill River basin which flows to Hudson Bay, and the waters of the Arctic basin which flow to the Beaufort Sea via the Clearwater, Athabasca, Slave and Mackenzie rivers.

Wildlife in the predominantly jack pine forest includes moose, black bear, wolf, fox, lynx, spruce grouse, ruffed grouse,

Canada jay and chickadee. The trail is located near the community of La Loche in the northwestern part of the province, and goes in a northwest direction from Wallis Bay on Lac La Loche, also known as Methy Lake, to the Clearwater River. Good camping sites close to a water source are at the south end of the trail on the shores of Rendevous Lake and near the Clearwater River. Return is by the same route.

More Information: Saskatchewan Parks and Renewable Resources, 3211 Albert Street, Regina, Saskatchewan S4S 5W6, (306) 787-2700.

La Ronge Provincial Park

The wilderness park in northern Saskatchewan's Precambrian Shield is covered with a dense forest and surrounded by many lakes including Lac La Ronge. White-tailed deer, moose, wolf, lynx, beaver, muskrat and snowshoe hare are some of the mammals that can be observed. Bird species in the park include the raven, ruffed grouse, spruce grouse, great horned owl and red-winged blackbird. Rainbow trout, lake trout and Northern pike are found in the park's lakes.

Walk: The Nemeiben Lake interpretive trail is a 1.5-km (0.9-mile) loop through boreal forest and Canadian Shield landscape.

Hikes/Backpacking: The 15-km (9.5-mile) one way Nut Point Hiking Trail traverses muskeg, rock ridges and several stands of jack pine. The trail leads to Nut Point at the tip of a peninsula jutting into Lac La Ronge. Return is by the same route.

More Information: Park Superintendent, La Ronge Provincial Park, Box 5000, Resources Branch, La Ronge, Saskatchewan S0J 1L0, (306) 425-4245.

Meadow Lake Provincial Park

The 1,543-km^2 (596-square-mile) area of Meadow Lake Park lies almost entirely in the valley of the Waterhen River in the Missouri Coteau, the eastward facing escarpment which rises

60 to 150 meters (200 to 500 feet) and separates the second and third prairie steppes. The park's rolling terrain encompasses, moraines, kames, and eskers. A transition zone near the Mustus Lakes separates the park into northern and southern sections of the boreal forest. Jack pine, birch, aspen, poplar and white spruce predominate in the southern section. The northern section is covered with black spruce and jack pine. Great blue herons, California gulls, ring-billed gulls, pelicans, golden eagles and bald eagles are seen in the park. Black bears, coyote, grey wolves, lynx, moose, elk and white-tailed deer are among the mammals that inhabit the park. The lakes and rivers contain a wide variety of fish including whitefish, walleye, pike, rainbow trout, brook trout, and cohoe salmon.

Walks: The park's nature trails include the 1.8-km (1.1-mile) White Birch loop through a mixed forest and bog, and the 2-km (1.2-mile) Kimball Lake trail past a burned area and beaver activity to Kimball Lake Beach.

Hikes: The Vivian Lake trail offers 1.5-km (0.9-mile) and 7-km (4.3-mile) loops through a mature spruce stand.

Backpacking: The Mustus Chain trail, a 20-km (12-mile) loop around Mustus Lake, has an overnight shelter at the halfway point.

Camping supplies can be obtained at stores located in and just outside the park.

More Information: The Superintendent, Meadow Lake Provincial Park, P.O. Box 70, Dorintosh, Saskatchewan S0M 0T0, (306) 236-3382.

Moose Mountain Provincial Park

Covering 388 km² (150 square miles) in the southeastern plains region of the province, Moose Mountain Park is a thick forest of white birch and aspen poplar on an elevated plateau which contrasts with the surrounding grassland region. The park's knob and kettle terrain has a topographic relief of 90 to 120 meters (300 to 400 feet) and there are more than 1,200 small lakes in the depressions. The veery, ovenbird, northern waterthrush and other songbirds, great blue heron, turkey vultures and various waterfowl are some of the birds that can be observed in the park. Mammals inhabiting the area include white-tailed deer, elk, moose, mink, beaver, coyote, porcupine and snowshoe hare.

Walk: The 2-km (1.2-mile) Wuche Sakaw interpretive trail explores Moose Mountain Park's wildlife and plantlife.

Hikes: The Beaver Lake trail offers 3.6-km (2.2-mile) and 6-km (3.7-mile) loops through a mature deciduous forest. The Little Kenosee trail's 3.7 km (2.2 miles) and 5.6 km (3.4 miles) loops also traverse the deciduous forest.

Backpacking: The park has recently begun promoting backpacking and there are 32 km (20 miles) of trails with two rest shelters. A trail map is available from the park. There are also cutlines and old access roads in the park that are suitable for backpacking, and a topographical map, needed for hiking these routes, can be purchased at the park office.

Supplies can be obtained at stores in and near the park.

More Information: Moose Mountain Provincial Park, Box 100, Carlyle, Saskatchewan S0C 0R0, (306) 577-2131.

Duck Mountain Provincial Park

Lying on the Duck Mountain Upland of the Manitoba Escarpment with elevations reaching 750 meters (2,500 feet), Duck Mountain Park covers 240 km² (93 square miles) adjacent to the Manitoba border and is the most southerly park in Saskatchewan's forest and lake belt. The heavy, mixed forest comprises aspen, spruce, jack pine, balsam fir, black spruce and tamarack. Abundant wildlife includes bear, deer, moose, elk and beaver.

Walks: Among the interpretive trails exploring the park's forests are the 1.7-km (1.1-mile) Woodland trail, the 1-km (0.6-mile) Red Squirrel trail and the 4-km (2.4-mile) East Bay trail.

Hike: The 7-km (4.2-mile) Pelly Point trail is a wilderness route.

Backpacking: Several areas in the park have routes that can be used for backpacking. The interior fireguard road along the park's perimeter is approximately 48 km (30 miles) long. The 152 km (95 miles) of snowmobile and cross-country skiing trails range in length from 3 to 35 km (2 to 22 miles), are equipped with several shelters and form interconnecting loops for hiking trips of varying length. In the southern portion of the park, the Boggy Creek Valley, a glacial meltwater channel reaching 120 meters (400 feet) deep, is an interesting hiking trip. The route is not marked and topographical maps are needed.

Groceries and camping supplies are available at the park.

More Information: Duck Mountain Provincial Park, Box 39, Kamsack, Saskatchewan S0A 1S0, (306) 542-3482.

Wildcat Hills Wilderness Area

Located in northeastern Saskatchewan, the 162-km^2 (62-square-mile) Wildcat Hills Wilderness Area encompasses the Pasquia Hills which are part of the Manitoba Escarpment, the rise between the first and second prairie steppes. The northern and eastern slopes rise steeply approximately 540 meters (1,800 feet) from the muskeg of the Manitoba Lowlands and reach an elevation of 822 meters (2,700 feet) at their highest point.

Hikes/Backpacking: A 32-km (20-mile) forestry access trail begins where the Overflowing River crosses the highway and follows roughly parallel to the river. The trail stops short of the Man River, and return is by the same route.

Changes in elevation are gradual, making the area a difficult one in which to orient yourself. Visibility is seldom beyond the surrounding trees and skill with a map and compass is essential.

More Information: Saskatchewan Parks and Renewable Resources, 3211 Albert Street, Regina, Saskatchewan S4S 5W6, (306) 787-2700.

View of Grace Lakes in Nipawin Provincial Park. (Saskatchewan Government Photograph)

Nipawin Provincial Park

Nipawin is a wilderness park in the forest and lake country of northern Saskatchewan. Wildlife includes white-tailed deer, moose, woodland caribou, elk, bear, several species of grouse and ptarmigan.

Hike: The Over the Narrow Hill trail leads 7 km (4.2 miles) along a glacial esker ridge.

Backpacking: The park has a network of approximately 110 km (68 miles) of historic trails. Although a large fire several years ago burnt over most of this area, it still provides interesting hiking.

Forest-inventory maps at a scale of 4 inches to the mile, can be acquired locally.

More Information: Nipawin Provincial Park, Box 130, Smeaton, Saskatchewan S0J 2J0, (306) 426-2082.

Greenwater Provincial Park

Greenwater Park occupies 184 km^2 (71 square miles) of the great rolling foothills of the Pasquia Hills and is covered with a thick forest of deep green spruce and silver aspen glades.

Walk: The Highbush interpretive trail is a 2.8-km (1.7-mile) loop that parallels Greenwater Creek through a mature mixed forest of aspen and spruce.

Hikes/Backpacking: The park has a number of snowmobile trails, old logging roads and cutlines that can be hiked, and one trail shelter that can be used by hikers. Topographical maps are necessary to hike in the park and are available at the park office.

Supplies can be acquired at stores in and adjacent to the park.

More Information: Greenwater Provincial Park, Box 430, Porcupine Plain, Saskatchewan S0E 1H0, (306) 278-2972.

Grasslands National Park

The original mixed-grass prairie of North America, protected nowhere else on the continent, is preserved in Grasslands National Park in southern Saskatchewan. Wildlife found here includes the pronghorn antelope, prairie rattlesnake, sage grouse, ferruginous hawk and prairie falcon. Encompassed in the park are the Kildeer Badlands where Sir George Mercer Dawson made the first recorded discovery of dinosaur remains in 1874, and a formation known as a "sinking hill," a fault-like formation 60 meters (200 feet) wide and 10 meters (30 feet) deep which is believed to be sinking 30 cm (12 inches) every year.

The area was used by Sitting Bull and his Sioux followers as refuge from the United States Army after the Battle of Little Big Horn in 1876. A few homesteaders tried farming here, but could not make a go of it. The surrounding area was then used for ranching operations.

Parks Canada is presently acquiring the land to establish Grasslands Park and visitor facilities have not yet been established.

Walks/Hikes: Visitors are encouraged to hike throughout the sections already acquired. Old trails used in the past by ranchers offer easy hiking to explore the prairie and view wildlife.

More Information: The Superintendent, Grasslands National Park, P.O. Box 150, Val Marie, Saskatchewan S0N 2T0, (306) 298-2257.

Guidebook Sources

Prince Albert National Park Trail Guide, by Donna Pletz and Marg Tarleton, describes the park's trails. Available from: Friends of Prince Albert National Park, Box 11, Waskesiu Lake, Saskatchewan S0J 2Y0; $5.

6

Manitoba

FOR ALL ITS settled image of bland, comforta-
ble wheat fields, over half of Manitoba is as rugged as it was in
the days of the fur-trading *voyageurs* and as wild as the charge
of Métis into herds of buffalo. Only the southern and
southwestern areas, less than two-fifths of Manitoba's 649,839
km² (251,000 square miles) is flat prairie farmland. The
three-fifths of the province to the east and southeast of Lake
Winnipeg lies within the Precambrian Shield characterized by
very rugged terrain with numerous lakes, wooded ridges and
rocks protruding from a surface denuded of soil by glacial
action.

The highest hills in the province are along the Manitoba
Escarpment which forms the edge between the Manitoba Plain,
the first prairie steppe, and the Saskatchewan Plain which is the
second prairie steppe. The escarpment extends from the

*Average daily minimum and maximum temperatures in
Manitoba*

		May		June		July		August		Sept.		Oct.	
		L	H	L	H	L	H	L	H	L	H	L	H
Winnipeg	°C	5	18	11	23	14	27	12	26	7	19	1	11
	°F	41	64	51	73	57	80	54	78	45	66	34	52
The Pas	°C	3	18	8	22	12	25	10	23	4	17	1	10
	°F	36	60	46	69	53	76	50	73	40	61	29	47

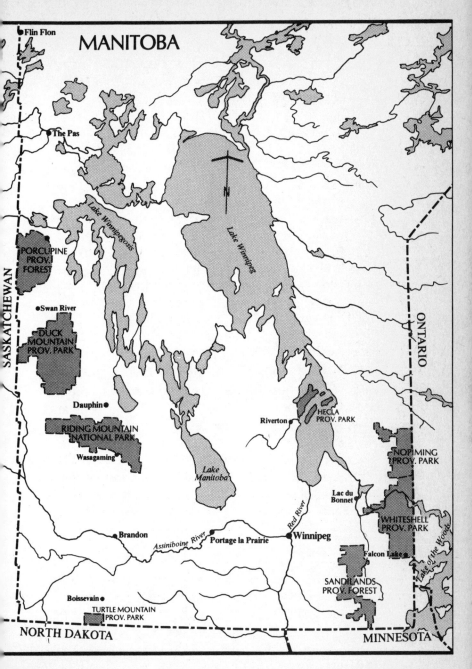

Flin Flon

MANITOBA

The Pas

SASKATCHEWAN

Lake Winnipegosis

PORCUPINE
PROV.
FOREST

• Swan River

DUCK
MOUNTAIN
PROV. PARK

Dauphin •

RIDING MOUNTAIN
NATIONAL PARK

Wasagaming

Lake Winnipeg

Lake Manitoba

Riverton •

HECLA
PROV. PARK

ONTARIO

NOPIMING
PROV. PARK

Lac du
Bonnet

WHITESHELL
PROV. PARK

Brandon •

Assiniboine River

Portage la Prairie •

Red River

Winnipeg

Falcon Lake •

Lake of the Woods

Boissevain •

TURTLE MOUNTAIN
PROV. PARK

SANDILANDS
PROV. FOREST

NORTH DAKOTA

MINNESOTA

Pembina Mountains near the United States boundary, northward to the Pasquia Hills just south of the Saskatchewan River, and encompasses the Tiger Hills, Riding Mountain, Duck Mountain and Porcupine Mountain. At an elevation of 831 meters (2,727 feet), Mount Baldy in the Duck Mountains is the highest point in Manitoba.

Manitoba has the most temperate climate of the three prairie provinces. Summer temperatures range from 10°C (50°F) at night to around 24°C (75°F) during the day. Average annual precipitation across the province varies from 41 to 53 cm (16 to 21 inches), and most falls during the summers.

More Information: Travel Manitoba, 155 Carlton Street, 7th Floor, Winnipeg, Manitoba R3C 3H8, or call in Winnipeg (204) 945-3777, or from elsewhere call toll-free 1-800-665-0040. Hostels in Manitoba are operated by the Manitoba Hostelling Association, 1700 Ellice Avenue, Winnipeg, Manitoba R3H 0B1, (204) 786-5641.

Birds Hill Provincial Park

Located close to Winnipeg, Birds Hill Park features a trembling aspen and bur oak forest, prairie grassland, and a man-made lake with sandy beaches. The park is a popular camping base for visitors to Winnipeg.

Walks: Among the park's self-guiding nature trails are the (2.1-mile) Cedar Bog trail and the Bur Oak trail.

More Information: Travel Manitoba, 155 Carlton Street, 7th Floor, Winnipeg, Manitoba R3C 3H8, (204) 945-3777, or toll-free 1-800-665-0040.

Grand Beach Provincial Park

A natural sand beach on the shores of Lake Winnipeg, Grand Beach Park is popular for swimming and sailing. It also offers visitors a nature trail.

Walk: The Ancient Beach self-guiding trail is a 2.5-km (1.5-mile) walk following the ancient beach of Lake Agassiz, the inland lake that covered most of southeastern Manitoba 8,000 to 13,000 years ago.

More Information: Grand Beach District Office, Grand Beach, Manitoba R0E 0S0, (204) 754-2212.

Riding Mountain National Park

Riding Mountain Park occupies 2,977 km² (1,150 square miles) of the Manitoba Escarpment, a rolling plateau that rises 450 meters (1,500 feet) above the surrounding prairie. At an elevation of 750 meters (2,460 feet), Riding Mountain is the third highest point in Manitoba. Forest cover in the park's high areas consists of white spruce, black spruce, jack pine, balsam fir, tamarack, trembling aspen and white birch. The base of the escarpment, the park's lowest and warmest region, is covered with a deciduous forest of hardwoods, shrubs, vines and ferns.

Riding Mountain National Park. (Parks Canada)

Black bear, wapiti, moose and white-tailed deer are among the larger mammals in the park. Beaver can be seen in almost every pond. Northern pike, walleye, whitefish, lake trout, rainbow trout and brook trout can be taken from the park's lakes.

Walks: Among the park's interpretive trails is the 1.9-km (1.1-mile) return Ominnik Marsh trail along a boardwalk through a marsh. The Burls and Buttersweet trail is a 2.2 km (1.3 miles) return walk through an unique eastern hardwood forest at the base of the Manitoba Escarpment. The Arrowhead trail is a 3.4-km (2.1-mile) return path exploring glacial features.

The 1-km (0.6-mile) return or 2.6-km (1.6-mile) loop Lakeshore Walk along the lake is wheelchair accessible. The 1-km (0.6-mile) Ma-ee-gun trail is designed for the visually impaired. It offers braille text and lets visitors experience sounds, smells, and textures of the mature boreal forest.

Hikes: Gorge Creek is a 6.4-km (3.9-mile) one way hike descending 320 meters (1,050 feet) along Dead Ox and Gorge creeks through the shale of the Manitoba Escarpment. On the 9.2-km (5.7-mile) return Moon Lake trail a variety of animal tracks can be seen. The Oak Ridge trail offers 3-km (1.8-mile) and 6.4-km (3.9-mile) loops through oak groves and meadows to a view of the Manitoba Escarpment.

Backpacking: Riding Mountain Park's 320-km (200-mile) trail network includes 15 backpacking trails ranging from overnight trips to routes suitable for excursions of up to five or six days. The 52.9-km (32.8-mile) North Escarpment Trail follows the Manitoba Escarpment through the northeast section of the park, and the 23.2-km (14.5-mile) South Escarpment Trail goes into the southeast part. The 21.6-km (13.5-mile) Grasshopper Valley Trail follows the shore of Audy Lake and crosses the semi-open meadows and fescue grass prairie of the Grasshopper Valley and eventually joins the Central Trail. The park's longest trail is the 69-km (43-mile) Central Trail across the western half of the park traversing vegetation ranging from white spruce stands to open rolling grasslands. There are three access trails along the route, and one side trail leading to secluded Gunn Lake which is surrounded by dry, rolling, semi-open ridges covered with short hazel and hawthorn brush. Primitive campsites are located at regular intervals.

Topographical maps can be purchased at the park office, and supplies can be obtained at stores in Wasagaming.

More Information: The Superintendent, Riding Mountain National Park, Wasagaming, Manitoba R0J 2H0, (204) 848-2811.

Duck Mountain Provincial Park

Lying on the rolling landscape of the Manitoba Escarpment, 1,274-km^2 (492-square-mile) Duck Mountain Park includes

Duck Mountain Provincial Park. (Manitoba Government Travel)

831-meter (2,727-foot) Mount Baldy, the highest point in the province. The boreal forest consists of white spruce, jack pine, balsam, aspen and birch. The park environment supports a major elk herd, moose, white-tailed deer, black bear, fox, lynx, coyote and timber wolf. The lakes and streams contain brook, speckled, rainbow, brown and lake trout, kokanee salmon, splake, muskellunge, pickerel, jackfish, whitefish, walleye and yellow perch. The park is a favorite place for anglers. Several lakes have been stocked with species not native to the area.

Walk: The Shining stone interpretive trail follows the shore of a peninsula in West Blue Lake.

Hikes/Backpacking: Hiking in the park is done following unmarked hiking routes along ridge tops and lake shores where there is backwoods camping.

More Information: Duck Mountain Provincial Park, Parks Branch, P.O. Box 239, Swan River, Manitoba R0L 1Z0, (204) 734-2321.

Turtle Mountain Provincial Park

Situated in the southwest corner of the province on the North Dakota border, 189-km² (73-square-mile) Turtle Mountain Park is at a higher elevation and has a different environment from the surrounding flat prairie. The forest cover consists of elm, birch and oak. Beaver, mink and muskrat are indigenous to the park. The park has 39 km (24 miles) of trails.

Walk: The Dead Lake interpretive trail, 1.5-km (0.9-mile) along a boardwalk, explores the death of a lake.

Hikes: The park's hiking trail network includes the 9-km (5.5-mile) Bower Lake trail, the 10-km (6-mile) Adam Lake trail, and the 5-km (3-km) Intermediate trail.

Backpacking: The James Lake Trail is a 15-km (9-mile) route with a backcountry cabin and shelter.

Supplies can be obtained in Boissevain, about 20 km (12 miles) north of the park. Topographical maps should be obtained from the Map Sales Office in Winnipeg.

Hecla Provincial Park. (Manitoba Government Travel)

More Information: Turtle Mountain Provincial Park, Parks Branch, Box 820, Boissevain, Manitoba R0K 0E0, (204) 534-7204.

Hecla Provincial Park

Hecla Island, covering 158 km² (61 square miles), is the largest island in Lake Winnipeg and the only one of the park's seven islands accessible by causeway. Rugged cliffs dominate the northern shore and most of the eastern shore is open fields. The interior is covered with a dense forest of spruce, aspen, balsam, jack pine and tamarack. The southern part of the island is a series of marshes containing rushes, cattails, duckweeds and water grasses where moose and deer come to feed. Hecla's marshes are located on the central North American flyway and fifty thousand northern migrant birds make it their summer home. Among the species observed are 15 varieties of ducks, Canada geese, snow geese, blue geese, pelicans, sandhill cranes, whistling swans, herons, bitterns and cormorants. The predatory bald eagle and golden eagle, and a multitude of hawks also inhabit the island.

Walks: Among the myriad of paths is the 1-km (0.6-mile) Hecla Village trail which includes pioneer remains of the island's Icelandic settlers.

Hikes/Backpacking: At present there are two routes that can be hiked including a 60-km (37-mile) trail on the eastern side of the island. The ground cover on Hecla Island is usually moist and rubber boots may be needed. Open fires are prohibited in the interior.

More Information: Hecla Provincial Park, Parks Branch, Box 70, Riverton, Manitoba R0C 2R0, (204) 378-2945.

Whiteshell Provincial Park

Lying on the Ontario border, Whiteshell Park covers 2,734 km² (1,056 square miles) of the Precambrian Shield. The primitive

Whiteshell Provincial Park. (Travel Manitoba)

forest is dotted with more than 200 lakes and streams containing Northern pike, suckers and pickerel. Wild rice grows in the bays of some of the lakes. Wildlife that can be observed includes moose, fox, coyote, lynx, deer, black bear, beaver, bald eagle, turkey vultures, spruce grouse and ruffed grouse.

Walks: Among the park's self-guiding trails is the 2-km (1.2-mile) Falcon Creek trail loop which explores man's influence on Whiteshell over the past 80 years. The McGillivray Falls trails offers 4.1 km (2.5 miles) or 2.4 km (1.4 miles) walks to a small Precambrian Shield drainage basin. The 9.6-km (5.9-mile) Pine Point trail explores the park's contrasts.

Hikes: The Hunt Lake Trail is a 16-km (10-mile) loop that leads north to Indian Bay and returns along the east shore of West Hawk Lake. The Amisk trail is a 4-km (2.4-mile) return route to the Rennie River below Inverness Falls. The Bear Lake trail is a 8-km (4.9-mile) route along rock ridges through jack pine stands.

The 66-km (40-mile) Mantario Hiking Trail traverses the Precambrian wilderness and skirts the shores of several lakes. Campsites are located at regular intervals. The trail is recommended for experienced backpackers.

More Information: Hecla Provincial Park, Parks Branch, Box 70, Riverton, Manitoba R0C 2R0, (204) 378-2945.

7

Ontario

ONTARIO has walking, dayhiking and backpacking opportunities in every part of the province. They range from easy trails close to cities to rugged wilderness treks for experienced backpackers. The Bruce Trail, along the Niagara Escarpment from Queenston to Tobermory, was the first long-distance hiking trail in Canada. Since its completion in 1967, independent trail associations have proliferated in southern Ontario and hundreds of kilometers of trails have been developed. Most of these routes pass through or close to towns where supplies are available, making extended trips possible. In northern Ontario, the majority of hiking trails are located in provincial or national parks.

Average daily minimum and maximum temperatures in Ontario

		May		June		July		August		Sept.		Oct.	
		L	H	L	H	L	H	L	H	L	H	L	H
Ottawa	°C	6.1	18.3	11.7	23.9	14.4	26.7	12.8	25.6	8.9	20.6	2.8	12.8
	°F	43	65	53	75	58	80	55	78	48	69	37	55
Toronto	°C	7.8	18.3	13.3	23.9	16.1	27.2	15.6	25.6	11.7	21.7	5.6	14.4
	°F	46	65	56	75	61	81	60	78	53	71	42	58
Thunder Bay	°C	2.8	14.4	8.3	20	11.1	23.3	10.6	22.2	6.7	17.2	1.1	10.6
	°F	37	58	47	68	52	74	51	72	44	63	34	51

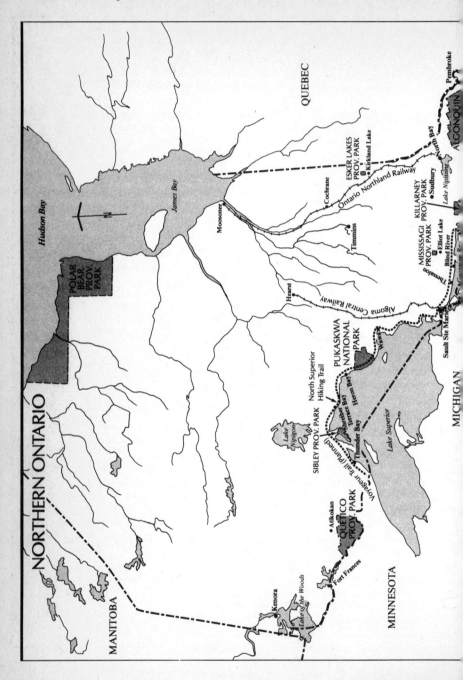

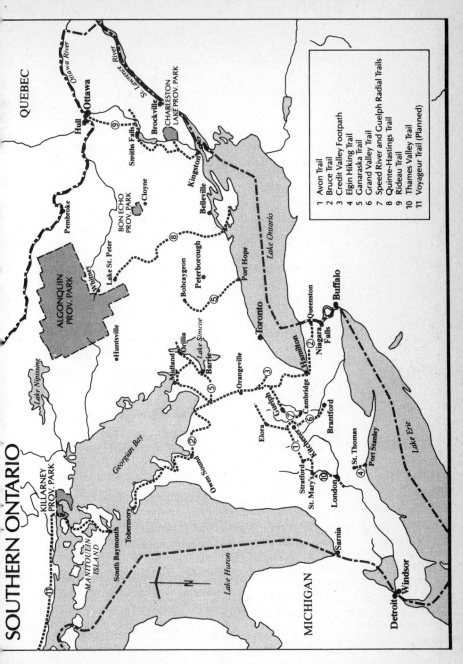

SOUTHERN ONTARIO

QUEBEC

MICHIGAN

1 Avon Trail
2 Bruce Trail
3 Credit Valley Footpath
4 Elgin Hiking Trail
5 Ganaraska Trail
6 Grand Valley Trail
7 Speed River and Guelph Radial Trails
8 Quinte-Hastings Trail
9 Rideau Trail
10 Thames Valley Trail
11 Voyageur Trail (Planned)

The geographic division between northern and southern Ontario is a line lying roughly along the Mattawa River, Lake Nipissing and the French River. Most of the 932,000 km² (360,000 square miles) of northern Ontario is underlaid by the Precambrian rock of the Canadian Shield. About one-third of the 129,500-km² (50,000-square-mile) area of southern Ontario is covered by a southern extension of the Precambrian Shield known as the Frontenac Axis. In the transition zone between the northern and southern forests, flora and fauna of both forest types occur together. The remaining two-thirds of southern Ontario is largely agricultural land and forests.

More Information: Ontario Travel, Queen's Park, Toronto, Ontario M7A 2E5, (416) 965-4008. From the U.S. and from Canada outside of Toronto, call toll-free, 1-800-668-2746. Topographical maps of Ontario can be purchased from: The Ministry of Natural Resources, Public Service Centre, Whitney Block Room 6404, Queen's Park, Toronto, Ontario M7A 1W3. Use Map Index 1 for ordering Ontario maps.

Hostels in Ontario are operated by the following organizations: Canadian Hostelling Association-Ontario East, 18 The Byward Market, Ottawa, Ontario K1N 7A1, (613) 230-1200; and Great Lakes Hostelling Association, 233 Church Street, Toronto, Ontario M5B 1Z1, (416) 368-1848.

Southwestern Ontario

Toronto Region Conservation Areas

Near Toronto, Canada's largest city, are conservation areas offering a variety of trails. Many offer interpretive programs.

The Kortright Centre for Conservation, which covers 4 square km (1.5 square miles) near Kleinburg, features 12 km (7.4 miles) of trails through forests, along a pond, and past a sugarshack. Also near Kleinburg, the 0.9 square km (0.3 square mile) Boyd Conservation Area offers a nature trail.

The 4.5-square km (1.7-square mile) Albion Hill Conservation Area, located 8 km (5 miles) north of Bolton offers 30 km

(18 miles) of trails through rolling terrain covered by hardwood bush and open parkland.

Bruce's Mill Conservation Area, named for its 120-year-old restored mill, features 12 km (7.4 miles) of trails through 0.9 square km (0.3 square miles) of mixed and hardwood forest.

Palgrave Forest and Wildlife Area, 10 km (6 miles) north of Bolton, covers 2.2 square km (0.8 square miles) of the Oak Ridges Moraine. Over 16 km (10 miles) of trails wind through the forest.

The Greenwood Conservation Area, covering 2.8 square km (1 square mile) north of Ajax, offers nature trails through woodlots, reforested areas and open spaces.

Within Metropolitan Toronto are trails along river valleys and ravines including the Humber, Don and Rouge rivers and Highland Creek. The walks are described in *Great Country Walks Around Toronto.*

More Information: Metropolitan Toronto and Region Conservation Authority, 5 Shoreham Drive, Downsview, Ontario M3N 1S4, (416) 661-6600.

Bruce Trail

The Bruce Trail, the longest and best-known footpath in Ontario, winds its way for 736 km (457 miles) along the Niagara Escarpment from Queenston on the Niagara River near Niagara Falls to Tobermory on the tip of the Bruce Peninsula in Georgian Bay.

The trail is the nearest long distance footpath to the Toronto area, and though it passes near some of southern Ontario's heavily populated areas, there are only occasional glimpses of urbanization. The Bruce Trail traverses a number of conservation areas, provincial parks and one national park that provide convenient access for hikers who want a short walk, day-hike or to backpack on the trail. Though extended backpacking trips can be taken, there are still long gaps without camping or shelters.

From the southern terminus at Queenston Heights Park along the Niagara Parkway, the Bruce Trail leads through the fruit lands of the Niagara peninsula, passes the historic Welland Canal, and crosses the Dundas Valley in the Royal Botanical Gardens near the city of Hamilton.

From Mount Nemo Conservation Area, the trail begins to climb along the escarpment and passes through the Crawford Lake Conservation Area, traverses the ski slopes at Glen Eden and the Kelso Conservation Area and crosses Highway 401 near Milton. North of the highway, the trail goes through Hilton Falls Conservation Area and continues north to Limehouse Conservation Area near Georgetown, and to Terra Cotta Conservation Area.

The trail winds northward through the Caledon Hills and the Hockley Valley, traversing Forks of the Credit Provincial Park near Belfountain, Glen Haffey Conservation Area, and Scott's Falls Provincial Park.

In the Dufferin Hi-Lands section, Mono Cliffs Provincial Park, Boyne Valley Provincial Park are crossed by the trail. Near Collingwood, the Blue Mountain ski resort area encompasses high bluffs and wide valleys. In this section, the Bruce Trail traverses Nottawasaga Bluffs Conservation Area, Devil's Glen Provincial Park and Petun Conservation Area.

In the Beaver Valley, a deep wedge in the Niagara Escarpment, the trail goes through Old Baldy Conservation Area, and along the valley's east rim and then along the west rim to the Owen Sound area. From Wiarton, the Bruce Trail follows the Georgian Bay shore, considered the footpath's most spectacular section, much of it on high cliffs through Bruce Peninsula National Park.

More Information: Bruce Trail Association, P.O. Box 857, Hamilton, Ontario L8N 3N9, (416) 529-6821.

Grand Valley Trail

This 250-km (155-mile) trail stretches from Rock Point Provincial Park on Lake Erie to the town of Alton. The route goes along the Grand River flood plain, woodlots and rolling hills. The area is a historic part of southern Ontario containing Mennonite and Scottish settlements.

Camping is available at the Elora Gorge, Conestoga, Pinehurst and Brant conservation areas and Rock Point Provincial Park.

More Information: Grand Valley Trail Association, Box 1233, Kitchener, Ontario N2G 4G8.

Avon Trail

The Avon Trail connects the Thames Valley Trail at St. Mary's with the Grand Valley Trail at Conestogo near Kitchener. The 100-km (60-mile) route goes to Wildwood Lake and then in a northeasterly direction to Stratford. From there the trail follows the Avon River and Silver Creek toward Amulree. Continuing in a northeasterly direction, the trail runs close to Wellesley and through Elmsville and the Waterloo Farmers Market. After following Martin Creek and part of the Conestoga River, it meets the Grand Valley Trail in the village of Conestoga.

Parts of the trail are on public roads, but most run through scenic farmland and woodlots. There is a side trail in the Stratford area. The only camping facilities are at Wildwood Park at St. Mary's.

More Information: Avon Trail Association, Box 384, Stratford, Ontario N5A 6T3, (519) 625-8097.

Thames Valley Trail

This trail follows the Thames River from the Byron Bridge at Springbank Park in the city of London, and extends upstream through the Fanshawe Conservation Area to the western limits of the town of St. Mary's. Most of the 60-km (37-mile) trail is on private rural land. The only camping facilities are in the Fanshawe Conservation Area northeast of London. At St. Mary's the Thames Valley Trail meets the Avon Trail and camping is available in Wildwood Park. Extensions of the trail from Springbank Park downstream to Wardsville are planned.

More Information: Thames Valley Trail Association, Box 821, Terminal B, London, Ontario N6A 4Z3.

Speed River Trail and Radial Line Trail

Both of these trails are maintained by the Guelph Trail Club. The Guelph Radial Trail runs from Guelph 28 km (17 miles) to Limehouse where it connects with the Bruce Trail. From Guelph to Georgetown it follows the route of the old Radial electric railway and passes through meadows and bush. The trail has a few steep sections.

The Speed River Trail follows the Speed River for 25 km (16 miles) from Guelph through Cambridge to Riverside Park near Preston where a side trail links with the Grand Valley Trail. Most of the trail goes through meadows. There are also sections of cedar and hardwood bush where Canada geese, herons and other wildlife abound. Neither trail has campsites.

The Guelph Trail Club also maintains the 5-km (3.1-mile) Hanlon loop trail through conservation land at the south end of Guelph, the 8-km (4.9-mile) Arkell loop trail through a variety of forests and meadows and the 4-km (2.4-mile) Starkey loop which leads to the area's highest point of land.

More Information: Guelph Trail Club, P.O. Box 1, Guelph, Ontario N1H 6J6.

Elgin Hiking Trail

The Elgin Hiking Club maintains two trail sections, a total of 35 km (21 miles) in length. The main trail winds along creek valleys, ravines, woodlots and hillsides of Kettle Creek from Payne's Mills to Port Stanley on Lake Erie. A side trail goes east from Union on the main trail to Shaw's Dairy. Overnight spots and additional trail sections are planned.

More Information: Elgin Hiking Trail Club, P.O. Box 250, St. Thomas, Ontario N5P 3T9.

Eastern Ontario

Rideau Trail

The Rideau Trail stretches 388 km (241 miles) between Kingston and Ottawa. Located in the broad corridor surrounding the historic Rideau Canal, the trail begins on the shores of Lake Ontario at the marshes of the Little Cataraqui, heads north to Sydenham and through bush country along the shores of Gould Lake and in Frontenac Park to the Perth Road. Foley Mountain Conservation Area at Westport and Murphy's Point Provincial Park are traversed, as well as the towns of Perth and Smith Falls before passing through the Richmond Farming district and the Ottawa/Carleton Conservation Centre. It enters Ottawa at Bells Corners and follows the Ottawa River Parkway to Richmond Landing.

Most of the trail is easy walking through meadows, bush and farmland. Campsites are located near the trail. A map kit is available.

More Information: Rideau Trail Association, Box 15, Kingston, Ontario K7L 4V6, (613) 542-5414.

Gatineau Park

Situated north of the Ottawa River, Gatineau Park in Quebec offers walking and hiking trails within close access to the city of Ottawa. The park is described in the Quebec chapter.

Algonquin Provincial Park

Created in 1893, Algonquin Park is the oldest provincial park in Ontario. The 7,600-km^2 (2,925 square-mile) park, located on the southern edge of the Canadian Shield, is a land of rounded hills, rocky ridges, spruce bogs, fast-flowing rivers and thousands of lakes, ponds and streams. The hills of the western two-thirds of the park are covered with hardwood forests of sugar maple, beech and yellow birch with groves of hemlock and scattered giant white pine. White pine, red pine and jack pine predominate in the drier and sandier eastern part of Algonquin.

Situated in the transition zone between southern broadleaf forests and northern coniferous forests, the park is the home of wildlife of both forest types. Northern birds such as the raven, gray jay and spruce goose can be observed with the rose-breasted grosbeak, brown thrasher and the scarlet tanager, which are southern birds. Among mammals, the wolf, moose, and fisher, which are northern animals, occur, as well as such southern species as the racoon and the white-tailed deer. Lake trout and speckled trout are found in the lakes.

Walks: Among the park's interpretive footpaths are the 1-km (0.6-mile) Lookout Trail to a magnificent view of the park, the 1.9-km (1.1-mile) Peck Lake trail loop exploring the ecology of a small Algonquin lake, the 2-km (1.2-mile) Beaver Pond trail on the theme of beaver pond ecology, and the 1.5-km (0.9-mile) which explores the flora and fauna of a typical northern bog.

Hikes: The 5.1-km (3.1-mile) Booth's Rock trail climbs to vistas of Algonquin scenery and returns along an abandoned railroad. The 11-km (6.8-mile) Mizzy Lake trail visits nine ponds and small lakes with good opportunities to view wildlife.

Backpacking: Algonquin Park's backpacking trails wind through the forest, and along lakes and rivers. The Western Uplands Trails has three loops: a 32-km hike to Maggie Lake, Oak Lake and Ramona Lake, a 55-km route to Clara Lake, Tern Lake and Rainbow Lake, and 71-km trek to Islet Lake, Brown Lake and Rainbow Lake. The Highland Hiking Trail has two loops: a 19-km trail around Provoking Lake, and a 35-km hike around Head Lake. Both trails have backcountry campsites. To alleviate overcrowding a maximum of 50 people a day are permitted to begin the Highland Hiking Trail and not more than 80 are allowed to start the Western Uplands Trail. Reservations for interior camping permits can be made by writing to the park, or by calling (705) 633-5538.

Camping supplies can be obtained at several stores and

outfitters within the park. There is a total ban on cans and bottles in the park interior. *Exploring Algonquin Park*, by Joanne Kates, includes descriptions of the park's trails.

More Information: The Superintendent, Algonquin Provincial Park, Box 219, Whitney, Ontario K0J 2M0, (705) 633-5572.

Ganaraska Trail

The Ganaraska Trail is planned to go through the hills near Port Hope on Lake Ontario, to Kawartha Lakes and the

Ganaraska Trail near Bethany, Ontario. (Ontario Ministry of Industry & Tourism)

Huronia resort area north of Lake Simcoe, and then along the Mad River to connect with the Bruce Trail at Glen Huron near Collingwood. The route crosses rolling farmland and goes over wooded hills.

About 257 km (160 miles) of trail have been completed. A little less than a quarter of the route remains to be blazed. Provincial parks and conservation areas with camping facilities are located adjacent to most sections of the trail. Emily Provincial Park at Omemee, Bass Lake Provincial Park at Orillia, and Devil's Glen Provincial Park at Glen Huron are recommended.

More Information: Ganaraska Trail Association, Box 1136, Barrie, Ontario L4M 5E2.

Frontenac Provincial Park

Located in the southernmost part of the Canadian Shield about 40 km (25 miles) north of Kingston, Frontenac Park covers 70 km^2 (27 square miles) of diverse lake and forest terrain. Rolling hills covered by deciduous forests lie in the northwest corner of the park. The middle section of the park is a transitional zone of broken ridges covered by mixed forests of pine, poplar, birch and red maple. The southern third of the park is a low area of sparse vegetation and numerous beaver dams. Beavers, porcupines, squirrels and chipmunks are among the mammals that inhabit the park. Many birds including the great blue heron and various song birds can be seen here.

Walks: The 1-km (0.6-mile) Arab Lake Gorge interpretive trail follows a boardwalk and explores the gorge's geology and ecology.

Hikes/Backpacking: A network of over 100 km (60 miles) of trails allows hikers to access most of the park's backcountry for dayhikes, overnight or longer trips. The Rideau Trail, described earlier in this chapter, is incorporated into the southern part of the park's trail system.

More Information: Park Superintendent, Ministry of Natural Resources, Frontenac Provincial Park, P.O. Box 11, Sydenham, Ontario K0H 2T0, (613) 376-3489.

Bon Echo Provincial Park

The scenic highlight of this 66-km² (25-square-mile) park in eastern Ontario is Mazinaw Rock. This 114-m (275-foot) spectacular cliff drops vertically to Mazinaw Lake and is the result of faulting. The name Bon Echo refers to the accoustical properties of Mazinaw Rock. Scattered along the rock at canoe level are scores of Indian pictographs.

Bon Echo Park is located on the Frontenac Axis, the narrow southern extension of the Canadian Shield and has both northern and southern plants and wildlife.

Walks: The Shield Trail is a 4.8-km (3-mile) interpretive walk on a part of the old Addington Road through rugged Canadian Shield landscape. The 1.4-km (0.8-mile) High Pines trail leads past tall pines, hemlock groves and seasonal ponds to a view of Bon Echo Rock. The 1-km (0.6-mile) Bon Echo Creek trail follows a winding creek bed as it enters lower Mazinaw Lake.

Hikes/Backpacking: The Abes and Essens Trail consists of three loops: a 4-km (2.4-mile) loop around Chutes Lake, and two 9-km (5.5-mile) loops around Essens Lake. A hike around all three loops is about 17 km (10.5 miles) in length and can be done as a long day-hike or an overnight backpacking trip. The trail has five interior campsites, all situated beside lakes. An interior camping permit, at $3 per night per person is required. Call in advance for reservations.

More Information: The Superintendent, Bon Echo Provincial Park, R.R. #1, Cloyne, Ontario K0H 1K0, (613) 336-2228.

Charleston Lake Provincial Park

Charleston Lake Park occupies 8.5 km² (2 square miles) on the Frontenac Axis, the southerly extension of the Canadian Shield, and combines northern land form with a southern climate. Wildlife typical of both regions inhabits the area. Loons, black rat snakes, great blue herons, turkey vultures, ducks and geese can be observed. More than 30 prehistoric sites and Indian pictographs are located in the park.

Walks: Among the park's nature trails is the Sandstone Island trail which explores a prehistoric campsite and abandoned farm remains. The Quiddity Trail includes a 256-meter (840-foot) boardwalk and a lookout over Charleston Lake. The Hemlock Ridge interpretive trail explores the park's forests.

Hikes/Backpacking: The Westside hiking trail system provides access to Tallow Rock Bay and Captain's Gap on the park's secluded west side where there are wilderness campsites. Quartzite ridges give excellent views of Charleston Lake and surrounding area.

More Information: The Superintendent, Charleston Lake Provincial Park, R.R. 4, Lansdowne, Ontario K0E 1L0, (613) 659-2065.

Northern Ontario

Killarney Provincial Park

The white quartzite La Cloche Mountains and clear lakes that vary in color from ink blue to turquoise make up this 344-km^2 (133-square-miles) park located on the shores of Georgian Bay. Visibility in the lakes, which are found high on the ridges as well as in the valleys, ranges from 9 to 20 meters (30 to 65 feet). The forest is a transition between northern and southern forest types. Deer, moose, bears, timber wolves, coyotes and bobcats are among the mammals that inhabit the forest. Ruffed grouse, white-throated sparrows, barred owls, blue herons and common loons can be observed. Many artists, including members of the Group of Seven, have painted in the park.

Walks: The park's three self-guided nature trails, Cranberry Bog, Chikanishing and Granite Ridge are loop routes that can be walked in less than three hours.

Hikes/Backpacking: The La Cloche Silhouette Trail is a 100-km (60-mile) loop through a variety of terrain including hemlock forests, beaver meadows and crystal clear lakes. The trail climbs to the summit of Silver Peak which towers

Killarney Provincial Park. (Ontario Ministry of Natural Resources)

360 meters (1,200 feet) above Georgian Bay. The trail also provides access to the exposed ridges which are a highlight of Killarney.

There are outfitters in the town of Killarney and the city of Sudbury to supply hiking needs. A Killarney Park user's map is available from the park office. An interior camping permit costs $3 per person per night. Cans and bottles are banned from the interior.

More Information: The Superintendent, Killarney Provincial Park, Killarney, Ontario P0M 2A0, (705) 287-2368.

Esker Lakes Provincial Park

Located in northeastern Ontario near the Quebec border, this 32-km^2 (12-square-mile) park is characterized by long serpentine ridges called eskers, great boulders known as erratics and kettle lakes. These features were formed as a result of the last Ice Age. The northern forest contains white birch, black spruce and jack pine. The park is the home of many large mammals including moose, wolves and bears. Among the many species of birds in the park are the great blue heron, hermit thrush, red-eyed vireo, loon and grouse. The lakes contain speckled trout, northern pike and yellow perch. In season you can pick raspberries, saskatoon berries, red currants, pin cherries and blueberries in the woods.

Walks: The Lonesome Bog Trail is a 1.5-km (0.9-mile) walk circling Sausage Lake that explores the bog ecology of a dying lake. The 1-km (0.6-mile) Prospector's Trail skirts Lake Panagapka and passes old mining equipment.

Hikes/Backpacking: The Trapper's Trail explores a rolling esker, glacial erratics and an ancient Ojibwa trapping ground, has three interlocking loops of 6.4 km (3.9 miles), 13 km (8 miles) and 20 km (12 miles), making it suitable for day-hiking or overnight trips. Rest shelters are located along the trail.

More Information: District Manager, Ministry of Natural Resources, P.O. Box 129, Swastika, Ontario P0K 1T0, (705) 642-3222.

Wakami Lake Provincial Park

Lying on the height of land separating rivers flowing to the Arctic Ocean and those flowing towards the Great Lakes and the Atlantic Ocean, 88-km² (34-square-mile) Wakami Lake Park encompasses Wakami Lake, an Ojibway Indian name meaning "water is clear and clean." The transition zone forest between the northern boreal forest and the southern Great Lakes-Saint Lawrence forest is inhabited by moose, mink, marten, fox and wolf. Birdlife includes bald eagles, ospreys, merlins and hawk owls. Hikers fishing from the shore of Wakami Lake can catch walleye, pike and whitefish.

Walks: The 2-km (1.2-mile) Transitional Forest trail is a loop route through a forest transitional zone. The Beaver Meadow

Discovery trail is a 2.4-km (1.5-mile) path that explores how beavers' activities have altered the forest. The Hidden Bog Trail, accessed at the 3-km (1.8 mile) point on the Height of Land Hiking Trail, is a 1-km (0.6-mile) route along a northern bog where the vegetation is slowly growing across the acidic water.

Hikes/Backpacking: The 75-km (46-mile) Height of Land Hiking Trail goes around the shores of Wakami Lake. The western shore of the lake is the height of land, the watershed divide between the Arctic and Atlantic oceans. Along the route, hikers can see remnants of the area's early commerce. There are 20 campsites along the trail, all located on the shores of the lake.

More Information: The Superintendent, Wakami Lake Provincial Park, 190 Cherry Street, Chapleau, Ontario P0M 1K0, (705) 864-1710.

Voyageur Trail

When completed, the Voyageur Trail will extend from South Baymouth on Manitoulin Island to Gros Cap west of Sault Ste Marie and then north along the shore of Lake Superior to Thunder Bay, a total distance of approximately 1,100 km (700 miles). A ferry service operated by the Ontario Northland Marine Services connects South Baymouth with the Bruce Trail at Tobermory.

Approximately 400 km (250 miles) of the trail have been completed including a 204-km (127-mile) section from Gros Cap to Blind River, a 16-km (10-mile) section through the La Cloche Mountains near Espanola and a 26-km (16-mile) stretch along Lake Superior's shore near Terrace Bay.

A guidebook for the Voyageur Trail is available and those who purchase it will be provided with descriptions of the new sections as they are completed.

More Information: Voyageur Trail Association, Box 66, Sault Ste Marie, Ontario P6A 5L2.

Lake Superior Provincial Park

Lake Superior Park has the highest average rainfall in Ontario due to the geographic effect of the high hills in the park. The elevation of this 1,550-km² (600-square-mile) park ranges from 180 meters (600 feet) at the shore of rugged Lake Superior to 600-meter (2,000-foot) mountains. As air rises over the mountains the moisture in the air cools and condenses as rain.

The park's forest is part of the transition zone between southern deciduous and northern boreal forest. The hilltops are covered with yellow birch and sugar maple. Spruce, balsam fir and tamarack grow in the lowlands. Brook, lake and rainbow trout may be caught in the park's lakes.

Lake Superior Park offers more than 100 km (60 miles) of hiking trails.

Walks: Among the park's walks are the 0.4-km (0.2-mile) Agawa Rock Indian Pictographs trail to the site of rock paintings, the 1.2-km (0.7-mile) Crescent Lake trail through a stand of maple, birch and white pine, and the 1.6-km (1-mile) Trapper's trail loop along the shore of Rustle Lake.

Hikes: Day-hiking opportunities in the park include the Orphan Lake trail which leads 6 km (3.7 miles) to a cliff overlooking Orphan Lake and climbs to lookouts over Lake Superior. The 8-km (5-mile) Awausee trail climbs the Awausee and offers views of the Agawa River Valley, Agawa Mountain and Lake Superior.

Backpacking: The most spectacular of the park's trails is the 41-km (25-mile) Coastal trail, a challenging route along the high cliffs and rocky beaches of Lake Superior. The 20-km (12-mile) return Towab trail leads to Agawa Falls, the highest waterfall in the park.

Supplies can be purchased in Wawa, Montreal Harbour or Sault Ste. Marie.

More Information: District Manager, Ministry of Natural Resources, P.O. Box 1160, Wawa, Ontario P0S 1K0, (705) 856-2284.

Pukaskwa National Park

Pukaskwa is a primitive wilderness area on 1,878 km² (725 square miles) of the Canadian Shield between the Pic and Pukaskwa rivers on the northeast shore of Lake Superior. Tip Top Mountain, the highest summit in the park, with an elevation of 630 meters (2,066 feet), is 450 meters (1,500 feet) above Lake Superior. The park's 80 km (50 miles) of coastline is characterized by exposed headlands, islands and islets, shoals, sand beaches, boulder beaches and coves. The wave-wash zone of Lake Superior contains arctic alpine plants. Pukaskwa's climate is classified as modified continental. Lake Superior modifies the weather and the coastal sections have cooler summers.

Moose, wolf, black bear and woodland caribou inhabit the park's boreal forest. Ravens, hawks, loons, chickadees, kinglets, nuthatches and warblers are among the birds that can be seen. The park's rivers contain speckled trout, yellow pickerel, pike and sturgeon. Lake trout, rainbow trout, coasters and whitefish thrive in Lake Superior.

Walks: The 1.6-km (1-mile) Southern Headland trail traces the history of volcanic rocks and ancient sea beds that formed the Canadian Shield. The 2.3-km (1.4-mile) Halfway Lake Trail explores a rock-rimmed lake in the boreal forest. The Beach Trail winds along a boardwalk through sand dunes and sandy beaches.

Hikes: Many visitors do a day hike on the Coastal Hiking Trail for 7.6 km (5 miles) one way from Hattie Cove to the White River.

Backpacking: The Coastal Hiking Trail meanders south over the rugged shield terrain for 60 km (37 miles) along the Lake Superior shore. The northern section of the trail is well used and generally clear, but the southern half is more remote and rugged.

Access to the park is by Highway 627 south of Heron Bay to Hattie Cove inside the park. The closest stores are in Marathon, 20 km (12 miles) away.

More Information: The Superintendent, Pukaskwa National Park, P.O. Box 39, Heron Bay, Ontario P0T 1R0, (807) 229-0801.

Sleeping Giant Provincial Park

Sleeping Giant Park lies on the 40-km-long and 13-km-wide (25-by 8-mile) Sibley Peninsula which juts southward into Lake Superior near Thunder Bay. The western shore of the 263-km^2 (101-square-mile) park is dominated by cliffs rising over 240 meters (800 feet) high. The eastern lowlands of the peninsula rise gradually from Lake Superior. The highlands in the middle are characterized by deep valleys, sheer cliffs and fast-flowing streams. The high cliffs at the southwest end of the park are known as the Sleeping Giant after an Ojibway Indian legend.

The Great Lakes mixed forest is composed of poplar, white spruce, birch, white pine, red pine and cedar. Cloudberry, arctic bistort and butterwort are among the plants found here and other places on the north shore of Lake Superior that do not occur elsewhere south of Hudson Bay. Moose, wolf, lynx, deer and bear inhabit the forest. Several species of gulls, ducks and ruffed grouse can be seen. Pike, pickerel, bass, brook trout and rainbow trout can be caught in the park's lakes and streams.

Walks: There are six interpretive trails at Sleeping Giant Park including the Sibley Creek trail which traverses a former timber cutting area, the Joe Creek trail which often has woodland flowers along the path, and the Thunder Bay Bogs trail exploring the effects of glaciation.

Hikes/Backpacking: The park's 80 km (50 miles) of interconnecting hiking trails includes the 40-km (25-mile) Kabeyun trail which follows the western and southern shores of the peninsula and circles the Sleeping Giant, offering good views in all directions. The longest distance between campsites is 13 km (8 miles). The several connecting trails enable hikers to do trips from one to five days. The park's eight other hiking trails provide access to the interior.

Supplies can be obtained in the town of Pass Lake bordering the park, or in Thunder Bay.

More Information: District Manager, Ministry of Natural Resources, P.O. Box 5000, Thunder Bay, Ontario P7C 5G6, (807) 475-1531.

Quetico Provincial Park

Quetico covers more than 4,660 km² (1,800 square miles) of Canadian Shield wilderness in northwestern Ontario. The rugged landscape is characterized by majestic cliffs, waterfalls and many lakes. The forest contains northern trees including black spruce, jack pine, trembling aspen and white birch, with some southern trees such as oak, elm, silver maple and yellow birch. Bald eagles, osprey, common loons and barred owls can be observed. There are good opportunities for catching lake

Quetico Provincial Park. (Ontario Ministry of Natural Resources)

trout, bass, yellow pickerel and northern pike in the many lakes. Among the park's highlights are 25 Indian pictograph sites. Many of the rock paintings are on impressive cliff faces.

Walks: Five interpretive trails ranging from 1.5 km (0.9 miles) to 2.5 km (1.5 miles) explore the park environment.

Hike: The 6.5-km Pines Hiking Trail which follows the Pickerel River to Pickerel Lake takes about two hours to hike.

Backpacking: The park has two backpacking areas. The 27-km (17-mile) Howard Lake Hiking Trail begins near the historic French River, winds along the south shore of Pickerel Lake and goes through the forest to Howard Lake. The trail can be hiked in ten hours but at a leisurely pace should take two to three days.

The McKenzie Lake area, in the northeast corner of the park, contains over 160 km (100 miles) of old logging roads now used for hiking. Specific routes are not marked and topographical maps should be used. Campsites are not designated along the logging roads and finding water may be a problem. Moose, wolves and black bears are frequently seen in both hiking areas.

An interior camping permit at $3 per person per night, is required. Cans and bottles are banned from the interior. Supplies can be obtained nearby in Atikokan.

More Information: Quetico Provincial Park, Ministry of Natural Resources, 108 Saturn Avenue, Atikokan, Ontario P0T 1C0, (807) 597-2735.

Polar Bear Provincial Park

Situated on 483 km (300 miles) of the shoreline of James Bay and Hudson Bay, Polar Bear Park is 24,000 km^2 (9,300 square miles) of subarctic and arctic landscape. The park includes the most southerly extension of arctic tundra in the world. Extending for several kilometers from the seashore are slightly elevated sand and gravel beach ridges caused by the uplift of the land and occasional severe storms. The coast is a mud-and-boulder flat several kilometers wide which is flooded by the tide twice a day. The shore located above the tidemark is a muddy belt of sedge, grass and rushes, with brackish ponds and numerous tidal creeks. In many places in the park the tundra is underlain by permafrost.

Polar bears, woodland caribou and white whales can be seen in the park during the spring and summer. Other mammals found in the park include seals, silver and arctic fox, timber wolf, otter and beaver. Snow geese, Canada geese, many species of duck including old squaw and king eider and arctic loons are among the water birds that can be observed. Land birds include white-crowned and tree sparrows, red polls, rough-legged hawks, willow ptarmigans, homed larks and Lapland longspurs.

The hundreds of kilometers of treeless beach ridges in the tundra section of the park near the coasts of Hudson Bay and James Bay are suitable for hiking. The 29-km (18-mile) old road from the abandoned Site 415 of the Mid-Canada Line radar station, across ridges and sedge meadows to sand dunes on the James Bay coast can also be hiked. During the summer hiking season the area has long hours of daylight. The most practical way of reaching Polar Bear Park is by air.

More Information: District Manager, Ministry of Natural Resources, Box 190, Moosonee, Ontario P0L 1Y0, (705) 336-2987.

Guidebook Sources

Exploring Algonquin Park, by Joanne Kates, describes the park and is a guide to its hikes. Available from Douglas and McIntyre, 1615 Venables Street, Vancouver, British Columbia V5L 2H1; $9.95 (for mail orders include postage of $1 plus 50 cents per book).

Great Country Walks Around Toronto, by Elliott Katz, is a guide to public transit accessible walks in the natural areas along Toronto's rivers, ravines and on the shores of Lake Ontario. Available from Great North Books, Box 507, Station Z, Toronto, Ontario M5N 2Z6; $2.95.

8
Quebec

JACQUES Cartier, the French explorer, climbed the wooded slopes of Mont Royal on Montreal Island in 1535 and gazed at the beauty of the vista before him. This sense of discovery, Quebec's beauty and unique *joie de vivre* can be enjoyed in the province.

Quebec's area of 1,540,595 km² (594,860 square miles) is greater than the combined areas of France, Germany and Spain. Its three main geological regions are the Canadian Shield stretching north of the St. Lawrence River to Hudson Bay, the Appalachian region south of the St. Lawrence and the St. Lawrence Lowlands between the Canadian Shield and the Appalachian region.

The Canadian Shield forms an immense rolling plateau with

Average daily minimum and maximum temperatures in Quebec

		\multicolumn{2}{c}{May}		\multicolumn{2}{c}{June}		\multicolumn{2}{c}{July}		\multicolumn{2}{c}{August}		\multicolumn{2}{c}{Sept.}		\multicolumn{2}{c}{Oct.}	
		L	H	L	H	L	H	L	H	L	H	L	H
Montreal	°C	8	18	14	23	17	26	16	24	11	19	5	13
	°F	47	64	57	74	62	79	60	76	52	67	41	55
Quebec	°C	6	16	12	22	15	25	14	23	9	18	4	11
	°F	43	61	53	72	59	77	57	74	49	65	39	52
Gaspé	°C	2	12	8	19	12	24	9	23	6	19	1	12
	°F	36	53	46	67	54	76	49	73	43	66	34	54

a coniferous forest and many rivers and lakes. Quebec's Appalachian region, an extension of the Appalachian Mountain chain of the eastern United States, is a succession of plateaus and plains. The Chic-Choc Mountains in the Gaspé, with an average height of 900 meters (3,000 feet), are a continuation of the 600-to-900-meter (2,000-to-3,000-foot) Sutton, Stoke and Megantic ranges of the Eastern Townships region southeast of Montreal.

Most of Quebec experiences a temperate climate with hot summers and cold winters. Average rainfall during the summer months is around 11 cm (4 inches) per month. Quebec's mild autumn temperatures provide comfortable hiking weather while the forests are a dazzling kaleidoscope of blazing colours; the backcountry is at its peak of beauty and should not be missed.

More Information: Tourisme Quebec, P.O. Box 20000, Quebec, Quebec G1K 7X2, or call toll-free 1-800-363-7777.

Ottawa/Hull Area

Gatineau Park

Situated just north of the Ottawa/Hull area, Gatineau Park covers 356 square km (138 square miles) of wooded mountains and lakes at the confluence of the Ottawa River and the Gatineau River.

Walks/Hikes: Gatineau Park's trail network includes the 3-km (1.8-mile) Larriault Trail which begins near Lake Mulvihill, winds along the 250-meter (820-foot) high Eardley Escarpment overlooking the Ottawa Valley, and skirts a waterfall. The 2.5-km (1.5-mile) King Mountain Trail is an interpretive path from Black Lake to the top of King Mountain which has good views of the Ottawa Valley and is the site of Canada's first triangulation point, a reference mark for surveying. The Lusk Cave Trail leads 5 km (3.1 miles) to a marble cave, considered rare in the hard rock of the Canadian Shield. From the cave you can return to the road or continue another 9 km (5.5 miles) to Taylor Lake.

More Information: Gatineau Park, National Capital Commission, 161 Laurier Avenue West, Ottawa-Hull, Canada K1P 6J6, (819) 827-2020.

Montreal Area

Oka Provincial Park

Situated on the north shore of Lake des Deux Montagnes, 50 km (31 miles) from Montreal, Oka Park's 18 square km

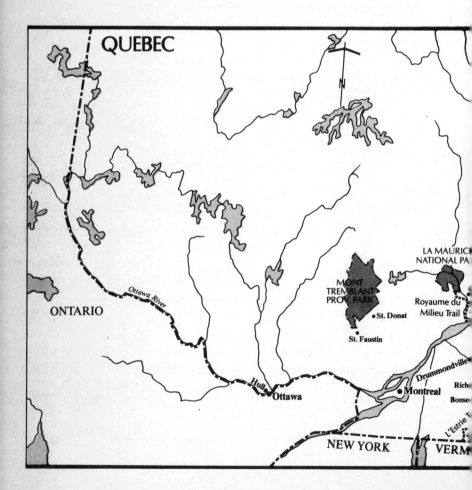

(7 square miles) offers a variety of trails and a sandy beach. The park is also traversed by a 30-km (18-mile) bicycle path stretching from St-Eustache to the town of Oka. The area is famous for Oka cheese made by Trappist monks of the La Trappe monastery, located just outside the park.

Walks/Hikes: The park's 30-km (18-miles) of trail include the 2.5-km (1.5-mile) Montée du Calvaire leading to a lookout on le Calvaire d'Oka where there are several chapels dating from the 1740s. The 5-km (3.1-mile) Colline trail leads to the

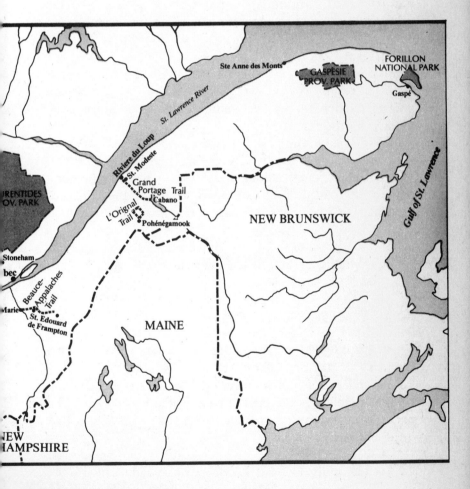

mountain's summit and explores local ecology. The 9-km (5.5-mile) Grand Baie trail skirts the shores of a bay of Lac des Deux Montagnes.

More Information: Oka Provincial Park, Box 447, Oka, Quebec, J0N 1E0, (514) 479-8365.

Mont-St-Bruno Provincial Park

Mont-St-Bruno reaches 198 meters (650 feet) high, and stands out from the surrounding flat terrain. It is a geographic phenomenon known as a Monteregian Hill. Other examples are Montreal's Mont Royal and nearby Mont-St-Hilaire and Rougemont.

Situated only 24 km (15 miles) from downtown Montreal, Mont St-Bruno Provincial Park's 6 square km (2.3 square miles) encompasses five lakes, a mixed hardwood forest and a variety of birdlife.

Walks/Hikes: The park's network of 30 km (18 miles) of trails offers 7 suggested circuits ranging from 4.6 to 9.1 km (2.0 to 5.6 miles) in length. Along the trails are a nature centre at a restored mill called Le Vieux Moulin, remains of the passing of the glaciers from the last Ice Age, and lookouts offering good views.

More Information: Mont-Saint-Bruno Provincial Park, 330, chemin des 25 Est, Saint-Bruno-de-Montarville, Quebec J3V 4P6, (514) 653-7544.

Mont Tremblant Provincial Park

Created in 1894, Mont Tremblant Park covers 1,248 km^2 (480 square miles) in the northern Laurentian Mountains, and is 139 km (86 miles) north of Montreal. At 967 meters (3,175 feet), Mont Tremblant is the highest peak in the Laurentians. The park's lakes and rivers contain northern pike, walleye, speckled trout and lake trout.

Walks: The park's self-guiding nature trails include the 2.7-km (1.6-mile) Lac des Femmes trail which explores the geographic features of the Laurentians. The 1.5-km (0.9-mile) Lac aux Atocas trail leads to a variety of the waterways found in the Laurentians. The 1.6-km (1-mile) L'Envol trail traverses the park's maple and yellow birch forest.

Hikes: Most of the park's day-hikes lead to panoramic viewpoints. The 3.3-km (2-mile) La Roche Trail and the connecting 2.5-km (1.5-mile) La Corniche trail lead to views of the Lac Monroe valley.

Backpacking: Mont Tremblant Park offers 85 km (53 miles) of backpacking trails. The 51-km (31-mile) Grand Randonee trail is a circuit from Lac Monroe to La Cachée that can be hiked as a loop or as a one way hike of 22 or 29 km (13.6 or 18 miles). There are four bunkhouses along the trails in addition to backcountry campsites. In the park's La Pimbina area, a 37-km (23-mile) trail goes from Lac aux Rats and skirts Lac des Sables.

Supplies can be obtained in St-Faustin or St-Donat.

More Information: The Director, Mont Tremblant Park, Box 129, St-Faustin, Quebec J0T 2G0, (819) 688-2336.

La Mauricie National Park

Straddling the Laurentian Plateau and the St. Lawrence Lowlands, this 544-km^2 (210-square-mile) park consists of low rounded hills, narrow valleys and many small lakes. The Laurentians were rounded by glaciers during the Ice Age and moraine deposits are widely scattered in the park. The transition forest consists of northern coniferous trees and the deciduous forests of the St. Lawrence Lowlands and is inhabited by moose, deer, black bear, wolf, coyote, lynx, fox and beaver. Anglers can fish for speckled trout, lake trout, northern pike and small-mouth bass in the park's lakes. More than 143 species of birds have been observed in the park, 116 species nest there.

Walks: Among the park's nature walks is the 3-km (1.8-mile) Family Trail at Riviere-a-la-Peche, and the 1.2-km (0.7-mile) Lake Edouard and Lake Etienne trails. The

Lac Larouche, L'Estrie Trail. (Jean-Pierre Panet)

0.5-km (0.3-mile) Ruisseau Bouchard trail is accessible for the handicapped.

Hikes: Day-hiking trails in La Mauricie Park include the 6-km (3.7-mile) Plantation Circuit, the 14-km (8.6-mile) Bouchard-Pimbina-Benoit-Isaie Lakes trail, and the 6.4-km (3.9-mile) Bouchard and Pimbina Lakes trail.

Backpacking: The 45-km (28-mile) Isaie and à la Pèche Lakes trail is a three-day route along the shores of several lakes.

Food supplies are available in St. Jean-des-Piles and Grand-Mère. Topographical maps can be obtained at the park office.

More Information: The Superintendent, La Mauricie National Park, P.O. Box 758, Shawinigan, Quebec G9N 6V9, (819) 536-2638.

Appalachian Mountains

L'Estrie Trail

Le Sentier de l'Estrie is a 130-km (80-mile) route in the Appalachian Mountain chain in the Eastern Township region southeast of Montreal. The trail goes between Kingsbury near Richmond to Sutton. Going in a southerly direction from Kingsbury, the trail parallels the Rivière au Saumon and Gulf Brook and goes over 465-meter (1,975-foot) Mont des Trois Lacs. The trail then goes through Mount Orford Provincial Park, passing over 858-meter (2,815 feet) Mount Orford, then over a ridge of Mount Chagnon, along the ridge of the Sutton Mountains to near Bolton Sud.

The trail has campsites and supplies can be acquired in towns near the route.

More Information: Les Sentiers de l'Estrie, Box 93, Sherbrooke, Quebec J1H 5H5, (819) 563-6200.

Quebec City Area

Jacques Cartier Provincial Park

Wooded peaks rise 450 meters (1,500 feet) above the swift flowing river in the spectacular Jacques Cartier Valley. Situated in the Laurentian Massif's highest section, Jacques Cartier Park includes the mountainous plateaus bordering the valley where the river flows through gorges up to 600 meters (2,000 feet) deep.

Located 40 km (25 miles) north of Quebec City, the park's forest of coniferous trees surrounded by stands of white birch is the home of moose, caribou, black bear, wolf and lynx. Speckled trout are found in the park's lakes and streams.

Walks: Interpretive nature trails are available at the interpretive center near the park entrance, and at Le Perdreau.

Hikes: The 15-km (9.3-mile) des Draveurs trail follows the rim of the Jacques Cartier Valley as it carves its way south through the park.

Backpacking: The park's trail network includes two backpacking trails, Le Chemin du Boucheron and Lac a la Chutes which skirt lakes and ascend over mountain summits. Shelters and primitive campsites are available.

More Information: Jacques Cartier Provincial Park, 9530 rue de la Faune, P.O. Box 7200, Charlesbourg, Quebec G1G 5H9 (418) 622-5151.

Saguenay Provincial Park

The dramatic scenery of the Saguenay River flowing through a 1,500-meter (4,900-foot) wide valley with cliffs rising 500 meters (1,600 feet) above the water is preserved in this

Jacques Cartier Provincial Park. (Quebec Tourist Branch)

provincial park. Covering 288 square km (111 square miles) on both sides of the river, the park stretches from Baie des Ha! Ha! near Chicoutimi to the confluence with the St. Lawrence River at Tadoussac. At the lower Saguenay near Tadoussac, the river is a fjord gouged by the glaciers of the last ice age.

The Saguenay River, reaching up to 600 meters (2,000 feet) deep, is the breeding ground of the beluga whale. Near the river's confluence with the St. Lawrence River other marine life including porpoises and finback, humpback, pilot and blue whales may be seen. At Tadoussac are sand dunes and beaches.

Walk: The Méandres à falaise trail is a 1.6-km (1-mile) loop along the Rivière Eternité.

Hike: The Statue trail is an approximately four-hour return hike to 518-meter (1,700-foot) high Cape Trinité where a large statue of the Virgin Mary built in 1881 overlooks a panoramic view of the Saguenay Valley.

Backpacking: The 25-km (15-mile) Capes trail leads from near where Rivière Eternité flows into Baie Eternité, along the ridge of mountains with many views of the Saguenay Valley and ends at the village of l'Anse Saint Jean. Along the trail are backcountry campsites and two huts. Reservations are required for the huts.

More Information: Saguenay Provincial Park, 3415 boul de la Grand-Baie Sud, Ville de la Baie, Quebec G7B 1G3, (418) 544-7388.

Beauce-Appalaches Trail

This 31-km (19-mile) trail is situated in the Beauce region, a northern extension of the Appalachian Mountains southeast of Quebec City. From the town of Ste-Marie-de-Beauce on the Chaudière River, the trail goes east past the town of Saint-Edouard de Frampton and crosses the Etchemin River. The trail traverses agricultural terrain and mixed forests of maple, cedar and pine.

Hiking the entire trail takes about three and a half days. There are five shelters and several campsites along the trail.

More Information: L'Association du Sentier Beauce-Appalaches, c/o Association Touristique du pays de l'Erable, 800 Autoroute 20, Bernier, Quebec, G0S 1C0, (418) 831-4411.

Gaspé Peninsula

Île Bonaventure and Percé Rock Provincial Park

This park encompasses two famous landmarks: Percé Rock near the town of Percé, and Île Bonaventure 3.5 km (2.1 miles) offshore in the Gulf of St. Lawrence.

Percé Rock, one of Quebec's most popular tourist attractions, has been immortalized by many artists. Stretching 510 meters (1,673 feet) long, 100 meters (328 feet) wide and 70 meters (230 feet) high, Percé Rock derives its name from the 30-meter (98 feet) wide archway pierced in it by the sea. At low tide you can walk to Percé Rock, otherwise there are boat tours.

Île Bonaventure, 4.1 square km (1.6 square miles) in area, is known for its migratory bird population. Over 200,000 birds nest here. Among these are 50,000 gannets, believed to be the world's largest colony of this species. The island has a conifer forest and many wildflowers, and is reached by boat from Percé.

Walks: Île Bonaventure has four nature trails. The 2.8-km (1.7-mile) Colonies trail is the shortest and suited for seniors, young children and groups. Along the 3.5-km (2.1-mile) Mousses trail are opportunities for observing flora. The 3.7-km (2.2-mile) Paget trail explores wooded areas and fields. The Chemin du Roy trail leads 4.9 km (3 miles) along cliffs past Baie des Marigots and near historic houses.

More Information: Île Bonaventure and Percé Rock Provincial Park, 4 rue du Quai, P.O. Box 310, Percé, Quebec G0C 2L0, (418) 782-2240.

Forillon National Park

At the eastern end of the scenic Gaspé Peninsula, which separates the Gulf of St. Lawrence and the Baie de Gaspé,is Forillon Park, 238 km² (92 square miles) in area. The peninsula's eastern coast is dominated by 180-meter (600-foot) limestone cliffs and the southern shore facing the Baie de Gaspé has pebble beaches and small coves interspersed by rocky headlands. The hills in the interior reach almost 540 meters (1,800 feet). The plant life comprises deciduous trees and arctic alpine plants. Harbor seals and several species of whales can be seen in the waters near the park. White-tailed deer, moose, red fox, black bear, Canada lynx and beaver inhabit the interior, and over 220 species of birds visit the park every year. Speckled trout are abundant in the lakes and streams.

Forillon National Park. (Claude Letarte, Sentier-Qqébec)

Walks: Une Tournee dans les Parages is a 3-km (1.8-mile) interpretive trail in the Grand-Grève area with exhibits on the farming and fishing at the turn of the century. The 1-km (0.6-mile) La Chute trail leads to a secluded waterfall.

Hikes: The 8-km (4.9-mile) Le Mont Saint-Alban trail circles the summit of Mont Saint Alban offering good views. The 8.8-km (5.4-mile) Les Graves explores pebble beaches on the Bay of Gaspé coast and sites that are centuries old.

Backpacking: The 16-km (10-mile) Les Lacs trail leads to the park's highest peaks and several small lakes and has a shelter in addition to wilderness campsites. The 16.9-km (10.5-mile) Les Cretes trail goes along some of Forillon's mountain peaks from the Penouille area to Petit Gaspé, and offers good views of the peninsula.

A Guide to Forillon National Park describes the area. Food supplies can be obtained in the surrounding villages of Gaspe, Cap aux Os and Cap des Rosiers.

More Information: The Superintendent, Forillon National Park, P.O. Box 1220, Gaspé, Quebec G0C 1R0, (418) 368-5505.

Gaspésie Provincial Park

This 802-km² (310-square-mile) park encompasses the Chic-Chocs (also spelled Shickshocks) Mountains, a northern extension of the Appalachian chain. The highest mountains of this range are known as the McGerrigle Group of peaks and include 1,270-meter (4,166-foot) Mont Jacques-Cartier, the highest peak in southern Quebec.

Peat bogs are found on the valley floors, and on mountain slopes are mixed stands of spruce and birch. The park's wildlife includes caribou, moose, deer, black bear and beaver.

Mont Albert is a plateau with treeless precipitous slopes forming a 20-km² (8-square-mile) table at an elevation of 1,151 meters (3.775 feet). At the base of the mountain is a boreal forest and on the upper slopes is a thin forest composed of trees less than 2.5 meters (8 feet) high. Alpine tundra, thick shrubs, moss, lichen and alpine flowers are found at the summit.

Walks: The 1.4-km (0.8-mile) each way Le Roselin trail leads to Lac aux Americains. The 5.2-km (3.2-mile) each way Les Cailloux trail climbs Mont Richardson.

Hikes: On Mont Albert a 16-km (10-mile) trail loops across the plateau. On Mont Jacques Cartier a 4.7-km (2.9-mile) trail ascends and loops around the summit. In the Lac Cascapedia area a 12.4-km (7.7-mile) loop trail climbs Pic du Brule.

Backpacking: Trails for overnight or longer trips lead from the Mont Jacques Cartier day-hiking trails, along Lac aux Americains to the Mont-Albert area. A network of backpacking trails wind from the Lac Cascapedia area west over a number of mountain summits to Mount Logan. Shelters as well as backcountry campsites are located along the trails.

More Information: Park Superintendent, Gaspésie Provincial Park, P.O. Box 550, Ste-Anne-des-Monts, Quebec G0E 2G0, (418) 763-3301.

Guidebook Sources

A Guide to Forillon National Park, by Maxime St-Amour, describes the park and includes information for hikers. Available from Douglas and McIntyre, 1615 Venables Street, Vancouver, British Columbia, V5L 2H1; $9.95 (for mail orders include postage of $1 plus 50 cents per book).
Country Walks Near Montreal, by William G. Scheller, is a guide to walks in the natural areas in and around Montreal. Available from Appalachian Mountain Club, 5 Joy Street, Boston, Massachusetts, 02108, U.S.A.; $8.95.

9

New Brunswick

THE LINK between the Atlantic provinces and the rest of Canada, New Brunswick has an area of 73,432 km² (28,354 square miles) and is part of the Acadian Highland, a rolling plateau intersected by ridges of great hills in both the north and south, with elevations reaching over 600 meters (2,000 feet). The Gaspésie Hills and the northern Appalachian Highlands separate the province from Central Canada. About 88 per cent of New Brunswick is covered with forest nurtured by heavy rainfall. The Acadian mixed forest of red spruce, balsam fir, sugar maple, and birch covers all but the province's northwestern corner which has a boreal forest of white spruce, black spruce and jack pine. New Brunswick has 2,250 km (1,400 miles) of coastline on the Bay of Fundy, Northumberland Strait, Gulf of St. Lawrence and Chaleur Bay.

The interior of New Brunswick has a continental climate of

Average daily minimum and maximum temperatures in New Brunswick

		May		June		July		August		Sept.		Oct.	
		L	H	L	H	L	H	L	H	L	H	L	H
Fredericton	°C	4	17	9	22	13	26	12	24	8	20	2	13
	°F	39	63	49	72	55	78	54	76	46	68	36	56
Saint John	°C	5	14	9	18	12	21	13	21	9	18	5	13
	°F	41	57	48	65	54	70	55	70	49	64	41	55

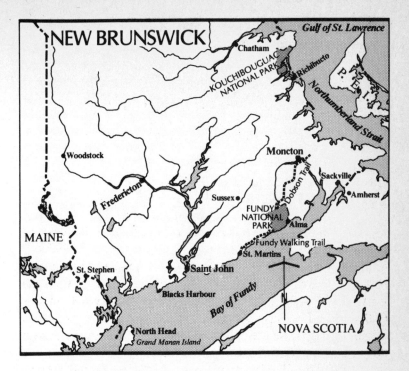

hot summers and very cold winters, while the coast has more temperate weather due to the moderating influence of the ocean.

More Information: Tourism New Brunswick, P.O. Box 12345, Fredericton, New Brunswick E3B 5C3. Call toll-free in New Brunswick 1-800-442-4442, in the rest of Canada and in the United States 1-800-561-0123.

Dobson Trail

This 60-km (37-mile) wilderness trail between the city of Moncton and Fundy National Park was named after Dr. Arthur Dobson who developed the idea and directed its completion. The Dobson Trail traverses the rugged landscape approaching the coast of the Bay of Fundy and is located on privately owned and leased crown woodlands. The route goes through Acadian mixed forest, open fields and near marshes. Some of the points of interest are the McFarlane Covered Bridge, the look-off at Prosser Ridge, the Hayward Pinnacle and an abandoned gold mine.

Two Appalachian-type shelters are situated on the trail and camping at other locations along the route is off the trail near springs and brooks. The trail crosses several good back roads but does not pass any towns, or close to stores where supplies can be bought. Provisions must be carried or cached at road crossings. Campfire permits should be obtained from: The New Brunswick Forestry Service, 33 Pacific Avenue, Moncton. Blackwood Lake is the best fishing spot on the trail. Brook trout may be caught in the brooks along the trail but the fish tend to be small. A fishing permit is required.

The Hillsboro-21-H/15-West topographical map covers most of the trail. From the terminus of the Dobson Trail at the Fundy Park boundary, the Laverty Trail leads to the park headquarters.

More Information: The Dobson Trail, R.R. #3, Petitcodiac, New Brunswick E0A 2H0, (506) 756-2281.

Fundy National Park

Skirting the Bay of Fundy for 13 km (8 miles) and extending inland for 15 km (9 miles) over a rolling forested plateau, Fundy National Park is 207 km² (80 square miles) of virtual wilderness. The area is famous for its tides which reach 16 meters (53 feet) and are among the highest in the world. The coastline is characterized by a line of majestic cliffs which range in height from 9 to 60 meters (30 to 200 feet) and are divided at intervals by deep valleys with streams that flow into the Bay of Fundy. The plateau, a remnant of an ancient mountain range, averages 300 meters (1,000 feet) above sea level and is cut by valleys with steep rocky walls and waterfalls.

The park's valleys and rounded hills are covered by the Acadian mixed forest, and along the coast where the summers are cool the forest cover consists of red spruce and balsam with some yellow spruce and white spruce. The plateau, which has warmer summers, is covered with sugar maple, beech and yellow birch.

Moose, white-tailed deer, beaver and snowshoe hare are some of the mammals that can be observed. A large number of bobcat inhabit the park but are rarely seen. The shoreline of the Bay of Fundy is along a migration route and in the spring and autumn large numbers of migrating birds stop at the park. Of the 185 species of birds observed 87 nest in the park. Birds that can be seen include the common loon, red-throated loon, great blue heron, bald eagle, spruce grouse and ruffed grouse. Anglers can find speckled trout in almost all the park's streams and lakes.

View of Point Wolfe from the Coppermine Trail, Fundy National Park. (Barbara Linke-Sinclair, Parks Canada)

Fundy Park's trail system presently comprises 120 km (75 miles) of trails.

Walks: The variety of walking paths, ranging from 0.5 to 4.4 km (0.3 to 2.7 miles) include trails leading to the Bay of Fundy coast, to waterfalls and through forests.

Hikes: The 3.3-km (2-mile) Coastal Trail to Herring Cove offers sea cliffs and vistas of the bay. Other hikes lead to waterfalls and through wooded river valleys.

Backpacking: Five of the park's trails have backcountry campsites for overnight or longer trips. The Fundy Circuit is a 50-km (31-mile) three- to four-day backpacking route through the park.

The trail network connects with the Dobson Trail which leads from the northern park boundary to the city of Moncton, described separately in this chapter.

Camping supplies are available in the town of Alma.

More Information: The Superintendent, Fundy National Park, P.O. Box 40, Alma, New Brunswick E0A 1B0, (506) 887-2000.

Kouchibouguac National Park

Situated on 26 km (16 miles) of the shoreline of the Northumberland Strait, this 238-km^2 (92-square-mile) park has sand dunes formed by the sea and wind, secluded beaches, salt marshes, bogs, swamps, and an Acadian mixed forest. The protected ponds, rivers, lagoons and bays of Kouchibouguac Park are resting places for waterfowl during their spring and fall migrations and more than 200 species of birds have been recorded. The shoreline has a large population of sand pipers, plovers, terns, gulls and kingfishers. The swamps, fields and woodlands are inhabited by crows, ravens, hawks, ospreys, ruffed grouse, woodcocks, woodpeckers and sparrows. Among the mammals that live in the park are moose, deer, black bear, bobcat, red fox, racoon, porcupine, beaver, otter and snowshoe hare. Bass, eel, smelt, trout flounder, clams, crabs and lobster may be found in Kouchibouguac's waters.

Kouchibouguac National Park. (T. Grant, Parks Canada)

Walks: The 3.4-km (2.1-mile) Claire-Fontaine trail follows the banks of Rankin Brook. The 5.1-km (3.1-mile) Conservation Trail passes marshes and creeks with abundant birdlife.

Hikes: The 11-km (6.8-mile) Major Kollock Creek Trail traverses the mixed Acadian forest, cedar swamps, small bogs and open fields.

Backpacking: The 14-km (8.6-mile) Kouchibouguac River trail follows the bank of the Kouchibouguac River, known as the "river of the long tides," to Kelly's Beach where there are many coves. A primitive campsite is situated along the trail.

More Information: The Superintendent, Kouchibouguac National Park, Kouchibouguac, Kent County, New Brunswick E0A 2A0, (506) 876-2443.

Mount Carleton Provincial Park

Situated in northern New Brunswick, Mount Carleton Provincial Park offers rugged terrain and a variety of forest types, wildflowers, birds and mammals. Mount Carleton, which reaches 820 meters (2,693 feet), is the highest peak in the Maritime provinces. The park features eight trails totalling 45 km (28 miles).

Walks: The 2-km (1.2-mile) Pine Point Trail follows the edge of the point of land in Lac Nepisiquit. The 1.8-km (1.1-mile) Williams Falls Trail is a loop route to the waterfalls.

Hikes: Among the park's hikes are the 6-km (3.7-mile) Mount Bailey Trail which leads to a view of the area. The 9.6-km (5.9-mile) Mount Carleton trail is a loop route to the mountain's summit.

Backpacking: Backcountry campsites are located off the Mount Carleton Trail.

More Information: Mount Carleton Provincial Park, Tourism Manager, P.O. Box 180, Saint Jacques, New Brunswick E0L 1K0, (506) 551-1377:

Anchorage Provincial Park, Grand Manan Island

The largest of the Bay of Fundy Isles, situated off the southwest coast of New Brunswick near the Maine border, Grand Manan Island is 35 km (22 miles) long and 10 km (6 miles) wide at the widest point. The eastern side of the island has several villages and long, sandy beaches. The uninhabited western side, where the famous dulse seaweed is harvested, is characterized by craggy 90-meter (300-foot) cliffs.

Walks/Hikes: Over 240 species of birds, including the sea-diving puffin, make Grand Manan their home. Deer and rabbit can also be seen. Weather on the island is unpredictable and hikers should be prepared for cool weather and periods of fog.

Grand Manan has a number of well-marked hiking trails both along the coast and through the interior. At the southern end there is a scenic trail along the cliffs with excellent views of the coastline between the South West Head Lighthouse to Bradford's Cove Pond. From Dark Harbour on the western side, a longer trail follows the coastline to Big Pond and then crosses the island's interior to a highway on the eastern side. There are also many old logging roads that can be hiked. Anchorage Provincial Park occupies 1.4 km² (0.5 square miles) on the island and includes two fresh-water lakes and offers a 3 km (2 mile) hiking trail.

Daily ferry service from Blacks Harbour to North Head on Grand Manan is provided by Coastal Transportation Limited, Box 26, Saint John, New Brunswick, E2L 3X1, (506) 657-3306. The superintendent of Anchorage Provincial Park can supply information on trails on the entire island.

More Information: Park Superintendent, Anchorage Provincial Park, Seal Cove, Grand Manan Island, New Brunswick E0G 3B0, (506) 662-3215.

Campobello Island

Famous as the former summer home of U.S. President Franklin D. Roosevelt, Campobello Island is situated in the southwestern corner of New Brunswick and is part of the Roosevelt-Campobello International Park. Adjacent to the park is Herring Cove Provincial Park which also offers short trails.

Walks: Roosevelt Park's 13.5 km (8.5 miles) of walking trails include the 1.2-km (0.8-mile) Fox Farm to Upper Duck Pond along a small estuary, and the 3-km (1.9-mile) Liberty Point to Raccoon Beach along hills and gullies with views of rocky headlands and cliffs. It is also possible to follow much of the shoreline along the beach.

More Information: Tourism Officer, Herring Cove Provincial Park, Welshpool, Campobello Island, New Brunswick E0G 3H0, (506) 752-2396.

10

Nova Scotia

SHAPED like a lobster, a native delicacy, Nova Scotia is 55,487 km² (21,425 square miles) almost completely surrounded by water—the Bay of Fundy on the south and the Northumberland Strait and the Gulf of St. Lawrence on the north. The province has 7,446 km (4,625 miles) of coastline. The Isthmus of Chignecto, less than 32 km (20 miles) wide at its narrowest point, joins Nova Scotia with the continental land mass. Cape Breton Island, linked to the mainland by Canso Causeway over the Strait of Canso, is well known for its spectacular scenery of rugged Atlantic coastline with a mountainous background. The northern part of the island is a wild, wooded plateau about 360 meters (1,200 feet) high. There are numerous trails along the scenic coastline and in the province's interior.

Nova Scotia has a moderate climate. The prevailing winds

Average daily minimum and maximum temperatures in Nova Scotia

		\multicolumn{2}{c}{May}		June		July		August		Sept.		Oct.	
		L	H	L	H	L	H	L	H	L	H	L	H
Halifax	°C	5	14	9	19	13	23	14	23	11	19	6	14
	°F	41	58	49	67	56	74	57	73	51	67	43	57
Yarmouth	°C	6	14	9	18	12	21	13	21	10	18	6	14
	°F	42	57	49	64	54	69	55	70	50	65	43	57

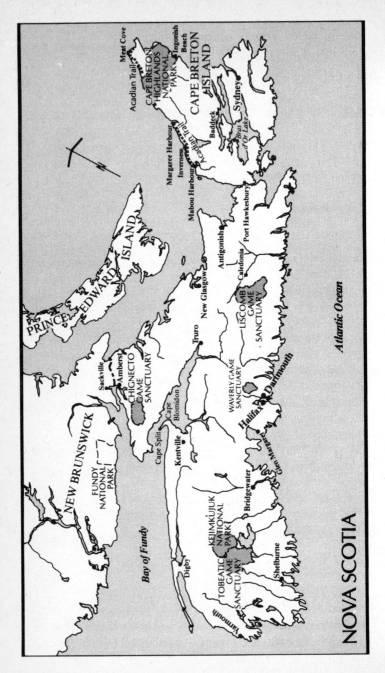

NOVA SCOTIA

from the west and northwest are modified by the ocean. Sea breezes from the Bay of Fundy or the Atlantic Ocean keep summer daily temperatures averaging around 21°C (70°F). In summer, banks of fog drift inland an average of 38 days during June, July and August, but rarely remain all day.

Average annual precipitation is 89 cm (35 inches). Spring arrives late in Nova Scotia but the autumn season is long.

More Information: Nova Scotia Department of Tourism, P.O. Box 456, Halifax, Nova Scotia B3J 2R5. Call toll-free in Canada 1-800-565-0000; in Halifax-Dartmouth (902) 425-5781; in the United States 1-800-341-6096; and in Maine 1-800-492-0643.

Topographic maps are available from: Nova Scotia Government Bookstore, 1597 Hollis Street, P.O. Box 637, Halifax, Nova Scotia B3J 2T3, (902) 424-7580.

Hostels are operated by: Canadian Hostelling Association, Nova Scotia Region, 5516 Spring Garden Road, P.O. Box 3010 South, Halifax, Nova Scotia B3J 3G6, (902) 425-5450.

Cape Breton Island

Cape Breton Highlands National Park

Bounded on the east by the Atlantic Ocean, and the Gulf of St. Lawrence on the west, Cape Breton Highlands National Park is on the Appalachian Highlands which reach 532 meters (1,747 feet), the highest point in Nova Scotia. The coastal cliffs on the western shore rise from sea level to 300 meters (1,000 feet) which contrasts with the gentle hills on the eastern shore. The picturesque 950-km^2 (367-square-mile) park has wooded hills, tundra-like highland bogs, treeless barrens, headlands and rocky and sandy beaches. The hills are covered with a thick Acadian forest of coniferous and deciduous trees. Balsam fir predominates at higher altitudes. Scrub growth and subarctic plants such as reindeer lichen grow on the central plateau.

Deer, moose, fox, lynx, beaver, marten and black bear are indigenous to the area. More than 185 bird species including sea birds such as gannets, puffins, terns and a variety of ducks and geese can be observed. Atlantic salmon can be found in the pools on the park's western side and brook trout in the

Cape Breton Highlands National Park. (S. Homer, Parks Canada)

many streams. The park's trail system is 100 km (60 miles) in length.

Walks: Among the park's variety of interpretive trails are the 1.9-km (1.2-mile) Le Buttereau oceanside trail where pioneer Acadians first tilled the soil, the 0.6-km (0.4-mile) wheelchair accessible Bog boardwalk trail through a highland plateau bog, the 0.8-km (0.5-mile) Lone Shielding trail exploring the area's Scottish history, and the 4-km (2.5-mile) Middle Head trail with views of Ingoniah Bay, Cape Smoky and wildlife including seabirds and whales.

Hikes: The park's day-hikes include the 9.6-km (6-mile) L'Acadien trail loop which leads to the top of Burnt Mountain with panoramic views of the Acadian coast. On the 7-km (4.3-mile) Skyline Trail loop is a headland cliff with views of the Cabot Trail, Gulf of St. Lawrence, pilot whales, bald eagles and boreal birds. The 11-km (6.6-mile) Coastal trail follows the ocean shoreline.

Backpacking: The 16-km (10-mile) return Fishing Cove trail leads along the Fishing Cove River to the ocean cove and a wilderness campsite. From here you can explore the beach and swim in either fresh or salt water.

The 25.8-km (16-mile) return Lake of Islands trails winds around several bogs, across the plateau barrens to a back-country campsite at Lake of Islands.

Food supplies are available near the park. Descriptions and maps of some of the park's trails are included in *Hiking Trails of Cape Breton Highlands National Park*, and *Hiking Trails in Nova Scotia*.

More Information: The Superintendent, Cape Breton Highlands National Park, Ingonish Beach, Nova Scotia B0C 1L0, (902) 285-2691.

Cape Smoky Provincial Picnic Park

Situated at Top of Smoky on the Cabot Trail 10 km (6 miles) south of Cape Breton Highlands National Park, Cape Smoky Park is in the center of an area that burned in 1968 when a smouldering campfire caused a large forest fire. The forest is now regenerating.

Hike: The 5-km (3-mile) Cape Smoky Trail leads to many lookouts along the coast to the north that offer spectacular views. The trail is described in *Hiking Trails in Nova Scotia*.

More Information: Department of Lands and Forests, P.O. Box 68, Baddeck, Nova Scotia B0E 1B0, (902) 295-2554.

Nova Scotia Mainland

Kejimkujik National Park

A gently rolling landscape with numerous lakes containing many islands and bays, characteristic of inland Nova Scotia, make up this 381-km^2 (147-square-mile) park. Kejimkujik is a Micmac Indian word meaning "place that swells" referring to the largest of the many lakes in the park.

The park's mixed forest consists of maple, oak, birch and white pine in the drier areas, and red spruce and balsam fir in the wetter areas. Among the birds that can be seen are the magnolia warbler, veery, pileated woodpecker and barred owl. American bittern and common yellowthroat nest in the large, treeless bogs bordering many lakes. Rare birds like the ospery and hooded merganser nest in secluded areas of the park. The park's waters contain brook trout, yellow perch and white perch.

Walks: Among the park's 12 walking trails are the 2.2-km (1.4-mile) Beech Grove loop trail through a variety of forests. A cassette tape explains the route's woodlands and wildlife. The 1-km (0.6-mile) Flowing Waters goes along the Mersey River, the 3-km (1.8 mile) Peter Point trail is a good area for bird watching, and the 3-km (1.8) Jakes Landing to Merrymakedge Beach trail includes a 0.9-km (0.5-mile) wheelchair accessible section along the shore of Kejimkujik Lake.

Hikes: For a longer day hike do part of a backpacking route.

Backpacking: Kejimkujik's longest hike is the 65-km

(40-mile) Liberty Lake route, stretching from Big Dam Lake to the Mersey River Bridge, a four- to five-day trip. The 20-km (12-mile) Big Dam/Frozen Ocean hike consists of the first

Kejimkujik National Park. (Peter Hope, Parks Canada)

10 km (6 miles) of the Liberty Lake route, returning by the same route. The 26-km (16-mile) Channel Lake is an overnight loop trail.

Supplies can be obtained in Caledonia, Maitland Bridge and other nearby communities. Several of the park's trails are described in *Hiking Trails in Nova Scotia*.

More Information: The Superintendent, Kejimkujik National Park, P.O. Box 36, Maitland Bridge, Annapolis County, Nova Scotia B0T 1N0, (902) 682-2772.

Kejimkujik National Park Seaside Adjunct

The 22 square km (8.5 square mile) Seaside Adjunct of Kejimkujik National Park straddles the tip of the Port Mouton Peninsula between Port Joli Bay and Port Mouton Bay, about 100 km (60 miles) from the inland portion of the park. The adjunct encompasses two white sand beaches, secluded coves, lagoons and exposed headlands. The mixed forest is home to mammals common to Nova Scotia such as white-tailed deer, snowshoe hare, raccoon and porcupine. From the shore you can see harbour seals, eider ducks, cormorants, sandpipers, yellowlegs and piping plovers. The Tundra-like vegetation includes heath plants such as cranberry and bog rosemary.

Walks: Two rough trails provide the only access into the area. From Southwest Port Mouton, an old gravel road leads 8 km (5 miles) to the shore on Black Point. From the community of St. Catherines River, an old cart track provides a 3-km (1.8-mile) access to the western part of the adjunct.

More Information: Kejimkujik Seaside Adjunct, 19 Fort Point Road, Liverpool, Nova Scotia B0T 1K0, (902) 354-2880.

Other trails on the Nova Scotia Mainland

Three trails totalling 24 km (15 miles) allow hikers to explore the scenic Blomidon Peninsula. The trail to Cape Split features spectacular views of the Bay of Fundy from 45-meter (150-foot) cliffs. The nesting grounds of many seabirds can be seen on a nearby island. The second trail on the peninsula is to Scots Bay Beach where hikers can observe tidal-zone life. A third route leads from Borden Brook in Blomidon Provincial Park across the peninsula to Scots Bay.

The 19-km (12-mile) Old St. Margaret's Bay Road is an old coach road leading east from Big Indian Lake near Route 333 to Glen Margaret. Several cabins near Big Five Bridges Lake, in addition to campsites in the Nine Mile River Area, are available for hikers.

At Glen Margaret, a 14-km (9-mile) trail leads to Fourteen Mile House on Route 3. The path follows the flat land along the Hosier River for 8 km (5 miles) and then turns inland to Hubley's Lake. There are numerous campsites and sources of fresh water along the route. A 10-km (6-mile) trail from Glen Margaret goes southwest through mostly flat terrain to Dover on Route 333.

These trails and others are described in *Hiking Trails in Nova Scotia*.

Guidebook Sources

Hiking Trails in Nova Scotia, by the Canadian Hostelling Association, is a guide to many of the trails in Cape Breton Highlands National Park, Kejimkujik National Park, the Acadian Trail and a number of trails outside the parks. Available from the Canadian Hostelling Association, Box 3010 South, Halifax, Nova Scotia B3J 3G6; $9.95.

Hiking Trails of Cape Breton Highlands National Park details 28 hiking trails in the park. Available from Les Amis du Plein Air, Box 472, Cheticamp, Inv. Co., Nova Scotia B0E 1H0; $4.95.

Walk Cape Breton is a guide to a number of trails on Cape Breton Island. Many follow the coast along cliffs or beaches. Available from Cape Breton Development Corporation, P.O. Box 1750, Point Edward, Sydney, Nova Scotia B1P 6T7; (write to obtain current price).

11

Prince Edward Island

PRINCE Edward Island, the "Garden of the Gulf," is a gentle place of rolling farmland and small woodlots bounded by hundreds of kilometers of sandy beaches. Only a few beach areas are crowded with tourists, leaving hikers to enjoy the rest in solitude. The crescent-shaped island has a total area of 5,654 km² (2,184 square miles), making it Canada's smallest province, and is separated from the mainland on three sides by the Northumberland Strait.

The terrain is low and rolling. The highest point on the island, the Caledonia Triangulation Station at the southeast end, is only 152 meters (500 feet) above sea level. The soil contains little rock and is a distinctive red color. The irregular coastline has large bays and inlets, high cliffs and long sandy beaches with rocky coves. Small wildlife is abundant on the island and includes beaver, mink, muskrat, fox, weasel, squirrel and racoon. Bird species include hawks, owls, falcons, black

---

Average daily minimum and maximum temperatures in Prince Edward Island

		May		June		July		August		Sept.		Oct.	
		L	H	L	H	L	H	L	H	L	H	L	H
Charlottetown	°C	4	14	10	19	15	23	14	23	11	19	6	13
	°F	40	57	50	67	59	74	58	74	51	66	42	55

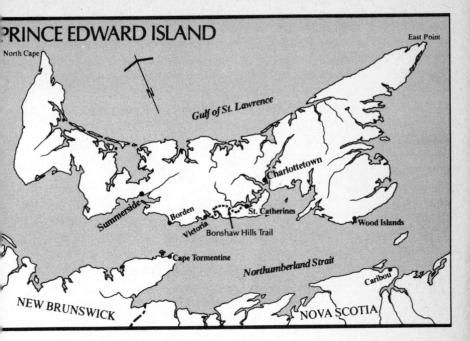

ducks, Canada geese and teal. Anglers can fish for brook trout, rainbow trout and Atlantic salmon in the island's streams.

More Information: Prince Edward Island Tourist Information Centre, P.O. Box 940, Charlottetown, P.E.I. C1A 7M5, (902) 368-5555 (from New Brunswick and Nova Scotia call toll-free 1-800-565-7421) from the rest of North America 1-800-565-0267.

Prince Edward Island has a temperate climate; extreme and sudden changes in temperature are rare. The island is free of fog as it is sheltered from the Atlantic by Nova Scotia and Newfoundland. Summer days are generally warm, with an average high of 22.6°C (73°F). Nights are cool due to sea breezes. Overnight condensation usually keeps vegetation damp until around 10 a.m. Average annual precipitation is 110.5 cm (43.5 inches). The cooler autumn temperatures are also pleasant for hiking.

Two ferry services connect Prince Edward Island to the mainland. The service from Cape Tormentine, New Brunswick to Borden, P.E.I. is operated by Marine Atlantic, P.O. Box 250, North Sydney, Nova Scotia B2A 3M3, (from Ontario, Quebec call toll-free 1-800-565-9411; from New Brunswick, Nova Scotia and Prince Edward Island call toll-free 1-800-565-9470; from Newfoundland call toll-free 1-800-563-7701; from the rest of Canada call (902) 794-7203; in the continental U.S., excluding Maine, call toll-free 1-800-341-7981; in Maine dial toll-free 1-800-432-7344. The other ferry service is run from Caribou, Nova Scotia to Wood Islands, P.E.I. by Northumberland Ferries Ltd., P.O. Box 634, Charlottetown, P.E.I. C1A 7L3, (902) 566-3000 or toll-free 1-800-565-0201.

Prince Edward Island National Park

Red sandstone cliffs, sand dunes, marshes, ponds, and 40 km (25 miles) of saltwater beaches dominate Prince Edward Island National Park's 32 square km (12 square miles) on the Gulf of St. Lawrence. The magnificent white sand dunes contrast with the clear blue ocean. In July and August, water temperatures average 20 degrees C (70 degrees F), giving Prince Edward Island beaches some of the warmest salt water north of the Carolinas.

Walks/Hikes: The parks trails, which range from 1 to 8 km (0.6 to 5 miles) in length include the 2.1-km (1.3-mile) Bubbling Spring Trail loop through spruce woods with a bird lookout over Long Pond, and the 1-km (0.6-mile) Reeds and Rushes Trail on a floating boardwalk over Dalvay Pond. Both trails are in the Dalvay Stanhope area.

Starting near Green Gables House in the park's Cavendish section are the 1-km (0.6-mile) Balsam Hollow Trail along the Babbling Brook made famous in the Anne of Green Gables story and through author Lucy Maud Montgomery's involvement with the area, and the 1.6-km (1-mile) Haunted Wood Trail through Montgomery's childhood environment which inspired her writing. Also in this area is the 5.5- to 8-km

(3.4- to 5-mile) Homestead Trail through farmland and along the shore of London Bay.

More Information: Park Superintendent, Prince Edward Island National Park, Box 487, Charlottetown, Prince Edward Island C1A 7L1, (902) 672-2211.

Strathgartney Provincial Park

Strathgartney Park is situated in the central Queens County Hills and offers scenic views of the West River. A forest of beech, sugar maples and yellow birches is encompassed in the park.

Walk: The 1.3 km (0.8-mile) traverses the park and neighboring Strathgartney Homestead.

More Information: Department of Tourism and Parks, P.O. Box 2000, Charlottetown, Prince Edward Island C1A 7N8, (902) 892-3420.

Bonshaw Hills Trail

The Bonshaw Hills Trail extends for 32 km (20 miles) from the West River Bridge near the town of Saint Catherines, to the beach at the town of Victoria. From the bridge, the trail follows the West River and crosses woodlots including a stand of remnant white pine and hemlock near Appin Road. The route goes through old fields, on country roads and along the beach at Victoria. There are scenic views near Strathgartney and Hampton. The distances between road crossings range from 0.5 to 8 km (0.25 to 5 miles). Camping is available at Strathgartney Provincial Park 3 km (2 miles) off the trail on Highway 1.

More Information: Bonshaw Hills Trail Club, c/o Department of Tourism, Parks and Conservation, P.O. Box 2000, Charlottetown, P.E.I. C1A 7N8.

Beach Walks

Prince Edward Island has many kilometers of long sandy beaches suitable for walking. As the island's beaches are tidal they are Crown Land, and the areas below high tide can be used for hiking.

The island's beaches are washed by warm gulf waters because the island is sheltered from the Atlantic by Nova Scotia and Newfoundland, and is not affected by the cold northern currents or the Gulf Stream.

If you're planning a hike on Prince Edward Island's beaches, choose a section of coastline that has either no rivers or where the rivers can be forded. One suggested route is a hike from Nail Pond to North Cape at the northwestern tip of the island.

More Information: Department of Tourism, Parks and Conservation, P.O. Box 2000, Charlottetown P.E.I. C1A 7N8.

12

Newfoundland

NEWFOUNDLAND may well have been the first part of North America to be seen by Europeans. The Vikings certainly knew of it a thousand years ago and it has had white settlement for almost four hundred years. But most of its shores are still as rugged as they were when the first Viking splashed ashore, the interior still teems with caribou and bear and its rivers still flash with trout and salmon. The island of Newfoundland, with an area of 112,293 km² (43,359 square miles) is a continuation of the Appalachian Mountain chain. The Long Range Mountains on the northern peninsula rise abruptly from the west coast. At Gros Morne Mountain, the island's second highest peak, reaches 795 meters (2,651 feet). Newfoundland's rugged southern and eastern coasts are laced with islets, filigree bays and coves.

Ferry service from North Sydney, Nova Scotia, to Port-aux-Basques, Newfoundland, is operated by Marine Atlantic, P.O. Box 250, North Sydney, Nova Scotia, B2A 3M3.

Average daily minimum and maximum temperatures in Newfoundland

		May		June		July		August		Sept.		Oct.	
		L	H	L	H	L	H	L	H	L	H	L	H
St. John's	°C	2	10	6	15	11	21	12	20	7	16	3	11
	°F	35	50	42	59	51	69	53	68	45	61	37	51

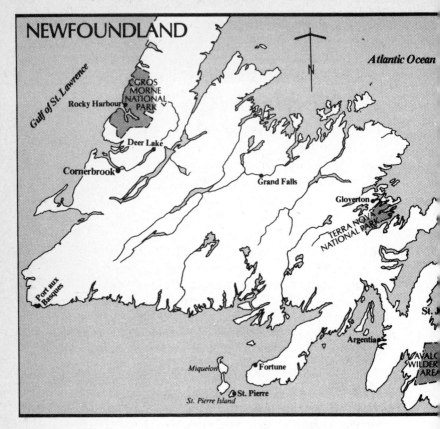

Reservations are required and can be made in several ways. From Ontario and Quebec, call toll-free 1-800-565-9411; from Newfoundland and Labrador call toll-free 1-800-563-7701; from New Brunswick, Nova Scotia and Prince Edward Island call toll-free 1-800-565-9470; from the rest of Canada call (902) 794-7203; in the continental U.S. outside of Maine call toll-free 1-800-341-7981 and in Maine dial toll-free 1-800-432-7344.

More Information is available from: The Department of Tourism, Confederation Building, St. John's, Newfoundland A1C 5R8, or call toll-free 1-800-563-6353. For information on topographical maps of Newfoundland, write: Mapping Division, Lands Branch, Department of Forest, Resources and

Lands, Howley Building, Higgins Line, St. John's, Newfoundland A1C 5T7. Hostels in the province are operated by the Newfoundland Hostel Association, P.O. Box 1815, St. John's, Newfoundland A1C 5P9, (709) 754-0210.

The island of Newfoundland lies directly in the path of storms moving northeastward up the Atlantic coast and during the winter has a heavy snowfall. In early summer floating ice moves southward producing fog and cool weather on the island. Newfoundland experiences frequent high winds, and on the east coast precipitation is heavy. St. John's experiences rain or snow an average of 201 days per year and has an average total precipitation of 137 cm (54 inches) per year.

Terra Nova National Park

Canada's most easterly national park, Terra Nova is located on the Appalachian Mountain Range and is 400 km² (155 square miles) of deep valleys, rocky fjords, rolling crested hills, spongy peat bogs, inland ponds and a deeply indented shoreline. The cold Labrador current gives the area cool, wet summers. Icebergs, a variety of whales and seals can occasionally be seen off the coast during the summer. Seabirds observed in the park include great black-beaked gulls, common terns, herring gulls and black guillemots. Land birds that can be seen at the ponds include thrushes, sparrows, warblers, woodpeckers and willow ptarmigans. Moose were introduced to the island by man in 1878 and are sighted frequently. Beavers, otters, snowshoe hares and black bears can also be observed. Fishing for brook trout and Arctic char in the ponds, streams and lakes is excellent. Saltwater fish in the area include cod, mackerel, herring, lumpfish and caplin. Blue mussels, barnacles and periwinkles can be found on coastal rocks while crabs and lobsters thrive in deeper water. The park has over 100 km (60 miles) of hiking trails.

Walks: Among the park's more than 10 walking trails is the 2.5-km (1.5-mile) Green Head Cove trail which is an easy walk along the coast of Southwest Arm. The Malady Head path

Icebergs off Terra Nova National Park. (Parks Canada)

leads 2 km (1.2 miles) to a lookout 200 meters (650 feet) above the sea with views of the Arm and Alexander Bay. The 4-km (2.5-mile) Louil Hills loop trail leads to a panoramic view of the park's northern end and the Atlantic Ocean. The Buckley Point trail is a 4-km (2.5-mile) walk along the inner Newman Sound coastline past a small beach.

Hikes: The Backbone trail goes 10.5 km (6.5 miles) from Newman Sound to Southwest Arm. The 5-km (3-mile) trail to Dunphy's Pond, the park's largest pond, passes Juicy's Pond and through several old burn-overs. The trail has a view of Clode Sound and the southern portion of the park.

Backpacking: The 20-km (13-mile) Coastal Trail begins at the Newman Sound campground, crosses Big Brook and follows the south shore of Newman Sound to the primitive campsites at Minchin's Cove and South Broad Cove.

Topographical maps can be purchased at the visitor centre. A grocery store is located near Newman Sound inside the park.

More Information: The Superintendent, Terra Nova National Park, Glovertown, Newfoundland A0G 2L0, (709) 533-2801.

Gros Morne National Park

Comprising the highest and most spectacular portion of the Long Range Mountains, Gros Morne Park lies on 1,805 km^2 (700 square miles) of Newfoundland's west coast on the Gulf of St. Lawrence. Gros Morne Mountain at 814 meters (2,672 feet) is the second highest mountain in the province. The coastal Long Range Mountains are cut by huge fjords with cliffs rising 600 meters (1,968 feet) above the water. The shoreline has almost every type of beach, from those covered with large boulders, to fine sandy beaches. The coastal tidal pools support

Gros Morne National Park. (Odile Dumais)

crabs, starfish, chitons, mussels, barnacles, periwinkles, hermit crabs, sea urchins and sea anemones.

The barren top of the Long Range Mountains have a severe climate, producing a tundra-like vegetation. Dense forests of balsam fir, black spruce, larch, white birch, mountain ash and red maple cover the lower slopes of the mountains. The Serpentine Tableland south of Bonne Bay is a barren landscape which contrasts with the well-vegetated hills nearby. As the park is located on the coast, hikers should expect some rain.

Moose, caribou, black bear, arctic hare and red fox are some of the wildlife that inhabit the park. Birds which are characteristic of the upland plateau, such as eider duck, common and arctic terns, dovekies, herring gulls and great black-backed gulls and ptarmigans, as well as many southern forest birds including the blue jay, black warbler and white warbler can be observed in the park. Several species of whales, porpoises and seals can be seen off the coast. Anglers can fish for salmon and brook trout in the park's fresh water, and mackerel and cod in salt water.

Gros Morne Park has over 70 km (43 miles) of hiking trails through varied terrain including isolated areas of the coast and into the Long Range Mountains.

Walks: The popular Western Brook Pond Trail is a 3-km (2-mile) route across Coastal bogs and low limestone ridges to the Western Brook Pond boat tour and a beach near Stag Brook. The 2-km (1.2-mile) each way Shallow Bay Trail follows the Stanford River. A boardwalk on the first part of the 2-km (1.2-mile) Berry Head Pond Trail loop allows people with limited mobility to enjoy the pond.

Hikes: The 9-km (5.5-mile) Green Gardens Trail leads to the coast where sea stacks, volcanic pillow lavas, a sea cave accessible at low tide and secluded coves with waterfalls can be explored. Hikers can walk along the beach and cliff-top meadows.

The Bakers Brook Falls Trail is a 10-km (6-mile) return hike to the waterfalls. The 6-km (3.7-mile) each way Lomond River trail leads hikers and salmon fishermen down to the river.

Backpacking: The James Callaghan Trail begins south of Rocky Harbour and crosses boreal forest, bog, alpine tundra and rock barrens to the summit of Gros Morne Mountain where there are views of Bonne Bay, the Tableland and the Long Range Mountains. A primitive campsite is located near the top of the mountain. The direct route is 4 km (2.5 miles) long, and a spur trail into the Ferry Gulch ascending the northeast side of the mountain makes the trip 7 km (4.5 miles) long.

Although there are no marked trails in the Long Range Mountains, hikers can explore with a map and compass this spectacular area of deeply glaciated canyons and freshwater fjords situated 600 to 800 meters (2,000 to 2,600 feet) above sea level. The 35 km (22 mile) route through the Long Range Mountains can be reached from Western Pond Brook or via the James Callaghan Trail. A larger system of hiking trails and primitive campsites in Gros Morne Park is planned.

Best Hiking Trails in Western Newfoundland describes the park's trails.

More Information: The Superintendent, Gros Morne National Park, P.O. Box 130, Rocky Harbour, Newfoundland A0K 4N0, (709) 458-2417.

Avalon Wilderness Reserve

The Avalon Wilderness Area is situated on 1,070 km² (413 square miles) of the Avalon Peninsula in eastern Newfoundland. The terrain is barren with scattered clumps of timber and is underlain with Precambrian rock. The barrens are covered with a low-growing, wind-pruned spruce and fir known as tuckamore, ship Laurel and Labrador tea.

Walk: Riverhead Trail, 5 km (3 miles) in length, leads over barrens and bogs and into a caribou calving area.

Hike: The 10-km (6-mile) Biscay Bay Trail takes you along the Biscay River, a salmon river popular with anglers, to Seven Islands. Caribou can usually be seen here.

Backpacking: The Daniel's Point to Holyrood Pond Trail is a two-day hike across the reserve's southwest corner.

A number of roads and trails built for access to hydro dams in the area are suitable for hiking. Extended cross-country trips are possible through the largely barren area. Hikers may encounter problems with soft and boggy terrain in some areas and the tuckamore is nearly impossible to walk through. *Trails of the Avalon* describes some of the area's trails. A permit is required for hiking in the Avalon Wilderness Reserve.

More Information: Environment and Lands, Parks Division, P.O. Box 8700, St. John's, Newfoundland A1B 4S6, (709) 576-2431.

Guidebook Sources

Best Hiking Trails in Western Newfoundland, by Keith Nicol, describes 18 trails in the Port-aux-Basques, Stephenville, Corner Brook, Gros Morne National Park and Northern Peninsula areas. Available from: Breakwater Books Ltd., P.O. Box 2188, St. John's, Newfoundland A1C 6E6; $10.95.

Trails of the Avalon: Hiking in Eastern Newfoundland, by Peter Gard and Bridget Neame, is a guide to trails in the St. John's, Conception Bay, Southern Shore and Western Avalon areas. Available from: Gallows Cove Publishing, Site 82, Box 15, SS 3, St. John's, Newfoundland A1C 5K4; $13.95 (add $2 for postage and handling).

Index

Printed in Canada